ALFISSIMO!

ALFISSIMO!

The postwar four cylinder twin-overhead camshaft
ALFA ROMEOS

1900
Giulietta
Giulia
Alfetta
New Giulietta

DAVID OWEN

OSPREY

Published in the winter of 1979 by
Osprey Publishing Limited
12–14 Long Acre, London WC2E 9LP
Member company of the George Philip Group
Reprinted spring 1980

British Library Cataloguing in Publication Date
Owen, David, b.1939
Alfissimo!
1. Alfa-Romeo automobile
I. Title
629.22'22   TL215.A35

ISBN 0-85045-327-5

Editor Tim Parker
Design Peter Wrigley
Filmset and printed by BAS Printers Limited,
Over Wallop, Hampshire

Contents

Preface

Deep-sea yacht racing has been likened to standing under a cold shower, tearing up five-pound notes. Do the same in a noisy, dirty factory workshop under a leaking roof, and using hundred-pound notes instead of fivers, and you have a fair approximation of what it can feel like to be a car manufacturer. From almost the very beginning of the automobile age, the business of making cars has been a hard, demanding and commercially very dangerous business to engage in.

With the passing of the years, this has become more and more true. The market has grown ever more competitive, costs of labour and machinery have climbed, the technicalities of design and development have become ever more sophisticated. This has produced great improvements, to be sure: cars are now relatively cheaper, faster, more economical, more roadworthy and more reliable than ever before. But the process has lost us something too. As clever market research and shrewd design creeps closer and closer to the ideal, cars are losing their old individuality. They are growing more and more alike. As they become more efficient, so they become more predictable—the quirks of character and behaviour, and the *tradition* of a design which at one time marked out cars from a particular maker, are almost gone. Nowadays, mergers and takeovers have joined with this process to make the badge on the front of the car virtually meaningless. The model may be thoroughly desirable and worth while, but in terms of its philosophy, its engineering and its soul it might just as well be blessed with half a dozen other symbols on its radiator grille.

Happily, every rule has at least one exception. And while the super-sophisticated, super-luxury car builders can still afford individuality, there is still at least one company in the harsher cut-and-thrust of the mass market which still gives its customers more than their fair share of that hard-to-find commodity: Alfa Romeo, whose glorious name seems to have been founded, when one looks back over its history, by breaking every possible commercial rule in succession. After a beginning which would have caused all too many companies to sink without trace, the company was rescued only to find itself staggering from crisis to crisis during the inter-war years under the burden of a heavy racing programme and a series of designs already being hit by competition from less carefully designed opposition. Bombed and driven into hiding during the war years, the company lingered on into the hungry forties, still committed to combining sporting quality with the realities of mass production—a recipe which had spelled disaster for so many of their one-time competitors.

Yet Alfa Romeo is still very much with us—against all the rules.

Put an aficionado behind the wheel of one of today's Alfas while securely blindfolded, and if it were possible for him to try the car out without seeing it, he would still know exactly what car it was from the feel of the steering, the layout of the controls, the handling and the roadholding, the very *feel* of the vehicle. Nor is this really surprising, for all these qualities have been passed down from model to model through an enduring family pedigree.

Even a model like the Alfasud, which has a basic design having more in common with its contemporaries from other companies than with the larger models in the Alfa range, has this recognizable Alfa quality. But this continuity is most marked in the bigger cars, the Alfettas and the new Giulietta, which are still classic Alfas to a surprisingly large extent. Take engine design, for example. In a market where technical sophistication is the major yardstick, these cars manage to hold their own in a world where change has become a commonplace, with an engine design which has been left virtually unchanged over the last thirty years. An engine design, moreover, which owes its basic layout and philosophy to an Alfa design which first saw the light of day more than sixty-five years ago, soon after the dawn of the Motor Age.

Why? Answering this question is not easy. To search for clues means taking a close, detailed look at the story behind today's most thoroughbred Alfas, the classic twin-cam range which was born more than thirty years ago in a bomb-shattered factory in a defeated and war-ravaged country; a look at how and why those first Alfas were designed and built the way they were, and at how and why they developed over more than three decades. But as is the way with any subject where an enduring tradition is a factor, this involves making a start much earlier still. So strong is this thread of continuity running through any part of the Alfa legend, that the story behind today's *Alfissimo* Alfas have their true beginnings more than seventy years ago. Here is that story . . . .

Prologue

In the early years of the motor car, a dispassionate observer might have been forgiven for thinking that the automobile was destined to be little more than a passing fancy. After all, compared with the silent, unfussy electric carriage, the internal combustion engine was noisy, smelly, complicated, temperamental, unreliable and thoroughly uncivilized. True, the combination of batteries and electric motors left something to be desired in terms of range and speed—but, given time, it must have seemed far more likely that these drawbacks would have been eliminated by careful development than that the petrol engine could be tamed into a respectable and trustworthy mechanical servant.

But if the first cars did not entirely inspire confidence, then some of the companies making them were positively terrifying in the ways they went about their business—pinching one another's designs, making often inadequate designs under licence (or not) rather than producing improved versions of their own, hit-or-miss marketing, inadequate financing, non-existent spares. All the worst possible mistakes, forgivable—or rather survivable—only because of the increasing and largely unsatisfied demand for cars, *any* cars.

Yet there *were* companies who went too far, even for those undemanding days. In 1906, Alfa's predecessors first set up shop in Milan, and the result was a disaster. It was difficult to see how the company could conceivably have got off to a worse start—they were producing the wrong cars at the wrong time in the wrong country, with the wrong man at the helm. They were fortunate in only one respect—they were doing all these things under the wrong name, so that the taint of failure would not be associated with the company for ever more.

The original title was the eminently forgettable set of initials S.A.I.D., standing for Societa Anonima Italiana Darracq. As this name implied, the company began as the brainchild of the shrewd but eccentric French motor manufacturer Alexandre Darracq. What it did *not* imply, was that S.A.I.D. would be used as a commercial dumping ground for Darracq's older and smaller models in a more remote and less exploited market than existed in most countries of Western Europe at the time.

Unfortunately, this was one occasion where Alexandre Darracq's commerical judgement led him wildly astray. Times were changing quickly, even in the undemanding and unsophisticated Italian market—so while a dumping operation might have worked in the years before 1906, by that time it was already too late. Even in the days when the mighty Fiat concern was just a gleam in the eye of an Italian cavalry officer named Giovanni Agnelli, the seeds of the Italian fascination with motor cars had already been sown. The fact that all cars had to be imported didn't mean that Italians didn't know a good car when they met one—rather the opposite, since they had the pick of the world market to choose from, without home-industry loyalties to distract them. Perhaps because of this, an imported car had a value as a status symbol, which, for the time being, no home-produced car could hope to match, unless it was a very good one.

The problem was that the Darracqs aimed at the Italian market were *not* good cars, by the standards of the time. There were two models chosen from the company's range—an 8–10 horsepower single-cylinder car and a 14 horsepower twin—and they were underpowered for the conditions they met with south of the Alps.

So as a commercial venture, S.A.I.D. was doomed from the start, and the crash was not long in coming; by 1909 the company was on the point of closure. But there were many people in Italy who would have been sorry to see it go—the idea of setting up car production in Italy was still a good one, provided that this time it was done properly, and building on the remnants of the S.A.I.D. organization would still be a great deal easier than starting again from scratch at a later date.

So a rescue operation was needed: Cavaliere Ugo Stella, who had been Darracq's managing director at S.A.I.D., called in the help of the Milan bankers. With the aid of a loan from the Banca Agricola Milanese, Darracq was bought out and the company reconstituted with just half of its original share capital. But Ugo Stella had more ambitious plans up his sleeve—and for these he needed some new cars. So he called in a surveyor-turned-car-designer called Giuseppe Merosi, who had worked for Fiat and for Bianchi.

Just as important was a new name: any reputation which S.A.I.D. might have built up in its brief existence would do far more harm than good, so it was replaced with another set of initials which would accurately reflect the change of ownership and, hopefully, lead the way to an entirely new and more successful commercial career. The name eventually chosen was the Societa Anonima Lombarda Fabbrica Automobili—to be known from the day of its birth, on 24 June 1910, as A.L.F.A.—or Alfa—of Milan.

Choosing the name was easy—building the cars to carry it was a great deal more difficult. At first Merosi played for safety, choosing reliability rather than performance as the top name on his list of priorities. The first Alfas were splendidly engineered cars, massive and solid and well proportioned, but even the most fanatic supporter of the marque would hardly call them exciting. There

Giuseppe Merosi, Alfa's first designer, was originally trained as a surveyor—seen here with an experimental compressor for the Italian Army, which helped provide work for the fledgling company through World War One

were two cars, with a 4-litre engine for the larger 24HP Alfa, and a 2.5-litre version for the 12HP.

The engines were modern in some ways: all four cylinders were cast in a single block with a fixed cylinder head and side valves. Certainly they were better prospects than their predecessors—the 4-litre unit turned out four times the power of the larger of the two Darracq units used in the S.A.I.D. cars. But as far as the promise of performance was concerned, the biggest difference between the Alfas and the Darracqs was that the new cars really did deliver the goods.

This was a good beginning—good enough to bring in the customers which S.A.I.D. had so disastrously lacked. But it *was* only a beginning. Performance could, and would, come later. After only a year's production, when the Alfas had reached the total of fifty cars sold, Merosi set to work on the first racing version. One advantage of the heavy bodywork fitted to the production cars was that removing the body panelling to leave the bonnet, steering wheel, bucket seats, petrol tank and spare wheels of the sports car of the times produced

28 - VIII 1906

12786

After the war, Merosi went on to bigger and better things: though his RL designs—like this Castagna-bodied version of the RL Super Sport—used pushrods rather than overhead camshafts

a dramatic increase in performance. Very small adjustments to the engine's breathing produced equally encouraging increases in power—and the reliability which the cars already possessed added up to the best possible pedigree for racing success.

So was born the Alfa 24HP Corsa. With a narrowed and shortened chassis and stripped bodywork, its weight was cut by 250 lb, and its top speed was increased to 70 mph. Two of the cars were entered in the 1911 Targa Florio, where one led the race until the driver dropped out, blinded by the appalling weather conditions in which the race was run; the other retired with engine trouble.

Other 24HP Corsas were entered, with varying success, in other events. But engine design was improving all the time, and there was definitely a limit to the performance which could be achieved, even in a much lighter car, with Merosi's side-valve design. Increasing the power by building a larger engine simply increased the weight as well. Increasing the speed of the engine would be far more effective.

Fiat had already been working along these lines when Merosi himself had been one of their racing department's development team. The Fiat solution had been to put two rows of inclined valves in the roof of the combustion chambers, driven by camshafts mounted above the cylinder head. Merosi adopted a compromise solution for his next Alfa design however—this was a larger and more powerful version of the 24HP car, called the 40–60, which was introduced in 1913.

This car used the frame, axles, running gear and semi-elliptic suspension of the 24HP, but the engine was a still larger four-cylinder unit of just over 6 litres capacity. The biggest difference was that the inlet and exhaust valves were mounted in two rows side by side above the cylinders, just as in the racing Fiats, except that in this case the valves were mounted vertically. This brought them much closer to the point where the fuel-air mixture was put to work, but the vertical arrangement meant that the valves took up more space than could be fitted above the piston crown, so that the combustion chamber had to be widened over the top of the cylinder block proper.

In fact, the 40–60 engine was no faster in its running than its two smaller sisters—but the new valve gear was a much more efficient arrangement, and the power delivered by each cubic centimetre was half as great again as that produced by the 12HP's engine. Added to this, the engine was a very flexible one, and its reliability was every bit as good as the smaller units. When stripped for racing, the car amounted to another 24HP Corsa, with an extra sixty per cent power bonus.

Not surprisingly, the 40–60 acted as a shot in the arm for Alfa's racing efforts as well as providing a valuable foothold in the larger, more luxurious sector of the production car market. On their first sporting trial, two of the cars took first and second places in their class in the Parma to Poggia hillclimb, a tough thirty-three-mile sprint up to the foot of the Cisa Pass, which was used as a test run for many new Italian competition cars. The following spring, two more cars were entered in the Coppa Florio race of 1914. Run for the first time over the Grande Madonie circuit in the mountains of northern Sicily, where the Targa Florio was run, this was a much tougher event altogether. Each lap was almost three times as long as the Poggia hillclimb. Surfaces varied from loose gravel to mud and potholes, surroundings from sheer rock-faces to thousand-foot precipices. By any standards, this was one of the most formidable challenges in the whole world of motor racing, and it was hardly surprising that neither of the Alfas succeeded in winning. What *was* surprising what that two almost standard production cars took second and third places with almost contemptuous ease.

Almost in spite of themselves, Alfa were building up a formidable sporting reputation. Ironically, a company which had been set up, and re-formed, as a purely commercial and sober business, was proving itself just as successful in racing as any group of fanatic competition enthusiasts. But having found that the virtues of careful, logical design and a high degree of reliability which had been so important in rebuilding the reputation so casually squandered in the S.A.I.D. days gave them a powerful advantage over their competitors, the Alfa management were quick to realize the implications. Nothing succeeds like success.

The logical next step was to increase the racing efforts—so far, the racing Alfas had been almost casual conversions from ordinary production cars,

Vittorio Jano, 'poached' from Fiat's racing department, succeeded Merosi in charge of Alfa's racing efforts—he was responsible for the first of the production twin-cam Alfa Romeos

but now the company was about to make a bid for the most specialized and the most expensive racing of all. Single-seat Grand Prix racing was the name of this new game, and for this kind of competition no modified production car had the slightest hope of success—nothing less than a brand-new, highly sophisticated, specially designed racing car would do. This would cost a great deal of time and money, and even then nothing was certain—all could come to naught, or worse, with a humiliating defeat to crown years of expensive effort. But if the stakes were high, then so were the potential rewards—no other racing result could hope to match the prestige of winning a major Grand Prix.

So it was that Giuseppe Merosi was given *carte blanche* to develop an entirely new Alfa which would win Grand Prix races. In some ways, this task was a good deal simpler in those early days—chassis and suspension design was still a fairly crude business, and here Merosi was able to save time and cost by using the already well-proven frame, axles and springs from the 24HP Alfa. But the big problem was clearly going to be the engine.

The Grand Prix formula from the beginning of 1914 specified a capacity limit of 4.5 litres, and a maximum weight of 2400 lb. So Merosi designed another four-cylinder engine, with a bore of 100 mm and a stroke of 143 mm—in effect, this was a slightly longer stroke version of the 24HP engine, which increased its capacity from 4084 cc to 4490 cc. But the biggest changes were at the top of the engine. Developing the maximum possible

Antonio Ascari, Alfa works driver, at the wheel of one of the P2 Grand Prix cars which, designed by Jano, provided the company with their first racing World Championship

power meant higher compression and more efficient breathing, and combining these two requirements created more problems. It was now obvious that overhead valves were musts. But Merosi's vertical valves made for a large and awkwardly shaped combustion chamber, which had two severe limitations—it prevented the use of a high enough compression ratio, and the flame front which spread when the charge of fuel–air mixture was ignited by the spark plug could not expand evenly and efficiently. Both of these problems would limit the power output of the new engine severely—what was the answer?

Merosi found the solution by going back to his own experience at Fiat, and in doing so set a tradition that has endured at Alfa to this day. The most efficient shape for the combustion chambers,

from the point of view of allowing the flame front to spread as evenly and quickly as possible, is a hemispherical shape with the spark plug at the top centre position. But because the walls of the chamber are set at an angle, this also provides enough space for valves to be set in them, *provided* those valves are set at an angle of around forty-five degrees, rather than vertically, as in Merosi's 40–60.

In order to allow as much mixture into the cylinders as quickly as possible, Merosi opted for four valves per cylinder, since this arrangement gave a larger valve area for a combustion chamber of a given size. He set them in two rows, each canted at an angle of forty-five degrees to the vertical, which left space in between them for two spark plugs to be set, one behind the other, down the centreline of each combustion chamber. Each row

of valves was driven by an overhead camshaft, rather than one located low down in the crankcase and actuating the valves through pushrods and rockers. The overhead camshafts were driven by sprockets and chains.

In theory, this was a very promising design. But the basic configuration of the engine was less than half the story—after all, Fiat had arrived at a similar solution more than seven years before. For all that time, they had been working on the painstaking detail development which would make all the difference between an engine with good potential

Jano produced a smaller six-cylinder version of his twin-cam design to power the long range of production models which began with the 1500 series—this is the Sport Speciale version of 1928

and a real race-winner. Everything centred on the power output figures: fitted with twin down-draught carburetters and domed pistons to provide a 5.55 to 1 compression ratio (compared with the 4.1 to 1 of the production cars), the engine was bench-tested in the spring of 1914. The power peak was 88 brake horsepower at 3000 rpm—compared with the earlier designs, this was a considerable step forward, but as a potential GP contender, it was simply not yet in the running.

There were worse problems to come. The engine's power output might have been enough, had it been fitted into a specially light and sophisticated chassis. But this was where Alfa's preoccupation with toughness and reliability proved a drawback—the chassis of the production 24HP which was used for the Grand Prix car had already had to be shortened to bring the car's weight within the 2400 lb weight limit. But it was only *just* within the limit, at 2310 lb dry, and several of its future opponents were already lighter and more powerful.

For reasons like these, Merosi's Grand Prix Alfa of 1914 was doomed, as a race-winner, before it ever turned a wheel in earnest. Everything was overtaken by the outbreak of war, and Italy had far more urgent problems to deal with. Alfa too had more serious difficulties on the way.

The Great War brought another sharp change in the Alfa story. The company had just been getting on its feet after the S.A.I.D. débâcle, when the war cut the ground away from underneath it by removing the market for its cars. Diversification was the only chance—Merosi himself turned from designing Grand Prix engines to adapting his existing and well-proven 12–15HP unit to more mundane purposes. By redesigning the pipework, he was able to use the two innermost cylinders as a power unit and the two outer cylinders as air compressors, in a portable unit for army use.

Unfortunately, contracts for the compressors could not keep Alfa going on their own, and some of the shareholders grew worried. One of them was the last of the Darracq family to retain his shares in the firm—Albert, nephew of the Alexandre who had started it all. He sold his shares to the Banca di Sconto, who now began to worry in their turn. They had a large investment in a company which they could not sell easily, at a time when the economic climate was bound to get worse. The only remedy was to find sound backing to share the burden—but who would be interested in such a doubtful bargain in the middle of a world war?

The answer to that question was a shrewd civil engineer from Naples by the name of Nicola Romeo. At the age of 26, he had gone into business for himself, designing and building mining machinery. When the war began, he had been marketing compressors, which had won him huge government contracts—so huge that he was suddenly very wealthy, and very keen to find new factory space to keep up with his ever-increasing government commitments. He was also looking for good investments on which to spend some of his money, and eventually he called on the Banca di Sconto for advice. The final piece of the jigsaw fell into place: the bank sold Romeo its Alfa shares, he took over direction of the company, and put workers and workshop space to new uses in building compressors, tractors, aircraft engines and generators.

Oddly enough, Nicola Romeo was no more a car fanatic than Alexandre Darracq. Continuing wartime business had led to his taking over more and more shareholdings in the company, so that when peace came again in 1918 he was in total control of what had now been retitled the Societa Anonima Italiana Ing. Nicola Romeo. But the car business had dwindled to nothing, and there was likewise nothing in Romeo's character to suggest any interest in resurrecting it.

Yet peacetime turned the tables with a vengeance. Suddenly the requirements of the army came to a stop, and the huge wartime production meant that all the components which had made Romeo rich were now so many drugs on the market. With acres of factory space, new machine tools of every kind and a big workforce standing idle, he badly needed to find something to produce, which *could* be sold to an eager postwar public.

The answer, fortunately, was fairly obvious. Even in the vastly expanded Romeo organization there were enough ex-Alfa hands who knew all about car production—and as soon as the Italian economy swung back to peacetime requirements, cars were bound to be in desperately short supply for a long time. This was Romeo's trump card and, car fanatic or not, he was businessman enough to recognize it. He was also quick to realize that in the car-buying world, the Alfa name counted for a great deal more than his own did—so he finally decided to compromise. He renamed the company Alfa Romeo, using the Cross and Serpent badge from the old company, and set Merosi back at the head of the team, with a whole new world at their feet.

To begin with, however, changes would be a long time coming. For several years, there would be no spare money on the scale needed to design and

Another version of the six-cylinder twin-cam 1500, in this case with a close-coupled Zagato body

develop new cars, and it was to be 1920 before another production model design emerged from the Alfa workshops. This turned out to be a car called the G1, another long step on the road towards more size, luxury and weight, and as such it was one of the company's few real failures. Designed as a replacement for the big 40–60 model, it was the first six-cylinder Alfa. If it had a market, it was the super-rich, super-luxurious Edwardian market which had been largely killed off by the war, and in terms of the sporting enthusiasts who were now Alfa's main customers, the car was totally useless. For the home buyers, the G1 stayed asleep at the starting post.

To give Romeo his due, he learned his lesson quickly. Small-production luxury limousines were

out, and he had no longing for the ultra-cheap mass-production business at the other end of the price table. Sport, he knew well, was a splendid prestige-earner, and already Merosi had been set to work on a potential successor for the 1914 car. True, it had been resurrected from its temporary hiding place in a Milan drugs warehouse once the war was over, and it had been entered in two events in particular with encouraging results. As early as 1919, however, it had been fitted with a new cylinder head and given better breathing arrangements, which lifted the power peak to 102 bhp. It was to behave even more excitingly two years later at the Brescia Speed

The classic simplicity of Jano's mechanical sculpture—one of his twin-cam sixes today, in a restored 1750, the model which succeeded the 1500

Week of September 1921, in a 275-mile race called the Gran Premio Gentlemen. Giuseppe Campari drove the car brilliantly. Masetti, in the brilliant 1914 GP Mercedes, took the lead at the beginning, but Campari stayed with him, and amazed everyone by passing the German car at the halfway point in the race. Thereafter he held on to his lead to the bitter end—or almost, for the end was bitter indeed. With the end of the last lap in sight, water began to gush from the radiator, in such a torrent that it was obvious to Campari that the car would never last out to the finishing line. He pulled over and stopped, and Masetti shot past to win—the GP Alfa was wheeled away, its career over.

In spite of these encouraging successes, its competitors had been pre-war cars from other companies, who would by now have much more advanced designs taking shape in their workshops. If Romeo was convinced of the value of Grand Prix success as an aid to sales—and by now he was most definitely convinced—then the solution was clear. Merosi must make up for lost time, and design a car to suit the new Grand Prix formula for 1921, with a smaller capacity limit of 3 litres.

Despite the decrease in size, Merosi's own feelings about the G1 were that the future still lay with six cylinders rather than four, though with more modern valve gear than the L-head side valves he had used on that ill-fated car. All the same, he chose not to return to the hemispherical combustion chambers and twin overhead camshafts of the earlier Grand Prix car. Instead he returned to vertical overhead valves, but set in a single row made up of one inlet valve and one exhaust valve per cylinder, and driven from a camshaft mounted low down in the crankcase and actuated by

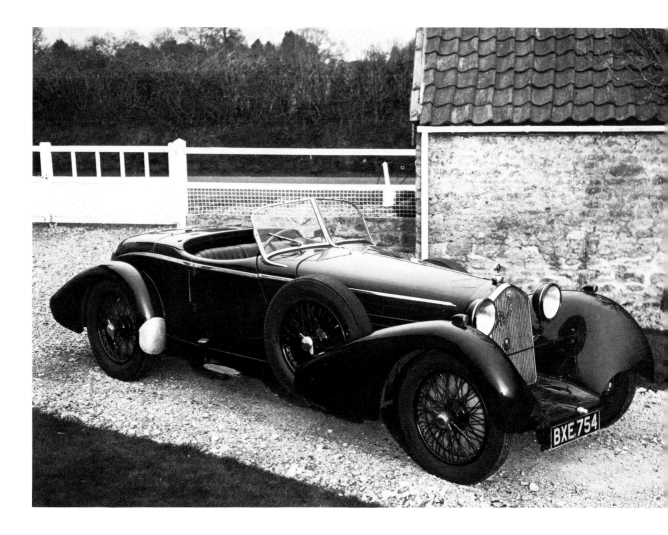

To satisfy the demand for bigger and more powerful cars, Jano turned the twin-cam six back into an eight, to power the 2300 series. This is the Lungo long-wheelbase version of 1933

pushrods and rockers. At the expense of slightly restricted breathing, this allowed a cylindrical combustion chamber that was slightly less efficient than the hemispherical shape but which avoided the reliability problems which were thought to be inevitable with overhead camshafts at the time.

Unfortunately, yet again the car's Grand Prix hopes were to be blighted before its career had even begun. Before the car was ready, the Grand Prix formula was changed—after only a year's racing—to 2 litres, and everyone had to start again from scratch.

By this time, however, the car had found a new role. Worried by the failure of the G1, Romeo badly needed a new model to take over from the

pre-war cars. So the RL, as the new design was identified, took on a new lease of life as a production car. After a rushed development programme and some tough testing, the first production cars were on show to the public by the autumn of 1921. Unfortunately, old habits die hard, and the RL could all too easily have gone the way of the G1. It was fitted with an even heavier body. Top speed of the standard version was less than 70 mph.

Fortunately though, its troubles were curable. Cutting the weight, tuning the engine and fitting a more sporting gearbox produced a transformation. Sport and Super Sport versions of the car sold in increasing numbers, and lifted Alfa Romeo well and truly clear of the early postwar doldrums. The racing versions of the car went one better, and really established the company as one of the great names in sports car racing—a Targa Florio version of the car won this epic motor race in 1923 with Ugo Sivocci at the wheel with Ascari second and Masetti fourth, and they came close to winning it again the following year, when Ascari was pipped on the post by Masetti's Grand Prix Mercedes.

These were the crowning victories in a sporting career which, together with the steady sales on the production front, made the RL the most successful Alfa so far. But in terms of its design it was a retrograde step, a stopgap which worked well within its own limits, but which marked an interruption in the steady evolution of an Alfa pedigree. And whatever else it was, it certainly wasn't a potential Grand Prix winner, so that perhaps that sudden change in formula had been a blessing in disguise.

What the RL did do, however, was gain time for Romeo and Merosi to have another try at the prize which had eluded them for so long. By now Merosi's ideas had swung back to the overhead camshaft layout of the 1914 car, and for his next racing design, the GPR (for Grand Prix Romeo), he was to return to the mainstream of Alfa development with another variation on the hemispherical combustion chamber theme. This car, afterwards known as the P1, was given a new six-cylinder engine. Instead of a cast block, he followed the increasingly popular practice among designers of racing engines by building up water jackets from sheet steel, fitted around the cylinder bores and bolted to a crankcase cast in light alloy.

This was a much smaller engine than the 1914 car—with 65 mm bores and a stroke of 100 mm, the total capacity was 1990 cc. Compression ratio was set at 7.5 to 1, and bench tests showed a power peak of better than 80 bhp. At the same time, greater care was taken to save weight in the car's construction—the inevitable channel-section girders were shortened and curved to allow a more compact and better-streamlined body than the earlier car, and the bodywork was built up from carefully shaped light-alloy panels.

The wheels were still hung on semi-elliptics, though this time they were also kept more firmly in contact with the road through the use of friction dampers. Braking was greatly improved too, with foot-pedal-operated drum brakes on all four wheels, reinforced by a transmission handbrake.

Unfortunately, the weight pruning was not nearly drastic enough. This time, the Grand Prix formula specified a minimum weight limit rather than a maximum one, which provided less direct incentive to lighten the car still further. All the same, the P1 was a couple of hundred pounds over this minimum, while many of the opposition cars, including the formidable Fiats, were close to the limit. The result was that although the Alfa Romeo P1 could top 110 mph fairly easily—itself an indication of how far things had progressed since 1914—the opposition was once again faster still, and the P1 would have its work cut out to win anything worth while.

In fact the car never had a real chance to win anything at all. Three cars were entered for the most important event, from an Italian point of view, on the whole calendar: the Italian Grand Prix, to be held at Monza in September 1923. But even before the race began, tragedy had struck the team, and with it Alfa's entire hopes of Grand Prix success. Skilled and experienced as he was, Ugo Sivocci found the new car too much for him in practice, with fatal results. He slid off the track at the sweeping Curva Vialone, and died in the resulting crash. Alfa Romeo scratched the team from the race, and the P1's career was over even more abruptly than that of the earlier GP car.

This was the end of the Grand Prix road for Merosi too. Twice he had seen all his hard work come to naught with cruel suddenness and finality. Yet his modified production cars were going from strength to strength, setting an enviable record with wins in every kind of short-distance sprint and long-distance endurance epic all over Europe. Rather than compete in an arena of which he had little direct experience, it seemed far more sensible to leave him to do what he could undoubtedly do very well—design honest, capable production cars and modify them to win races.

Romeo, however, was still committed to putting his company at the top of the racing ladder, and this meant finding someone with the expertise and the experience to do what Giuseppe Merosi could not do. As far as Italy was concerned, at that time this meant hiring someone from Fiat, but this was a course which would be fraught with difficulty. Romeo himself could hardly sneak into the Fiat racing workshops with a bundle of notes and try to lure away key experts. In the end, he found himself a most unlikely go-between: none other than Enzo Ferrari, then an up-and-coming new driver for the Alfa Romeo team. The position at Fiat, in spite of their previous success, had also been one of change and replacement. The Fiat Tipo 802 had been a name to conjure with in the racing world of the early 1920s, but like Merosi's RL, this had been designed for the 3-litre Grand Prix formula.

Unlike Merosi, however, the Fiat engineers had opted for eight cylinders rather than six, and once again they had stuck to the twin overhead-cam and

To avoid vibration problems with the long camshafts and crankshaft on the straight-eight, Jano virtually cut the engine in half and put the two halves back-to-back with the drive gears in the middle

Power, and still more power was needed to stay competitive in Grand Prix racing—this was the Tipo A of 1931, which had two tuned 1750 twin-cam sixes mounted side-by-side in the chassis

hemispherical combustion chamber configuration. When they too had been overtaken by the change in formula to 2 litres, they already had a reliable and successful engine to form the basis of their development. All they had to do was remove two cylinders, reduce the dimensions to 65 mm bore and 100 mm stroke, and tidy up the details, and they had a viable engine all ready for the new season's racing.

But perhaps the biggest difference between the two designs was that Merosi's P1 was Alfa's first-team weapon, while the Tipo 804 was very definitely a stopgap for Fiat. Their real white hope was the Tipo 805, which brought them back to their ideal of eight cylinders, with smaller bore and stroke

dimensions to bring them within the 2-litre limit.

By the time the P1 was being prepared for its first outing at Monza in September 1923, the 805s already had one Grand Prix appearance to their credit—at Tours in the French GP. As an aid to still greater performance, the engines had been fitted with vane-type Wittig superchargers. These blowers sucked in too much of the dust and gravel thrown up by the cars' wheels on the rough circuit, and the cars collapsed after showing undoubted promise. The conclusions were clear enough: superchargers were definitely a Good Thing, but not these particular superchargers. As often happens, there was a post-mortem in the works over who had been responsible for missing this obvious hazard, which had robbed the factory of an almost certain victory. Fornaca, chief of the design team, blamed Luigi Bazzi—and Bazzi was an old friend of Enzo Ferrari, who was now working for Alfa.

So angry was Bazzi that he left Fiat and went to work for Alfa Romeo. But useful as he was, he was not the expert that Romeo needed to build an entirely new car. Higher speeds, higher power and higher boost pressures from supercharging all meant much thinner safety margins in racing engines, and this was a job for a racing specialist rather than a sound production engineer like Merosi. But if Bazzi was not the man, he knew the man who was—Vittorio Jano.

Jano was then in his early thirties, and on the threshold of one of the most brilliant careers in engineering history. But he was careful to stick to established and well-proven ideas, rather than wasting time with radical and ultimately fruitless alternatives. Where his work scored over his rivals was in the quality of the detail design.

Ferrari's task, as emissary, was very difficult— why on earth should Jano leave a company then at the forefront of racing development for a struggling and much smaller concern with almost no Grand Prix racing experience at all? One reason might be the sheer challenge of the job—at Fiat he had inherited a professional organization where he was the leader of a group of experts. At Alfa Romeo, on the other hand, he would have to begin from the very beginning—but any successes the company might win would be due entirely to the team *he* had chosen and trained.

Jano's reply was guarded. He was interested in the idea of working for Alfa Romeo, of designing an entirely new racing car and then running the team responsible for entering it in the major Grands Prix throughout Europe—all of which Ferrari had passed on to Rosina Jano, as Jano himself had been out when Ferrari had made his secret poaching trip to Turin. But he would only agree if Romeo himself made a formal offer of the job.

So the impossible was achieved. Romeo sent team manager Giorgio Rimini to Turin to carry the formal offer of the post, Jano agreed, and inside a week he was hard at work for Alfa Romeo.

Once again, Jano was careful to stick to the configuration which was known to work, the engine arrangement which gave the best results in terms of efficiency and engineering elegance: the classic twin overhead-camshaft hemispherical-head layout. But the keynote of his work was the trouble he took over every detail which could help to ensure reliability as well as performance, and so well did he do his work that the same design would be performing brilliantly in racing cars, as well as production cars, more than twenty years later.

Jano's design for the engine of the P2, as the new car was called, was another straight-eight, like Fiat's 805. But the problem with eight-cylinder engines was that the length of the engine could cause problems with vibrations in the long crankshaft needed to transmit the power generated in the eight cylinders. So Jano supported the full counterbalanced crankshaft in no less than ten roller bearings. Even the camshafts, which had far smaller stresses to carry, were each carried in ten bearings—instead of the old chain-and-gear camshaft drive, they were now powered through spur gears and a vertical drive-shaft at the rearmost end of the engine.

There was good reason for all this special care to be taken: Jano had far-reaching plans for the engine. Not only was it to be fed by a powerful lobe-type blower, but it was intended to deliver maximum power at the unusually high (even by Fiat standards) speed of 5500 rpm. This meant centrifugal forces of enormous strength, acting to try to pull apart all the rotating parts of the engine—forces which Jano calmly calculated and allowed for in every step of the design. Breathing too was of prime importance: so he fitted larger valves, two per cylinder, tilted at 100 degrees to one another to fit them into the combustion chambers.

The rest of Jano's contribution to Alfa's hopes was in the effect he had on the workshops—his close personal check on every operation kept production problems and delays to the minimum. Everything which could be tested and proved beforehand *was* tested—the P1 was brought out of premature retirement to serve as a mobile test-bed for the specially designed supercharger, and the effect the blower had on the car was dramatic, boosting the power peak by a quarter, and pushing the top speed up to 118 mph!

In the same way, Jano's design for the car was not radically different from either the Fiat racing cars or even from the P1—the frame was built up from channel-section girders, and the wheels were hung on semi-elliptic springs, backed up by friction dampers. But the master's touch was evident in the *way* in which things were done—the frame was carefully shaped to cope with the stresses without having to carry additional weight. The body panelling was pared down in profile and plan to save frontal area and drag, and also to play its part in the all-important weight reduction. The effect of all this careful detail design was valuable indeed—even when carrying the extra weight of the blower, the car was still 200 pounds lighter than the P1!

Bearing in mind that Jano's design, while conventional in its basic approach, was still a completely new one from Alfa's own point of view, the car was ready in an amazingly short time. Jano moved to Milan in September 1923, just after the P1's disastrous non-debut, and by the following spring the first car emerged from the workshops, ready for testing. From the beginning, the results showed just how effective Jano's design was going to be. Right at the start of the car's development programme, the engine was producing a healthy 134 bhp, and the car was timed on its first event at Cremona at a speed of 123 mph.

This was a case, for Alfa's Grand Prix efforts, of third time lucky—with a vengeance. Jano's magnificent P2 went on to win the Grands Prix of Europe and of Italy in 1924, on their only two GP appearances that year. Even then, the careful development work went on: by the following

Much more successful was the straight-eight P3, one of the most beautiful racing cars of all time. This immaculately preserved example belongs to Alfa Romeo's own museum collection

season the engines were delivering 155 bhp, and they were entered for the French Grand Prix, the Italian Grand Prix and the Grand Prix of Europe. They won the second and third of these events—and they would have won the French race as well had Ascari not skidded off the track and been killed in the resulting crash, after which Jano withdrew the team from the race as a gesture of respect. Even so, the P2's results were enough to win for Alfa Romeo, in the company's second season of proper Grand Prix racing, the first-ever World Championship. Ever since then, every production Alfa wears a stylized laurel wreath around the badge in commemoration of the first (but far from the last) championship win.

Sadly, however, this was the end of the P2's Grand Prix career—already it was time for another change in the rules, and the authorities had decreed that Grand Prix cars for 1926 onwards would have to comply with an engine capacity of only 1.5 litres.

This did not turn out exactly as planned, since the decision proved unpopular with almost everyone connected with racing—in particular, the teams who were faced with the expense of developing entirely new designs due to an arbitrary shift in the rules, and the racing public, who felt that the smaller cars would lack the excitement of the previous years' racing cars.

So it was that the P2 would soldier on for several more years, though in private hands rather than in the official works team, for Alfa Romeo had taken the chance of withdrawing at the moment of greatest achievement to concentrate on other problems. Everything had gone by the board to allow Jano to concentrate on the P2: the sports car racing programme had been stopped, the RLTFs had been sold, and now the P2s followed them under the auctioneer's hammer. It was time to return to the more mundane problems of the cars that brought in the money.

Yet Jano's brilliance was to have an astonishing effect even here. For if the reliability of his racing engine was legendary, the same design should be virtually indestructible in the far less demanding context of day-to-day driving. In fact, he had been working on a successor to Merosi's RL series as far back as 1924, with the P2 barely off the drawing board. This was to be a car called, originally, the NR—for Nicola Romeo—and was to be based on the Grand Prix car to a quite unexpected extent.

This was a more ambitious idea than it sounded. The requirements of racing cars and road cars were in some ways very far apart indeed. Granted, racing cars were powerful and efficient, and they had to be reliable as well—all virtues which any car engine

Outclassed by their powerful Government-backed German opponents, Alfa were forced to develop a series of more and more ambitious Grand Prix cars to try and stay in the running: this is the only moderately successful 3-litre V16 of just before the war

would be better off for sharing. But the order of those priorities, and their character, was different in the two cases: racing car engines were small and highly stressed because they had to be, under the rules of competition, not because that was the best way to produce a given amount of power. And the reliability they needed was the reliability which let them last out the hundreds of miles of the longest of long-distance races, not the hundreds of thousands of miles of an average car's working lifetime—stripping down and rebuilding a racing engine in between events had become commonplace. So it was hardly surprising that for ordinary car engines, combining endurance with power was almost always done by using a larger engine, which could work at lower stress levels and hence with greater margins of safety.

So Jano's basic idea for the NR—or the 6C 1500, as it was soon to become—was unusual to begin with. He intended using the engine of the P2 racing machine to provide the basis for an ordinary, bread-and-butter production model. What was then even more suprising was that he left the bore and stroke dimensions almost unchanged, but removed two of the cylinders to make the engine a six instead of an eight. Opting for a six cut the engine's capacity to only 1.5 litres; it would obviously have to work a great deal harder for its living.

In one way, Jano made its task slightly easier. Although the car was built on a C-girder ladder-frame chassis much the same size as that of the RM, the RL's smaller four-cylinder sister, Jano managed to save fully half a ton, or one-third of the total weight, by careful engineering. This was just as well though—the RM's performance was hardly sparkling and the new car's power unit would be only three-quarters the size of the RM's 2-litre four.

Fortunately, Jano made it an efficient one. Slightly larger in the bore-to-stroke ratio than its parent, with bores a millimetre wider at 62 mm, and the stroke 3 mm shorter at 82 mm, it displaced a modest 1487 cc. The biggest difference between the engines, though, apart from the number of cylinders, was the number of camshafts. The new engine had a single overhead camshaft, actuating a single row of vertical overhead valves, each pair (inlet and exhaust) opening into the roof of a flat combustion chamber, with domed piston crowns and the spark plug set almost horizontally into the side of the chamber. The drive to the single camshaft, mounted high up at the very top of the tall engine, was exactly the same as the double-cam drive of the P2, using bevel gears and a vertical shaft at the back of the engine block.

As befitted a modest production car, the 6C 1500 had no plans for superchargers to be fitted, in the beginning at least. In standard form, the engine put out a creditable if hardly exciting 44 bhp. This power was put to use at the rear wheels through a four-speed manual gearbox and a torque-tube transmission—the wheels, for their part, were hung as before on a simple semi-elliptic spring suspension with friction dampers, and brakes on all four wheels were rod-operated drums.

The first 6C 1500s to be shown to the public made their appearance at the Milan Show in the spring of the P2's World Championship-winning season. But this was more an indication of good things to come, rather than an invitation to buy on the spot, since it would be another two years before the prototypes were followed up—two years during which production and sales of the RL and RM models finally tailed off. Even then, fully three-quarters of the 200 or so cars produced in 1927 were the long-wheelbase tourers, and the best that sports-minded buyers could do was opt for a standard-wheelbase chassis which could be fitted with a slightly more rakish body by one of the specialist *carrozzerie*.

This was an understandable but slightly short-sighted policy, because in character and appearance most of the production cars were now in danger of losing all apparent identification with Jano's brilliantly successful but highly specialized P2. What was urgently needed was a high-performance version of the 1500, to bridge this yawning gap and keep the enthusiast buyers from having to look elsewhere, while at the same time helping to transfer some of the P2's aura of success to their humbler sisters bearing the Alfa banner. So the introduction of the 1500 Sport the following year, 1928, was a very welcome step forward. This reverted to the twin overhead camshafts, double row of valves and the hemispherical combustion chambers of the P2—used for the first time on a production Alfa—in conjunction with a removable cast-iron cylinder head instead of the fixed light alloy head used in the normal 1500.

The actual improvement in power was fairly modest: peak power was up by 10 bhp, but this pushed the top speed up to 78 mph and—more importantly—the engine's design and potential for development now had much more in common with the P2. Already the car was capable of giving the RL a good run for its money, with an engine only half the size, and this was just the beginning. While keen drivers speedily made their feelings clear with order forms and cheques—to the point

984.A

where the Sport accounted for almost half the 327 cars built and sold in 1928—the works were already at work on something better still.

Just as the RL had been followed in its career by an RL Sport and an RL Super Sport, so now the 1500 was to complete a similar progression—and the 1500 Super Sport was to take an even bigger step back in the direction of its Grand Prix parent. Now the wheelbase was shortened to cut another vital 200 lb in all-up weight, while carrying a compact and businesslike two-seater body. The engine had its compression increased, and its power climbed to 60 bhp, which increased the top speed to just over 80 mph. But when fitted with an optional accessory, in the shape of a Roots blower geared at one and a half times engine speed and delivering a modest 7.5 lb of boost (compared with the 12 lb boost of the P2), the car produced 76 bhp at peak—an increase of almost eighty per cent over the standard 1500, and enough to give the blown version of the Super Sport an 87 mph top speed.

These were cars for the real sporting purists, and while they sold in small numbers compared with the other models, their influence on sales was out of all proportion. Their brilliant sporting appeal gave

Half the V16 made a 1·5 litre straight-eight which, fitted into this 'Alfetta' (little Alfa) dominated voiturette racing in the smaller class in the final seasons before the second war

Alfa Romeo's name a much needed boost on the road as well as at the track, and this was intensified when they began to be used in competition. The factory had officially withdrawn from racing after the P2's Championship win, but they were not above giving private owners gentle encouragement in entering the cars in sprints and hillclimbs over the length and breadth of Europe.

This was sound thinking: for the blown SS models still looked sufficiently like the slower versions for their success to be identified with the series as a whole. And while the memory of the P2's victories was beginning to fade from the fickle general public, they were continually being reminded of more and more 1500 wins in club races and trials on their own doorsteps. But this vital programme could not be left in the hands of the willing private owners for ever. It was clearly only a question of time before the factory was bound to reconsider its decision to leave the racing world, and make a return to sports-car competition at least.

And return they did—though, rather surprisingly, with a pair of RLSS cars until the works 1500s were ready. The two pushrod cars ran in the first-ever Mille Miglia of 1927, a challenge the company could ill afford to miss, even without the new cars. And the old models did fairly well: Brilli-Peri led the race at one stage in one of them, but they both dropped out before the end with mechanical problems. It was good to see the old firm back in the racing business, but something new and more competitive was clearly needed.

It wasn't long in coming. By the start of the 1928 season, the works drivers had an even hotter version of the 1500 Super Sport at their disposal: this reverted to the fixed head of the ordinary 1500 model, but still with the double overhead cams of the other sports versions. Larger valves improved the breathing, and the power peak was up to 84 bhp. Campari and Ramponi drove one of these cars in the second Mille Miglia, and proved that the works had been right to enter, and right to develop this special version of the car, by winning the race outright against much larger and outwardly more formidable opposition.

But one race still eluded all the works team's efforts at victory: the Targa Florio. Scene of the earlier Alfa successes with the RLTF sports cars, the Targa had now become a Bugatti benefit. In 1928,

After the war, the Alfetta returned to even greater glory, going on to win no less than four world championship seasons up to the company's final withdrawal from Grand Prix racing in 1951

Campari found his works 1500 was simply too short on power compared with the most competitive of the Bugattis. Other circuits saw encouraging wins by the little Alfas, but on a mountain circuit where acceleration out of the thousands of hairpin bends was of paramount importance, something with more power was required.

The next stage in the progression sounds simple enough. Jano simply widened the bores by another 4 mm, and lengthened the stroke to just one millimetre longer than that of the P2, at 86 mm, to produce a larger capacity of 1752 cc. In normal production terms, the results were even less noteworthy, since the engine was tuned to deliver only 2 bhp more than the standard 1500. Any improvement this might have produced in performance was cancelled out by an equally slight increase in weight, but in terms of the bread-and-butter market, this mattered scarcely at all. What *did* matter was that the sports versions now had a larger engine on which the various improvements could be made: the 1750 Sport inherited the twin-cam head of the 1500 Sport (the standard 1750 had the single-cam layout of the original 1500), while the 55 bhp power peak was only half the story. The top speed of both Sport versions was the same, at 78 mph—but thanks to the big increase in torque provided by the larger engine, the car's acceleration was greatly improved.

This process was taken several steps further in the later Super Sport and Gransport 1750s. These used the same short-wheelbase chassis as the 1500 Super Sport, and this gave coachbuilders like Zagato and Touring the chance to produce some of the classic sports cars of all time. By the standards of their time, by the standards of *any* time, these cars were beautiful, with a rakish purity of line and a grace rarely equalled before or since. To many people at the time—and to enthusiasts today—these cars were the ones which sprang to mind whenever the name of Alfa Romeo was mentioned.

Yet no cars can qualify as great designs on looks alone; fortunately the 1750 was more than just a pretty face. The unblown Super Sport gave way to the Gransport. The blown car, as sold to the customers, turned out 85 bhp and 90 mph, while the later Gran Turismo supercharged close-coupled sports saloon could cope with a relatively heavy body and still top 84 mph. The works cars, as before, went a considerable step further: the cars used in the 1929 season turned out 95 bhp from their fixed-head, large-valve blown engines, providing a top speed of 103 mph, and this was increased the following year to 102 bhp and 106 mph.

The cars followed their smaller sisters in the drama of their debut. Entered in the 1929 Mille Miglia in one of the works 1750s, Campari and Ramponi won outright for the second time. They notched up wins in events ranging from the Circuit of Mugello to the Grand Prix of Ireland, but oddly enough the 1500's history was to repeat itself in a slightly less happy way. Victory in the Targa Florio, still a Bugatti preserve, eluded them once again. Though the invaluable extra torque produced by the 1750's engine made the contest a much closer one, they still failed to catch the flying Molsheim cars.

Yet this was the only major disappointment. The 1750s won the Mille Miglia again in 1930, with Tazio Nuvolari turning in one of the epic drives of his life. His only real opposition came from his team-mate and bitter rival Achille Varzi, who had started ahead of him on the road. Nuvolari finally managed to catch the other 1750 after a terrifying race through the pre-dawn darkness on sidelights alone over twisting mountain roads, lest the flash of approaching headlights should give the game away to the unsuspecting Varzi.

The biggest news of 1930 from the engineering viewpoint, however, was the return of the P2. The racing organizers, faced with the total failure of the 1.5-litre Grand Prix formula which had seen the exit of Alfa Romeo from the racing scene at the end of 1925, had finally given way to public pressure and instituted a totally new kind of GP formula for the 1928 and 1929 seasons. Capacity limits of any kind were out, to be replaced by a minimum-weight limit, and ultra-powerful sprint specials were to be deterred by making each GP race at least 600 miles long.

It is difficult to imagine a formula better suited to the virtues of the P2s, still busy winning free-formula races regularly in the hands of Alfa works drivers running as private owners. Reliability was not a problem—nor was minimum weight, since the racing Alfas had traditionally had a weight problem. Some changes had already taken place to help the ex-works cars to keep up with the competition: Count Gastone Brilli-Peri's P2, for example, had had its cylinder bores widened by just half a millimetre, to raise the capacity from the original 1987 cc to 2006 cc.

But changes like these were modest indeed compared with what the factory had in mind. First of all, they bought three of the old team cars back from their new owners. They bored out the engines to the Brilli-Peri prescription, then they went on to strip off the bodywork, replace the axles with components from the 1750s, modify the springing by bringing the rear semi-elliptics closer to the wheels than before, and replace the steering and brakes with sports-car parts. New bodies were fitted, much lower and leaner than the originals and having more in common with an ultra-Spartan version of the sports car bodywork than the old P2 shape.

The new P2s were to have a brief but splendid career: entered for the GP of Bordino in April 1930, the new-old car took Varzi to a win on its first appearance, but there were problems, though none which could not apparently be cured: the new suspension arrangements had produced a slight decrease in the quality of the car's handling, and placing the supercharger between the carburetter and the engine, as had been done with the sports cars, did not result in the hoped-for power improvement. The supercharger was removed and relocated to feed the high-pressure air into the carburetter, and this boosted the power to a scorching 175 bhp at peak, making the car a formidable contender indeed.

Too formidable for some: when the idea was first proposed to use it as an ultimate Bugatti-crusher in the Targa Florio, even drivers of the calibre of Campari opted for a 1750 instead. Only Achille Varzi, full of burning ambition, was determined to handle the car within the tight and unforgiving confines of the Targa circuit, even against Jano's advice. In a sense, it was no more than Bugatti deserved: his cars were unashamed Grand Prix cars running in long-distance sports car races. But the difference was that the revamped P2 could never compete with the Bugattis on roadholding, so it would have to make up the difference with sheer power.

It was a glorious race, even by the standards of that extraordinary event. It was a measure of the brilliance of Ettore Bugatti's design that his cars proved so hard to beat even after several seasons of domination by so formidable a new challenger. But beaten they were in the end, though Varzi suffered a leaking fuel tank. This forced his mechanic to top up the tank from a can carried in the car while they were on the fast downhill sprint on the very last lap. The petrol, inevitably, was spilled, the fuel ignited, and the car swept down to the final straight with flames and smoke pouring from its tail like some angry, earthbound comet foretelling a world-shaking event.

What the P2's fiery trail announced, however, was the end of the long Bugatti domination of the Targa. Varzi swept on to win in record time, and if the revamped P2 had never done anything else, it would have been more than worth while for that one fact alone. In reality, its career was almost over, with only two third places at Brno and Pescara to come—but never again would a Molsheim car win the Targa Florio either.

It was time for the P2 to return to racing in a rather different form. When the 1750 had appeared in the car showrooms it had proved itself a more successful commercial prospect than even its predecessor had been. But the market trend was towards bigger, more luxurious and more powerful models. Nicola Romeo himself had retired from running the company in 1928, but his successors were just as keen that Alfa Romeo should win its rightful share of this increasingly popular area of the market.

Designing a larger car was easy enough. Just as the six-cylinder cars had been derived from three-quarters of the straight-eight P2 engine, so a return to eight cylinders, but with the dimensions of the 1750 rather than the 1500, would produce a capacity of 2336 cc rather than the 1987 cc of the P2. Apart from the advantages of having many interchangeable parts, this would provide valuable extra power from the increased size.

But this was no mere return to the old Grand Prix engine. Jano was even more concerned with long-term reliability in a prestige model like this, and the return to eight cylinders meant a return to the old problems of long crankshafts and camshafts, with consequent vibration problems. In the P2 he had guarded against this danger by providing adequate bearing support. Now he took things a stage further by changing the basic shape of the whole engine—he simply cut the eight-cylinder unit in half, and effectively turned the two four-cylinder halves around, so that the auxiliaries and camshaft drives were in the centre instead of at one end. This solved the vibration problem quite simply—instead of one long crankshaft serving all eight cylinders, the new engine had two short ones serving four cylinders apiece. Instead of two camshafts (this engine missed out the single-cam stage of the basic 1750 model, using hemispherical combustion chambers and two rows of inclined valves from the very beginning) it had four short camshafts, two for each bank of four cylinders.

The two halves of the crankshaft were joined together through a pair of helical gears, and these gears were also used in one case to power the gear-train which drove the four camshafts, and in the other to drive the pumps for oil and water and the supercharger on one side of the engine, and the

Above
*Some of the Alfas which didn't race were even more
interesting than those that did: the rear engined flat-twelve
Tipo 512 of 1940*

Below
*Another might-have-been: the 1940 version of the V16,
mounted at the front of the Tipo 162 Grand Prix project*

The thirties were difficult years on the production front too: the magnificent craftsmanship of the 1500s, 1750s and 2300s gave way to the more practical six-cylinder 2300s like this Mille Miglia coupé

dynamo on the other side. The cylinder blocks themselves were cast in light alloy, each block having its own cylinder head, and each cylinder being fitted with a hardened steel liner.

Even though each half of the crankshaft was now only as long as in a comparable four-cylinder unit, Jano took care to support each half in no less than five bearings. The whole engine boasted an impeccable standard of detail finish: the long camboxes, the manifold piping and the finned supercharger castings were polished to a fine brilliance, and the entire underbonnet layout was kept as tidy as

possible. The domed pistons and the H-section connecting rods were made from light alloy, to cut down on the rotating masses. Each of the four camshafts was carried in six bronze bearings, while the large valves were set in phosphor-bronze valve seats screwed into the cylinder heads.

For Alfa Romeo the 2300 was the top of the tree: with a single carburetter fed by 6 lb of boost from the supercharger, and working at 5.75 to 1 compression, the engine produced 138 bhp at 5000 rpm, or more power per litre than the works fixed-head 1750 Super Sport!

Just for once, the bodywork department managed to avoid overloading this magnificent engine. There were two versions: the short-wheelbase Corto version, which was little larger than the 1750, and the long-wheelbase Lungo variant.

With such a powerful engine, and such comparatively light cars to carry it, the new Alfa Romeos promised exciting performance. And what is more, they delivered it in full measure. The standard production versions of the new car were as fast as the works racing versions of the already competitive 1750.

In many ways, this was the most brilliant Alfa yet. Its future seemed assured, yet bitterly cold economic winds were blowing over the car market at the start of the 1930s. Many old and well-established names were about to vanish from the scene, and only the strength of Nicola Romeo's other companies, turning out trucks and aero-engines under the furious impetus of dictator Benito Mussolini's armament contracts, helped curb the worst threats to the car company's solvency. Even so, there were severe problems. Once again the Banca di Sconto found itself worrying about its large shareholding, and this time it was the Romeo group's biggest customer, the Italian Government, which stepped in and took over the shares to help keep the firm afloat. This removed short-term anxieties about the company's future, and allowed Jano to carry on with the development of his magnificent 2300. But with the recession affecting the whole of the Western World, and growing worse by the hour, how many people would be left with the means to buy the splendid new cars?

In the meantime, however, the competition programme went on a little longer. The 2300 offered magnificent material for the workshops to develop into a real race-winner, and eventually they did just that, although not quite in the form that previous experience might have predicted. The car was outstandingly flexible: thanks to the engine's wide torque band and the extra power, it could pull away smoothly from 10 mph in top gear. Its combination of hard semi-elliptic spring suspension with a flexible chassis and ultra-sensitive steering made it a precision instrument to drive.

The first competition version of the 2300 was ready early in 1931, with slightly higher supercharger gearing, larger valves and higher 6.5 to 1 compression, which raised the peak power output to 155 bhp. Its first appearance was in the Mille Miglia, but here the car failed to live up to its promise—not for any reason connected with its design, but because of tyre problems which plagued the entire Alfa Romeo team, including the smaller 1750s. The Targa Florio, where the tyres had been replaced by more suitable types, was a different story. Jano planned the whole effort like a military operation, with two-way radio communication between the pits and the refuelling station in the mountains, and long practice sessions before the race. And here the 2300 triumphed, with Nuvolari beating his arch-rival Varzi, who had swopped his Targa-winning P2 for the latest twin-cam Bugatti 51. It was a close-run battle though, and even the 2300's formidable power output did not enable it to leave the Bugatti behind. Only its better weather protection, in a race plagued by gales, rainstorms and mud, finally ensured an Alfa victory.

But on other occasions the 2300 did well on more equal terms. The 1932 Mille Miglia was won by Baconin Borzacchini in a 2300, and the cars seemed set for a bright future. But one factor above all was to stop their brilliant promise in its tracks, at least as far as production success was concerned: the price. Buying a brand-new 8C 2300 cost the would-be customer just about twice as much as a new 1750, at a time when money supplies were drying up all round. Even if it *was* twice as good—and there were many 1750 enthusiasts to call that into question—too few people had the spare cash to make the sales figures keep pace with production costs. The magnificent 2300 was destined to remain a very rare bird indeed—only 188 were ever made, a mere fraction of the total of the smaller models.

In the end, the 2300 very nearly killed Alfa Romeo stone dead. With production falling, costs climbing and even the well-tried smaller models coming to the ends of their production runs, the firm was quite simply running out of money. One of the reasons was the increasing amounts of money being spent on Grand Prix efforts—the old late-twenties racing formula had been replaced in 1931 by a simple stipulation that cars would have two-seater bodywork, carry no mechanics and race for at least ten hours at a time, and the rules could hardly have been aimed more fairly and squarely at the 2300. Just two weeks after Nuvolari had driven the 2300 sports-racing car to victory, Jano's men had produced a new version altogether, aimed at the new formula.

This had a tuned-up engine, fitted with a higher compression head, higher boost pressure from the blower, larger valves and sharper cam profiles to lift the power to 178 bhp. The engine was fitted into a chassis which had been shortened by three inches and fitted with a Spartan, pointed-tail two-seat racing body tapering down to a small radiator at the front end. The car could top 130 mph with ease, and on its first outing at the 1931 European Grand Prix at Monza, the new cars took first and second places. For ever afterwards, the stripped-down Grand Prix

Under Mussolini's rearmament plans, Alfa specialized in aero-engine production, and car production was limited for several years to prestige-earning racing and semi-racing cars like these different versions of the powerful 2900 series

versions of the 2300 were known as Monzas in honour of this victory.

Almost as soon as the Monzas had made their first triumphant appearance, events were overtaking Alfa's new contender. The lack of engine capacity limits was allowing a power race to develop, led by cars like the 4.9-litre Bugattis. Jano had no design for a similar large engine up his sleeve, but he had one idea which could be used as a stopgap, based on the Sedici Cilindri Maserati, which had appeared in 1929. This had combined two straight-eight 2-litre engines in a single V16 of 4 litres, harnessed through clutch, gearbox and transmission in the normal way. Jano however decided to use two separate engines mounted side by side in his new racing car, the Alfa Romeo Tipo A.

The engines used were 1750 engines, kept entirely apart, with the timing changed so that they turned in opposite directions so as to balance the torque forces. But this separateness was carried further: each engine had its own gearbox and clutch, through which it drove one of the rear wheels. Though the driver still had a single gear lever and clutch pedal to worry about, the complexity of the linkages made for difficult engineering.

In terms of sheer speed, the car worked very well. With 115 bhp from each engine, pulling a total weight of only eighteen hundredweight, its top speed was 150 mph and its acceleration was stupendous. But racing car development was approaching the point where the simple leaf-spring suspensions were unable to cope with the vastly increasing amounts of power being delivered by bigger and more efficient engines, and the Tipo A was a very difficult car to handle. It killed Arcangeli on its first test outing, when he failed to persuade it to stay on the Monza track at the Lesmo bend, and it took a driver of the calibre of Nuvolari to get the best out of it. Campari too handled the car to great effect, winning the 1931 Coppa Acerbo and beating the larger Bugattis to do it. At Monza in the September Grand Prix, they proved faster than their rivals until mechanical trouble eliminated both cars before the end of the race. But these exceptions apart, it was the Monzas which carried the Alfa Romeo banner to victory most frequently.

What was needed was an improvement on the stopgap of the Tipo A. Yet once again, Jano was experienced enough and shrewd enough to limit his objectives. He knew only too well, from experience with the Tipo A, that sheer power was not the answer. More power meant greater weight, while a high proportion of the extra power so arduously won was wasted through the sheer inability of the crude suspension systems of the time to cope with it. Instead, he began modestly indeed, by basing his new car on the elderly but still supremely reliable and efficient P2 engine design.

First of all, he took the engine in its Monza form and he lengthened the stroke from 88 mm to 100 mm, which brought the capacity up from 2336 cc to 2654 cc. This in turn meant a bigger charge of the fuel–air mixture would be needed on each stroke, so he fitted 34 mm diameter valves instead of the 29 mm valves used on the Monza— and *this* in turn meant tilting the two rows of valves over to fifty-two degrees each from the vertical, to provide room for the larger valves in the roof of the combustion chamber.

The single blower used on the 2300s and Monzas was now replaced by a pair of blowers, with dramatic result—a peak power output of 215 bhp at 5600 rpm.

One big change in the racing rules helped him a great deal: no longer did racing cars have to carry a duplicate seat for a non-existent riding mechanic. They could now be genuine single-seaters, which allowed the use of a much smaller, lighter, better streamlined body. The big problem was still one of height, however: if you put a driver in the centre of the car, then he has to sit on top of the propeller shaft, which effectively cuts out any real reduction in height and frontal area.

Jano reduced, rather than solved, this problem in an ingenious way. Instead of leading the power to the rear wheels through a propeller shaft and differential in the normal way, he put the differential next to the gearbox in the middle of the car—the differential gears were linked to *two* drive shafts, each one projecting backwards and outwards at fifteen degrees to the car's centreline, and driving one of the rear wheels through a simple set of bevel gears.

There were three advantages resulting from this unusual arrangement: because the differential was mounted on the chassis and not on the rear axle, the unsprung weight on the rear wheels was reduced to that of the wheels themselves, with their associated bevel gears, so that the roadholding of the car was improved. The divided-drive arrangement made maintenance work on the transmission easier. Finally, the angled drive shafts allowed the driver's seat pan to be lowered slightly in between them.

No expense and no effort were spared to reduce the weight of the car as far as possible: the light alloy cylinder blocks helped to reduce the weight of the power unit, and Alfa Romeo's aircraft-engineering experience proved useful in providing exotic light alloys for the chassis frame itself. Altogether, the savings were dramatic indeed; although the new Alfa's arch-rival, the 4.9-litre Bugatti, had an engine of almost twice the capacity, it only had a 40 bhp power advantage, and the Bugatti weighed more than 400 lb more than Jano's new contender, quite apart from the improved roadholding of the Italian car.

Nor was this all: like the 1750 and the 2300, the P3 (as the new car was officially designated, though it became equally well known as the Tipo B, or more simply as the Monoposto) was elegant and supremely graceful. Although the bodywork was designed with simplicity, streamlining and compactness as its chief priorities, there was still room for a shape which managed to suggest speed and agility from its subtle, supple curves even when it was standing perfectly still. Looking at pictures of the P3, it is almost impossible to imagine the car could ever be a failure with lines—and lineage—of that quality.

Nor was it. Nuvolari and Campari were entered to drive the new cars in the Italian Grand Prix of 1932—Campari came in third, behind Fagioli's scorchingly fast twin-engined Sedici Cilindri Maserati. But thanks to poor pitwork by the Maserati mechanics, and Jano's care with the P3's handling, it was the inimitable Tazio Nuvolari who won the race, at the wheel of the other P3.

The French Grand Prix was even better, with the Bugattis thoroughly trounced and the Alfa P3s coming home first, second and third. Likewise the German GP, and the Coppa Ciano. At the Coppa Acerbo, it was the P3s in first and second places, with a Bugatti third—and the Circuit of Avellino

saw almost the same result again, the only difference being the substitution of a Maserati for the Bugatti. At the Monza Grand Prix, the P3s came in first, second and fourth. The only events the car failed to win were at Brno and at Marseilles. The name of the game was total domination of Grand Prix racing, and it seemed that the P3 was on the verge of its greatest successes of all when disaster struck.

The problem was that while the company's efforts went from victory to victory on the racing tracks, in the commercial world failure was staring them in the face. Alfa Romeo had never thought of themselves as mass-producers, but in 1933 the production of all models would fall to only 408 cars—less than half the total of 876 cars produced and sold during 1929—at a time when economic conditions were far better.

No one wanted Alfa to die—not even their sporting rivals—but very few people had cash available to invest on the scale which would be necessary to tide the company over the fast-developing cash crisis, provide money for new models better suited to harsher market conditions, and support the increasingly costly competition programme. Those who *did* have that kind of finance available knew only too well that producing small numbers of high-quality but expensive cars at a time of genuine recession was second only to backing three-legged horses as a reliable way to lose large amounts of money quickly. Yet rescue was on the way: as the bills piled up and the reserves dwindled, the Fifth Cavalry came galloping up over the horizon—metaphorically speaking—in the unlikely person of Il Duce, Benito Mussolini, dictator of Fascist Italy.

Mussolini had limitless Government funds at his disposal—one of the advantages of being a dictator—and his motives for bailing out Alfa Romeo from their economic problems were complex. First of all, he was committed to reducing unemployment in Italy, to prove to the disapproving outside world that Fascism could solve problems which the democracies seemed to find impossible to cope with. Hitler would do this by building autobahns, weapons and aeroplanes; Mussolini would do the same. But Alfa Romeo had an extra bonus for a Duce hungry for international prestige—at that time the Italians had a stake in international motor racing which the Germans did

not have. If rescuing Alfa Romeo gave the company the opportunity to develop more racing cars which would bring them, and Mussolini's Italy, prestigious victories on the world's race tracks, then the money would be doubly well spent. Finally, there was the rest of the Romeo group: their First World War experience in building aero-engines and trucks would be essential in Italy's ever-expanding armaments programme, and such an asset could not be allowed to wither away for lack of money.

So the Government came to Alfa Romeo's aid. The Istituto Recostruzione Industriale took over the company's funds and poured in extra cash when and where it was needed; the company then had to listen to Government requirements, but otherwise it was free to carry on under its own management. From Jano's viewpoint, the biggest difference—apart from the fact that his own future was now secure—was that building racing cars now had a much higher priority than before. No longer was the racing programme a mere luxury, a sales aid which was to be stopped and started according to the sales figures for production cars. On the contrary, production designs could take something of a back seat—now their job was to keep the company's name in the public eye and, if possible, to repay some of the Government's cost in rescuing the company. But production and sales totals were no longer the matters of commercial life or death they had become for so many during the early thirties.

But this rescue had come just in time, on the racing front as well as the commercial. So bad had things become that the glorious promise of the P3s had been nipped in the bud at the end of the 1932 season. On orders from the management, they had been wheeled away into storage, and the Scuderia Ferrari, Enzo Ferrari's highly professional team which master-minded Alfa's works racing efforts, was forced to drop back on using Monzas and 2300s instead, at a time when the opposition was becoming more and more formidable.

Fortunately, this embargo on the use of the P3s did not last. Mussolini wanted all the prestige he could get in return for propping up the company, and having the Alfa name represented by older and slower cars was not the right way to go about it. So in July 1933, after the rescue operation was complete, the doors were unlocked and the cars brought back into competition. Sadly though, it seemed almost too late to recapture all the hopes which had been running so high at the end of the previous year. The rest of the season was marked

Left
Only on the very eve of war did anything like serious production recommence—with these different versions of the 2500 models

chiefly by wins for the P3s at the Coppa Acerbo, Comminges and Marseilles, but marred by a tragic accident at Monza which cost the lives of Campari and Borzacchini. The other tragedy, from the team's viewpoint, was the way that many of the events where the P3 could have shone to best effect had been missed because of their temporary absence from the tracks.

This was far from the end of the P3's career: but it was the end of the easy victories. From this point onwards, every win would have to be fought for against increasing opposition, especially from teams owing their backing to Europe's other great dictator, Adolf Hitler. Taking a leaf from Mussolini's book, he would spend vast sums of his own country's money on buying Grand Prix domination for Germany. It would take a long time, but in the end he would get his way. Auto Union and Mercedes-Benz would between them take Grand Prix racing to a pitch of performance and power and technical development it had never thought possible, and their mastery would be almost total. From 1933 onwards, Alfa's racing future looked bleak indeed.

In the interval, before the German challenge reached full maturity, the P3s would still do well. Even when the German invasion had taken place, there would be occasions when the car's toughness and agility, matched by its driver's indomitable courage and unbelievable skill, would overturn all the odds, as was the case with Nuvolari's magnificent win in the 1935 German Grand Prix. Even though his P3 had the largest engine developed for the car, with the bores widened to 78 mm to increase the capacity to 3822 cc and lift the power to 330 bhp, Nuvolari was still catching, and passing, superbly engineered cars with 100 bhp *more* power on tap!

That was a magnificent victory by any standards, a worthy crown to a career which had included wins in the Targa Florio and most of the major Grand Prix races. But by this time the P3 was already obsolete. With the technically very advanced German cars showing the advantages of new multi-cylinder engine designs, it was time for Jano to depart from the classic in-line, double overhead-cam engine, and catch up with an entirely new design.

So the P3 was followed into the Grand Prix arena by more sophisticated but less attractive and ultimately less successful Grand Prix Alfas. The Tipo C was a lower, rounder, more streamlined car with all-independent suspension. At first, the car used the 3.8-litre version of the P3's ultimate engine, but this was only a stopgap until the car's own 4-litre V12 was ready. This finally appeared in the 1936 season, delivering 370 bhp at peak; but by that time the German cars had moved on yet again, and the car's most spectacular victory was to be on the other side of the Atlantic, where Nuvolari used it to win the Vanderbilt Cup at the Roosevelt Field track in New York on 12 October 1936.

Yet in a sense this V12 engine still owed a great deal to the classic Alfa engine configuration. In essentials, it was made up of two 2-litre straight sixes coupled together in a sixty-degree Vee, and each of those straight-sixes had twin overhead camshafts, inclined valves, hemispherical combustion chambers and domed pistons. Because the cylinder bores were smaller, the valves were slightly smaller than on the latest versions of the P3 engine, but the angle at which the valves were set and the gear drive for the camshafts were the same as before, except that with the shorter engine the camshafts were now driven from the back of the block and not from the centre.

On the production front things were changing too. Racing cars might have to be rare birds, carefully and expensively assembled from the very best materials; this the Government financiers seemed happy enough to underwrite, for the sake of Italy's sporting reputation. But they clearly saw no need for production cars to aim at the same lofty ideals, and the biggest change to come from the new arrangement was a shift to higher output and lower costs per car.

Jano was set to work on designing an entirely new Alfa Romeo. Quality was still a high priority, but so was a reasonable selling price—and now the car would have to be engineered down to this price target, rather than simply built up from the best possible materials with the price being worked out almost as an afterthought. Commonplace now, this kind of thinking was still a major change for many companies in the thirties, who had gone on specializing in cars for the quality market, when other companies such as Ford, Austin or Morris had made fortunes going for real mass consumption.

Yet, even here, one thing was clearly not going to change, and that was the Alfa philosophy on engine design. Straight-eights were out, as being too big, too expensive and too complicated for this new generation of cars: what was specified instead was a six-cylinder engine which could provide the performance of the old straight-eight 2300, since clearly the most likely buyers, even for the newer cars, would be keen on all the Alfa virtues of power and speed.

So Jano produced a hybrid. The last development of the old 1500–1750 series had been the 1900, which had had its bores widened by another 3 mm to 68 mm, which raised the capacity to 1917 cc and produced 68 bhp in Gran Turismo form. With a top speed of 80 mph carrying a close-coupled Alfa saloon body, the car had a top speed of 80 mph, and was reasonably successful; 197 were sold during the crisis year of 1933. One feature of this car had been an improved light-alloy cylinder head, and this was adapted to serve as part of the new six-cylinder.

The dimensions were changed, however: the bore was widened another 2 mm to a round 70 mm, and the stroke lengthened to the 100 mm of the P3. This took the capacity up to 2309 cc, but so lightly was the engine stressed that in its basic Turismo form it developed the same power as the 1900 GT—68 bhp—although there was more torque to improve flexibility. Other changes included a cast-iron cylinder block and a camshaft drive of chain and helical gears, mounted for the first time at the front of the engine rather than at the back.

The chassis of the car was changed too: gone were the traditional channel-section girders to be replaced by welded steel box-sections. Even so, when fitted with a spacious six-seater body, the weight was more than 400 lb over the figure for the 1900, and the top speed dropped to 75 mph. What was more important was that the price came down too: the 6C 2300 Turismo cost just three-quarters the price of the 1900 GT, and less than half the price of the old 2300 models.

It was therefore hardly surprising that the new car was a big sales success. Introduced in 1934, the sales total for the remainder of that year was 199, or more than the previous 2300 model had sold in its four-year career. So popular was it that Alfa Romeo was once again persuaded to begin the traditional performance progression. Introduced during the same year was the Gran Turismo option, with a shorter wheelbase chassis, lighter bodywork

War conditions demanded new designs: like this down-to-earth Coloniale version of the 2500, produced from 1939 to 1942

(usually close-coupled sports saloon styles), higher compression, 76 bhp and a top speed of almost 80 mph—and once again this sold even more briskly, with 453 being turned out during that first year of production.

They even had their part to play in the sporting programme. Three tuned 6C 2300 GT cars with special slab-sided high-waisted bodies designed by Carrozzeria Touring were entered in the 24-hour Targa Abruzzo sports car race at Pescara on 13 August 1934. Matched against faster machinery, including some of the straight-eight 2300 Alfas, the reliability of the new cars proved decisive, and they ran as regularly as clockwork to finish first, second and third overall.

As Italy's colonial empire vanished, a few cars of the old 2500 series were turned out from the works—whenever aero-engine production and air raids allowed. This saloon/coupé has bodywork by Castagna

This was the kind of result to make any sporting production car sell well, and just to make the point doubly sure among the buying public, the Touring-bodied GT version of the 6C 2300 was thereupon named the Pescara in honour of that crushing victory. With still higher compression (7.75 to 1), power (95 bhp) and top speed (90 mph), they proved very popular, priced as they were well below the old 1900 GTs; forty were sold in the remainder of 1934 alone.

Sales on this scale made more improvements possible, and little by little the simple quality of the old vintage six- and eight-cylinder Alfas gave way to more complicated and sophisticated designs. The 2300 six boasted details like a movable idler wheel on the camshaft timing chain to allow fine adjustment of the chain tension, and hollow camshafts to help in channelling lubricating oil to the top of the engine. Now similar changes were being made to the rest of the car: the revised B series of the 2300 range, introduced in 1935, had slightly longer chassis frames and completely new suspension arrangements. Gone at last were the semi-elliptic springs, replaced by a suspension set-up derived from the latest of the Grand Prix cars. The front wheels were hung on coil springs, aided by hydraulic dampers, while the rear wheels were also independently suspended. On the racing cars the rear wheels were carried on swing-axles, with the springing provided by a transverse leaf spring—on the production cars the differential was mounted on the chassis and the wheels carried on swing-axles in the same way, but the springing was provided by torsion bars instead, with adjustable hydraulic shock-absorbers to vary the softness of the ride. The four-wheel drum brakes were now operated by hydraulics instead of the manual linkages of the A-series 2300s, and the body-styles of the new cars were much sleeker, more rounded and altogether much more modern-looking than their immediate predecessors. Though the weight of the new cars was increased, the top speed of each version was unchanged, and although the prices for the second series cars were around ten per cent higher than the 2300 A equivalents, they seemed certain to sell well.

And so they might well have done, had not outside events conspired to change Alfa's role yet again. Sixty-six of the earlier cars had been sold in the first part of 1935—but in the rest of the year only nineteen of the B-series cars were to follow them, while 1936 would see only ten cars of all models leaving the factory! The reason was that on 3 October 1935, Il Duce had taken a much bigger step on his chosen route to establish Italy as a front-rank Great Power: he started a campaign for a new Italian Empire in Africa with the invasion of Ethiopia. This meant putting Italian industry on to a war footing—particularly those parts of it wholly or partially under Government control.

In Alfa's case, the Government's requirements were simple: aero-engines and yet more aero-engines, to power the new generations of fighters and bombers which would spearhead Italy's armed forces. Soon nearly every corner of the Portello factory was given over to aero-engine production, and production of cars to sell to the public died away almost overnight. What space *was* left for car production would be used for strictly sporting and super-prestige designs—a complete reversal of the earlier shift of policy which produced the 6C 2300.

So, paradoxically, Jano was briefed to produce a newer, bigger, more powerful sports car purely for competition use rather than for series production. At the time, he had been working on a new, smaller model which was virtually an updated version of the 1500 of eight years before. Using the same stroke as its predecessor, but with wider 75 mm bores, this new 1500 achieved a similar capacity with four cylinders rather than six, and in its production form it had a similar single overhead camshaft wedge-shaped combustion chamber layout, using a single row of inclined valves. The car was slightly shorter and narrower, with a lighter body, so that the 50 bhp produced by the engine was capable of pushing it to a top speed of 68 mph. There was even a sporting version of the engine with the usual twin overhead camshafts and hemispherical combustion chambers on the stocks—a precursor for all the postwar Alfas to be described later—but both production and sports car were to be casualties of the vast rearmament programme.

Instead, Jano was set to work on a much bigger and more glamorous piece of engineering. This combined the chassis of the all-independent-suspension Grand Prix car, the 8C 35, with the P3 engine and a streamlined two-seater body to produce a sports car called the 8C 2900A. This was the largest and sleekest Alfa sports car yet, and fitted with the 2905 cc, 68 mm by 100 mm, 220 bhp version of the P3's straight-eight, it was light enough and streamlined enough to reach a top speed of 143 mph. But only five were made that year, and three of those went to Scuderia Ferrari, to be entered in the 1936 Mille Miglia. And once again it was a case of the works cars finishing first, second and third in a major international race on their very first appearance. Another 2900A won the Belgian 24-hour sports car race at Spa, and the team's hopes of winning Le Mans were only blighted by its cancellation due to strikes.

That same year of 1936 saw the virtual ending of the fighting in Africa, and a very slight easing of the furious pace of armaments production. Car-making began to expand again, very slightly at first, and the 2300 models were revised again in 1937. The Turismo version was renamed the Lungo and fitted with a massive six- or seven-seat saloon body. The

GT version was christened the Corto, and the smaller four-seat bodies and 76 bhp tuned engine allowed a top speed of 80 mph. The Pescara was renamed too: three of the cars were entered in the 1937 Mille Miglia, and two of them succeeded, in appalling weather conditions, in finishing first and second overall, so that the car was to bear the name of this new victory from 1937 onwards.

Even more exciting were some of the specially bodied cars, built on some of the more plentiful chassis turned out by the works as production began to increase again. There were open two-seaters on the Mille Miglia formula. But these were dwarfed by the updated 2900Bs—big, powerful, sleek, road-going versions of the competition cars, still using the 2.9-litre straight-eight now developing 180 bhp. The short-wheelbase Corto version, fitted with imposing two-seater bodies by Touring or Pininfarina, could manage 112 mph in standard tune, and even the Lungo close-coupled coupés could match this in more sober style.

Only thirty of this splendid design were ever made before production stopped in 1938, and as far as the road cars were concerned, they were to herald the close of the brilliant Jano years in the company's history. For in spite of a great deal of hard work, and a lot of originality, the longed-for triumph over the German cars was still eluding Alfa Romeo. In 1937 Jano turned out a new Grand Prix car to carry the V12 engine, now increased in size from the 70 mm by 88 mm 4 litres of 1936 to a 72 mm by 92 mm, 4495 cc unit and fitted with a higher compression head and two superchargers instead of one. With a slightly lighter body built on a lower and wider chassis, but using the same suspension as the earlier car, the new GP contender produced 430 bhp and a top speed of 190 plus.

This was promising, but time was vital—and even the racing cars still had to take second place to aero-engine demands, so that the car's first appearance was delayed until the Coppa Acerbo in August 1937. But the results were disappointing. The car was entered in the Italian GP in September, but Guidotti was forced to drop out of the race with rear axle failure.

For Vittorio Jano, this was the end of the long road which had begun with his move from Turin so many years before. He had insisted on supervising the car's running himself, rather than entrusting it even to the old-established professionalism of Scuderia Ferrari, and now he had to bear the brunt of failure. He was made the scapegoat for the company's continuing inability to beat the German cars, even though many of the decisive factors were

Left
All Alfa's postwar hopes were concentrated on the revamped 2500 they called the Freccia d'Oro—the Golden Arrow, with its careful streamlining and rounded fastback tail

Below
Another view of the Freccia d'Oro shows off to perfection how the Alfa designers were able to update a design almost a decade old

Eventually, demand for the 2500 (and production capacity) expanded to the point where the company was able to introduce more bread-and-butter versions, like this sober Farina-bodied saloon

totally outside his control. Yet the legacy he left his old company was to last them a long time, far longer than anyone could dream at the time.

In those last frantic years before the Second World War, the company carried on with the momentum built up during the Jano years. His successors in the Alfa racing department built two new racing engines—a 3-litre V16 and a 1.5-litre straight-eight—to what was essentially the same design. In each case, each eight-cylinder bank of engines was fed through two rows of valves inclined at 100 degrees to one another and actuated by two gear-driven overhead camshafts. The 3-litre 60 degree V16 was fitted into a revised version of the car which had been Jano's downfall, for the 1938 3-litre Grand Prix formula; entered for the Tripoli GP it put up fastest lap in practice, but did not enter in the race. Two cars took part in the Italian GP in September 1938 and finished second and fourth, and that was the best the new car was able to achieve before the outbreak of war.

The 1.5-litre voiturettes did much better, in a class of racing where Italian cars did at least stand a reasonable chance of winning. Officially the Tipo 158, the little cars were known almost universally as the Alfettas, and they provided a powerful consolation to the deepening Italian

gloom over the procession of German cars which were invariably the first across the finishing line in the major Grand Prix events. With 195 bhp available to provide a top speed of 143 mph, the carefully streamlined, all-independent-suspension 'little Alfas' were to provide powerful opposition to the Maseratis and ERAs which contested the increasingly exciting field of voiturette racing. Their greatest role of all, however, lay ten years and a world war in the future, when they would play their powerful part in establishing a total Alfa domination over Grand Prix racing far more complete than the company had ever enjoyed before.

For the time being though, it seemed to Alfa Romeo's many fans that the good days were truly over. Even on the production front, it seemed that Jano's successors were content to build on the foundations he had provided. The well-proven 2300 series was still soldiering on in 1939, but it was increasingly obvious that the engines were having a harder time pulling the increasingly heavy bodies along with any pretence of performance.

So the engines were bored out to 72 mm, which raised the capacity to 2443 cc, and provided an extra reserve of badly needed power. The largest variant, the six-seater Turismo saloon which weighed a ton and a half, could still manage 84 mph, and at the opposite extreme the short-wheelbase Sport version could top 95 mph. In between came a bewildering variety of bodies and styles, including saloons and sports saloons, coupés and cabriolets, each one produced in tens rather than hundreds. They were the last of the pre-war Alfa Romeos—smooth, sleek, sophisticated, fast, high-quality cars which symbolized the virtues which designers like Jano had always striven to provide. Yet in the view of his successor, Bruno Trevisan, the 2500 version was simply an interim model to tide the company over while he worked on something much more promising altogether.

This was to be an advanced road car called the S10, powered by a detuned version of the old sixty-degree V12 racing engine linered down to 3560 cc, providing 140 bhp in single-cam form. Top speed was to be just over 100 mph, and two prototypes were built—together with two of the usual Alfa twin-cam versions of the engine for use in competition versions of the car. Another prototype was the S11, with a new 2260 cc ninety-degree V8 engine delivering 94 bhp. Fitted into a sleek, aerodynamic, monocoque body, this too provided a 100 mph top speed, and once again a four-cam, hemispherical-head version of the V8 was built for racing use.

Nor was this all. There was the Tipo 162, a new front-engined Grand Prix car with a 3-litre 135-degree V16 with a common crankshaft (unlike the 316 engine, which had two separate geared crankshafts, one for each bank of cylinders) delivering 490 bhp—once again using the traditional layout. There was the Tipo 163, a closed coupé with an unblown Tipo 162 engine mounted behind the driver in the now common mid-engine position. And there was the Tipo 512, a rear-engined Grand Prix car which was actually built and tested—this used a blown flat-12 four-cam engine of 1.5 litres delivering 335 bhp, fitted into a tubular frame with all-independent suspension.

Had history happened differently, all this brilliant promise might have totally transformed Alfa's hopes on the track as well as in the market-place. But all were fated to take their place as might-have-beens in the story, as all the normal priorities of commerce and competition were elbowed aside by a much larger drama. Even as the last events of the 1939 season were being run, Europe was sliding into war—and before the 1940 season was finished, Italy

Most obvious difference between pre-war and postwar 2500 saloons and coupés was the much narrower radiator grille fitted on the postwar models

too would be drawn into the conflict. All the plans were torn up, or filed away for the duration—and, just as twenty-five years before, it was clear that peace would bring a totally different world.

Even if the future *was* totally obscured behind the gathering clouds of war, that in itself was a blessing in disguise—for the trials and problems suffered by the fledgling Alfa company in the First World War were to be trivial when compared with the catastrophes of the second. Bombing, blockade, defeat and destruction would all but put an end to the story once and for all. All the hopes for new designs would come to nothing, for the only hope of continuing production once the bullets had ceased to fly would be with the tried and trusted models from the past. Survival in the harsher postwar world would depend, far more than in 1918, on tearing up all the ideas planned for their successors, and starting again with a blank sheet of paper. Exactly what was drawn on that sheet of paper, and how it was developed over thirty years of ever fiercer competition, we shall cover in the rest of this book.

Chapter 1
PICKING UP
THE PIECES

The man behind most of Alfa's postwar models: Dr Orazio Satta Puliga, one-time Professor of Engineering at the Turin Polytechnic, who master-minded every Alfa model from the Alfetta Grand Prix car in its Tipo 159 version of the 1950s to the Alfetta production models of the 1970s

For Italy, the war went from bad to worse. A series of expensive military adventures had resulted in Italian forces having to be humiliatingly rescued by their German allies, and Mussolini had come to be more and more subservient to Hitler in the Axis alliance. By 1943, it was all too clear that any hopes the country may have had for glory, conquest or even a better future were as dead as the increasing casualties, and plans were afoot to depose the Duce and try to save something from the wreck.

The Alfa Romeo works had come in for their own share of damage, when RAF bombers had pounded Portello with tons of high explosive on the night of February 14 1943. In July Mussolini was deposed, and Italy began to sue for peace, but while negotiations stumbled onwards, the fighting continued. Back came the RAF on 13 August, when Milan's anti-aircraft defences had been sent south to defend the Italian mainland against raids from recently captured Sicily. This time the destruction was far worse: so badly were the workshops hit, and so obvious was it that the same raiders could return again and again as often as they wished with nothing to stop them, that it was decided to send the design staff away for their own safety.

The move, when it came, was short enough: a trip of only fifty miles to the north-west of the city, to the village of Melzo on the shores of Lake Orta, the westernmost of the great Italian lakes. It was the first move since the company had been founded, but it achieved its purpose. Safe from the threat of the bombing, they were able at last to think and plan for the future—provided anyone in Italy had a future after the war was over.

From the design point of view, the uncertain future was a real problem. Cars and customers had changed very dramatically after the First World War—would not this also be true of its successor? The return of peace might bring with it hitherto undreamed-of mass markets. Or perhaps, after the destruction of Europe, it would be many years before anyone could afford a car at all—they might either die out altogether for a time, or revert to the wealthy-buyers-only conditions of the early days.

All the Alfa designers could do was carry on along the lines the company had been following—when it was allowed to produce cars at all, that is—before the war began. The idea of producing slightly simpler, cheaper cars such as the 6C 2300 and its successors had been the right marketing policy at the time—so why not aim at carrying this a stage further? If the guess was wrong, and the demand was for small numbers of expensive cars, Alfa had plenty of experience in that field to fall back on.

But if marketing was more or less unchanged, the engineering ideas were already moving on. During the thirties, coachbuilt bodies had become heavier and heavier, despite encouraging experiments like the Weymann fabric bodies which had been fashionable for a time at the beginning of the decade. Steel body panels, like those fitted to the later production Alfas, also carried a heavy weight penalty, and producing adequate performance to match the public's ever-rising needs without providing bigger, heavier, thirstier and more expensive engines was to become more and more difficult.

There was an answer, however, as demonstrated by manufacturers such as Lancia, whose lovely little Aprilia was small, stylish and so light that it offered lively performance from a small engine. This was to combine the chassis and the body into a single integral design: this avoided duplication, since in the old days it was the chassis which provided the strength to hold the car together virtually unaided, while all the body had to do was cover the occupants, so that all its extra weight was wasted. Now, with body and chassis sharing both roles, much of the weight could be pared away without cutting the strength of the finished vehicle below what was needed.

Of course there were problems: designing this kind of body/chassis unit took a great deal longer than drawing up the old ladder-frame of channel girders which had served makers like Alfa so well for so long. But time was just about the only commodity not in short supply at Lake Orta during those late-war years, so the team set to work with a will. As they were going to draw up plans for a car which involved a completely new building method, they were able to borrow for once very little from the past. This was one design which would begin from the legendary blank sheet of paper.

Or almost. Once again the long tradition of engine design which characterized Alfa Romeo more than any other manufacturer—with the possible exception of Bugatti—was harnessed to produce an instant power unit for the car without the necessity to redesign anything. The team turned to the engine which lay most ready for use—the twin overhead camshaft six-cylinder unit used in the 6C 2500, which was still technically in production, as a handful of the last pre-war models still continued to trickle from the works throughout the war years. One change, however, they did make: capitalizing on the weight saving which the new body would bring, they cut the size of the engine from 2.5 litres to a straight 2 litres. By shortening the stroke from 100 mm to 80 mm, they reduced the capacity to 1954 cc—otherwise the figures were almost identical with the pre-war engine. The compression ratio, as before, was set at 7 to 1, and the engine was fed through a single twin-choke vertical carburetter. The inlet valves were fractionally smaller, as befitted the engine's reduced size, and though the engine block was still an iron casting, this time the crankcase as well as the cylinder head was made from light alloy.

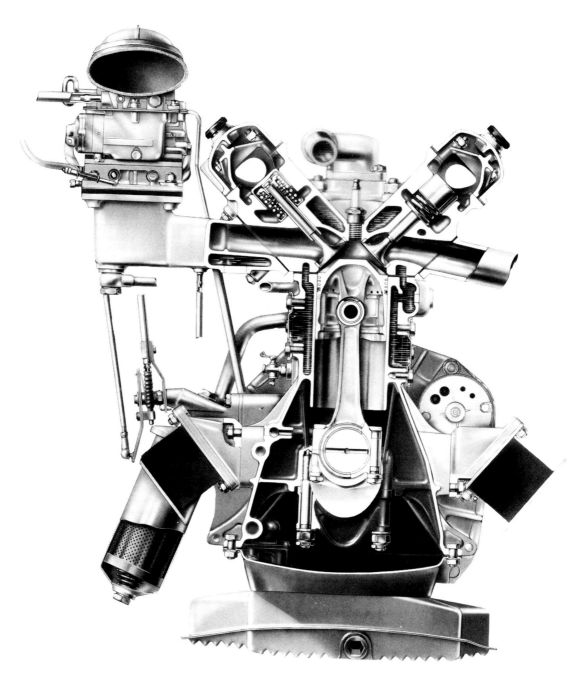

The classic Alfa four-cylinder twin overhead cam engine. This particular version is from the 2000 of the late 1960s–early 1970s, but the design is essentially the same from the 1900 to the Alfetta

But there were important differences in the way in which the engine was used. The modern trend has been for smaller engines, running faster to deliver more and more power for a given capacity than was possible with the long-stroke units of the past. And the fact that the Alfa engineers had chosen to reduce the capacity of the 2500 units by shortening the stroke was crucial: because the piston had a shorter distance to move on each cycle then, for a given engine speed, the maximum piston speed was lower. Or, to put it another way, for a given limiting piston speed, the engine could be made to run faster

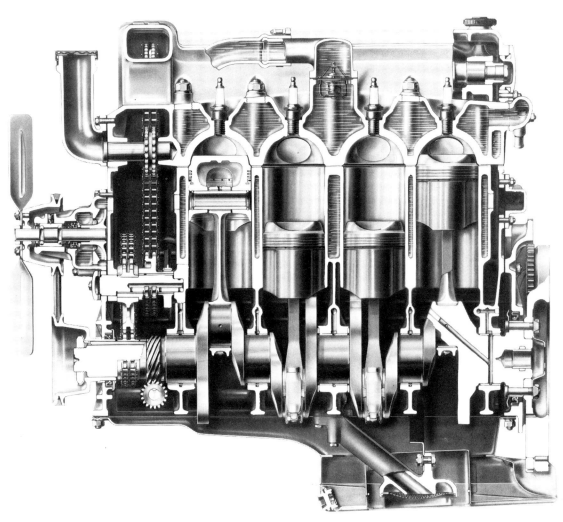

because of its shorter stroke. This made a vital increase in power possible—although the engine was only four-fifths the size of the 6C 2500 unit, the peak power was only 2 bhp less at 85 bhp, though significantly this figure was delivered at 5500 rpm, rather than the 4600 rpm of the pre-war car.

But if the engine shared its origins with the earlier cars, the body/chassis unit was a complete break with tradition. Instead of the welded longeron-and-cross-member chassis of the 2300 and 2500 series, the new car was built up on a flat floorpan, which was stiffened by a single cross-member joining the transmission tunnel and door-sill boxes, and further braced by two diagonally arranged boxes in a cruciform arrangement. This, then, formed the bottom face of a body box, reinforced by two more box-sections, one built up around the scuttle and dashboard at the front end, the other around the rear-mounted fuel tank.

Even the body shape was new: during the run of the 2300 and 2500 models, body shapes had become progressively more rounded and streamlined, but the new car took several steps forward in this

Chain-driven camshafts, hemispherical combustion chambers, five main bearings, wet cylinder liners: the classic Alfa prescription

direction. The outer skin was shaped in a gently sloping fastback style years ahead of its time, while the other benefit of the short-stroke engine was that it allowed a lower bonnet line, even with the air cleaner and carburetter air intake mounted on top of the camboxes. The bonnet line was also rounded at the front, with headlamps recessed into the panelling, and covers over the front and rear wheel-arches.

Though compact—eight inches narrower in track and more than eighteen inches shorter in wheelbase than the 2500 Turismo—the new design could accommodate five people: three on the wide front bench seat, two in the shaped but narrower rear seats. Suspension was independent front and rear, using transverse torsion bars, and one unusual feature was the placing of the gearbox between the rear wheels to help produce a more even distribution of weight between the front and rear wheels.

Just how much weight this type of construction saved was shown by the fact that the Gazzella, as the new car was to be named, provided almost the same interior space as the pre-war 2500, but the total weight of the car ready for the road was more than 1300 lb less! With virtually identical engine power, this meant the 80 mph top speed of the 2500 Turismo was increased by 19 mph. With a 2-litre engine providing a top speed just a whisker under the magic 100 mph figure, the Gazzella was aptly named indeed.

Working out the design details and assembling the first prototype helped pass the months of enforced exile for the Alfa engineers, while farther south the war blazed away as fiercely as ever. The car was finished and made ready for testing as soon as conditions allowed, while parts were assembled for another five development cars. All seemed set for another brilliant step forward in the Alfa story.

Sadly, it was not to be. As the fighting moved nearer, the area around Milan came under heavy air attack, as bombers and fighter-bombers hammered German communications. Even though the Wehrmacht forces in Italy surrendered to the Allies on 29 April 1945 with the city still firmly in their hands, the whole area had been stripped of its anti-aircraft defences the year before, and the results of the prolonged bombardment were soon all too obvious to the exiles who were making their different ways back to Portello.

As a major producer of aero-engines, the Alfa Romeo works had qualified as a high-priority target. Tons of high explosive had obliterated more than sixty per cent of the factory area, destroying machinery halls and workshops, spare parts and records. And it was in these piles of ruins that the fate of the brave new Gazzella was sealed—for while the men who created the new car had been sent away to safety, the heavy plant and machinery had had to stay right there in the firing line.

Most of the irreplaceable machines had been shattered: it would be a miracle if anything at all could be produced in the factory for a long, long time. The only possibility with a ghost of a chance of being made reality was to return to a familiar design, using existing parts with a minimum of complex fabricated assemblies. Starting a new car

The original rear suspension set-up for the 1900 used a Panhard rod for location, but was rejected as the system was not precise enough in its behaviour

Below left
The improved design used a wide, triangular-shaped arm, securely fixed to the top of the differential casing, to prevent unwanted sideways movement of the axle

project was out of the question, and starting something which was not only new but as unorthodox a trailblazer as the Gazzella, was far beyond the remotest hopes of anyone in the company—for the other requirements for its weight-saving body construction were specially set-up machine tools and solid financial backing for the expensive and time-consuming business of putting the design into production.

In some ways, the problems facing Alfa Romeo were similar to those which had faced the company in 1918. Then, as now, starting new projects had had to take second place to setting up production with well-tried old designs—designs like the 6C 2500, which had continued to emerge from the factory amid all the destruction and the furious demands of the wartime aero-engine programme. In 1943 there had been time enough, and men enough, to turn out ninety-one cars, nearly half of them Sport and Super Sport variants. Even in

1944, with all the upheaval, the heavy bombing raids and the uncertainty caused by the German occupation and the Allied advance, a total of eighteen Sport models had been finished—and even more miraculously, 1945 saw a trio of 6C 2500 Sports wheeled out of the half-ruined plant into a world which would seem to have left them behind for other, grimmer vehicles altogether.

On the other hand, the end of the second war brought a problem which had not existed in 1918: the physical destruction of the factory. So, as the Alfa workers began to reassemble at Portello after the fighting had stopped, the first priority was very clear indeed. Rebuilding the bomb-blasted workshops and mending or replacing the ruined machinery would occupy the entire work force for a long

time, but running as a close second was the need to get *something* into production as quickly as humanly possible. Human memory is fickle, and once the people of Europe recovered from the shock condition brought on by the war, they would need more cars more quickly than ever before. The lion's share in this new market would go to those companies who were the first to turn away from wartime weapons-production, and from the effects of some of those weapons; and turning out even pre-war models in a postwar setting would count for far more than any amount of pre-war reputation. The sporting glories of the thirties were already part of another world, on the far side of the abyss of six years of war.

Other questions—like future policy, future designs, future

Aerial shot of the old Alfa works at Portello, in industrial Milan. Originally founded on the edge of the city in open country, by the 1950s it was squeezed in between surrounding properties

marketing ideas, future competition programmes—were for the time being mere luxuries, and had to take second place to the necessity for commercial survival. So when the time came in 1946 for some of the work force to be turned from repairing walls and tinkering with broken machines to making cars, it was the trusty 6C 2500 series that came back to life. In that first year of postwar production, the figures were bound to be low—but with eighty Turismo saloons, sixty-eight Sport models and even fourteen of the two-seat coupé/convertible 100 mph-plus Super Sport as a reminder of past glories and a tonic for the future, the results were enough to be proud of.

Already, lessons were emerging for the future. Alfa's 2500 range divided into two very different sections: the large, relatively heavy, luxurious Turismo limousines, and the altogether sleeker and more exciting sports models. All were too big and too expensive to play a real part in the postwar market, but for the time being they would have to do—except that the customers were showing a very clear preference for the sports cars. So the pattern of production began to change, to reflect this choice: in 1947 only five Turismos would be made, but the number of sports models would shoot up to a distinctly encouraging 276.

Yet in a way the comparison is not quite a fair one. For all their virtues, the 1946 cars were very definitely pre-war models—apart from trifling alterations like the shifting of the gear-lever from the floor to the steering column as had been specified for the Gazzella, and the uprating of the rear shock-absorbers, these were identical to the models turned out in 1939. It was time for the next step: still too early to think of a completely new replacement for the 2500 better suited to the postwar market, but definitely time to switch to an updated postwar version of the company's mainstay in these difficult years.

So 1947 saw the emergence of an additional version of the 6C 2500 range, born almost a decade after the original design was first completed. This new car had a slightly detuned version of the pre-war Sport engine, with compression reduced to 7 to 1 (from 7.5 to 1) and the power peak dropped from 95 bhp at 4600 rpm to 90 bhp. This was a wise move in a Europe where petrol was still largely rationed, expensive and often of dubious quality, while the skilled attention needed to keep a highly tuned engine in peak condition was both rarer and more expensive than had been the case before the war.

But the bodywork was changed more dramatically. The chassis was essentially the same as that of the pre-war Sport, built up of a ladder-frame of welded box-sections, but this time a more modern close-coupled coupé body was welded to the chassis. With a long bonnet and long, sloping wings, two doors and small rear quarter-lights set into a sharply rounded-off tail, it looked sporty and well streamlined. Yet it was still a big car: so big that Alfa claimed it could carry not two passengers, nor two passengers and two children, but *five* full-size passengers. Three were catered for by an admittedly wide front bench seat and the now obligatory steering-column gear-change, and two were tucked away almost out of sight at the back.

In fact the new version of the Sport was heavier than its coachbuilt pre-war counterpart, by as much as 370 lb. So it was surprising, in view of the drop in engine power, that the top speed was identical at 97 mph; much of the credit for this must go to the very much more efficient streamlining of the postwar version. But the important point was that it looked different from its predecessor. In its lines and appearance, if not in its engineering, it was a 1947 model and not a 1939 one, and the Alfa management decided to make the distinction more obvious by giving it a new name to distinguish it from the rest of the 2500 range: it was called the 'Freccia d'Oro', or Golden Arrow, and it was a success from its first appearance. Not only did the customers queue up in their hundreds, but the independent body-builders begged for a chance to show their inventiveness on such a promising base. Unfinished chassis were made available to Touring, who turned out a neat and more compact still two-seater coupé, while Pininfarina, Boneschi and others turned out elegant (and sometimes less than elegant) cabriolet versions of the car.

The Freccia d'Oro was a shot in the arm for Alfa's production hopes—680 of these cars were sold, making it the single most popular model in the series, though updated versions of the Turismo 2500 and the Super Sport soldiered on alongside it into the 1950s. But in terms of Alfa's long-term postwar policy, it could never be more than a stopgap and a digression, a fortunate accident to tide the company over until the first real postwar Alfas were ready. Yet without it the new models might never have seen the light of day—as things were, they were only to make their first appearance five years after the war was over, and a full three years after the birth of the Freccia d'Oro.

There were good reasons for this, however. Alfa Romeo was a company which was still looking for its postwar role, and there were many who thought the best policy would be to carry on where developments had been brought to an abrupt stop in 1940. There were encouraging signs: as early as 1946, an embryo competition programme had begun with a new racing version of the 2500. Unlike the pre-war racing versions of this model, the new car did not use the standard production chassis, but a narrower and shorter version of it, fitted with a more compact version of the Freccia d'Oro body, which scaled just over half of the original's weight. With a tuned engine of 9.2 to 1 compression, fitted with larger valves, sharper cam profiles and three twin-choke carburetters, producing 145 bhp, the car was capable of 125 mph and achieved some encouraging results in the hands of works drivers and outside customers alike, including a third place overall in the 1948 Mille Miglia driven by Fangio and Zanardi, third in the 1949 Mille Miglia with Franco Rol, and second in the 1949 Targa Florio—then still in its early postwar round-the-island form.

But there was one good reason why things could never be the same for Alfa Romeo: the huge expansion of the aero-engine side of the company's activities, following the Government rescue in the early thirties, had been responsible for a vast increase in factory space, in machinery and in the number of workers employed at the plant. In

First of the truly postwar Alfas—the sober, yet neat and pleasing lines of the monocoque 1900 saloon

the crippling aftermath of the war, unemployment in Italy reached epidemic proportions. Apart from local pockets where successful businesses attracted droves of hopeful job-seekers, the economy was stagnant, and depression and discontent were ever-present facts of life for most of the population. So clearly, as a Government-backed, if not a Government-run, organization, Alfa Romeo had to take on a major role in providing work for as many Italian citizens as possible.

Even providing enough work for its own workers was a big problem. Before and during the war, more than ninety per cent of Alfa's work was in aero-engine production. Cars were little more than a public-relations gesture, representing only two per cent of the company's output. But under the terms of the peace treaty which ended the war for Italy, aero-engine production had to stop—in any case, no one in the postwar world would need engines for military aircraft on the scale of wartime production.

Seen in this context, the revival of the 6C 2500 was irrelevant. Turning out a few hundred cars a year by old-fashioned methods might occupy around 3000 people: but Alfa's own workforce numbered 15,000, and there was no way on earth that production of the car could ever be expanded enough to keep them all occupied, for there would never be sufficient potential customers for the finished cars.

But the 2500 could be used as a stepping-stone to something better: a car which, because it was designed and priced to appeal to a wider market, *could* be produced in much larger numbers and still go on selling, and one which would also make use of the most modern engineering and production methods to far outsell the increasingly big, expensive and luxurious models the company had turned out before (and after) the war. But there was no sense in Alfa Romeo descending all the way into the mass-production arena to compete with giants like Fiat and Ford with incomparably greater experience at this kind of car-making. What was needed was a compromise: a new kind of Alfa Romeo with enough of the traditional virtues for enthusiasts to identify with, and yet priced at a level which would attract buyers who before that time would have been unable to afford one of the Portello cars.

Compromises are always difficult: try to satisfy two different sets of requirements, and nine times or more out of ten you end up satisfying neither. So the new car would have to succeed in both areas: in the quality of its design and manufacture to satisfy the old guard of Alfa customers, and in the competitiveness of its price to win over the new buyers needed to increase the sales. There was nothing else for it: now the methods and the ideas which had been used for the interesting but ill-fated Gazzella would be needed again. A proper assembly line, turning out a light, modern design with up-to-date engineering and fiercely pruned costs, would be the minimum requirement. It was the key to survival—but at the time when the work began, the thoughts of the time and the expense, the new ideas and the carefully explored details which would be needed to bring it to fruition made it a daunting assignment indeed.

Fortunately, for the third time in the company's history, the right man for the job emerged at the time he was most needed. Since Vittorio Jano had left Alfa to go and work for Lancia, several hands had taken their turns at the helm of the design department. In 1937 Jano's assistant, Gioacchino Colombo, had taken over responsibility for the racing cars, and production car work had been looked after by Bruno Trevisan, a one-time air force officer and aero-engine designer for Fiat. He had been joined by a Spanish engineer named Wilfredo Ricart, who had taken over the design department in April 1940—but Ricart's contract had expired within a month of the end of the war, his last project for Alfa Romeo being the ill-fated Gazzella.

Ricart's successor was another aeronautical engineer, a lean, ascetic-looking young man called Orazio Satta Puliga. Satta had graduated in mechanical engineering from the Turin Polytechnic at twenty-three, and had later been assistant head of the Polytechnic's Aeronautics Laboratories. In 1938, at the age of twenty-seven, he had joined Alfa Romeo's design and experimental department, and following Ricart's departure he had been appointed manager of both departments. He had led the team which had produced the Freccia d'Oro, and he had worked on its competition version—and now, at the age of thirty-eight, he was about to tackle his greatest professional challenge yet.

Satta's first step was to design a new engine: or rather, since this was Alfa Romeo and a *new* engine was against all tradition, he was to update Jano's classic twin-cam layout to more modern standards. Some aspects of Jano's design were eternal engineering truths, which time could not alter—the basic efficiency of hemispherical combustion chambers was governed by the physics of combustion, and there was no point in changing them. In the same way, using the twin overhead camshafts was the logical method to actuate the twin rows of inclined valves which this shape of combustion chamber made necessary.

But if some aspects of the design were unchanging, others had been left behind by progress. Competition for increased performance among buyers had forced designers of the most ordinary and humble production cars to look at the ideas and techniques that had been used decades before in Grand Prix machinery. And just as the racing car designers had begun to turn from the big, lazy, slow-revving monsters of Edwardian days to the smaller, faster, more efficient designs of the 1920s, so the same thing was now continuing on a smaller scale in the production car world. Not that Jano's engines had anything Edwardian about them: but by the standards of the 1940s, they and their immediate successors were being left behind in the quest for power.

The limiting factor in increasing the speed which an engine could sustain without flying apart was the acceleration and deceleration which the pistons had to undergo at the beginning and end of each stroke, and *this* was governed by the maximum speed which the piston reached in the middle of its stroke. For a given engine speed, each piston would have a fixed time to complete its stroke— therefore, the longer the stroke, the greater the piston speed for a given engine speed and the greater the stresses. If an engine had to have a particular capacity to provide the power needed, then widening the cylinder bores and shortening the stroke would have the effect of allowing the engine to run faster without increasing stresses, and therefore help it to turn out more power.

There were other advantages to running engines at higher speeds. In the old days, a six-cylinder engine provided noticeably greater smoothness than a four-cylinder unit of equivalent size. But if the four-cylinder unit ran half as fast again, the number of explosions in a given time would be the same as the six; provided care was taken to balance the loads caused by the rotating masses, and given an engine mounting which gave sufficient insulation to cut the noise and vibration levels, the four-cylinder unit could do just as good a job, with far fewer moving parts.

Of course, this shift to wider bores and shorter strokes created other difficulties. Shortening strokes and reducing the number of cylinders made combustion chambers much larger, at the same time that speeding up the rotation of the engine increased the number of firing cycles per minute. All of this meant a very sharp increase in the charge of fuel–air mixture which had to be got into the combustion chamber in a given time, burned, and then expelled in the form of exhaust gases. So the shape of the combustion chamber became crucial from several points of view; from the breathing of the engine, since this governed the rate at which the gases could be persuaded in and out of the combustion space, from the speed and evenness of the combustion itself, since this affected the power which was extracted from the fuel, and from the point of view of cooling, since the passage of a greater amount of fuel in a given time meant a greater build-up of local heat which had to be got rid of efficiently.

This is how Jano's design (or, for that matter, Merosi's) qualified for another lease of life in a field where change was happening so quickly. Locating the spark plug in the centre of the roof of the hemispherical combustion chamber allowed the flame front to spread outwards and downwards evenly and smoothly, reaching the limits of the combustion space as quickly as possible. This meant that increasing the width of the bores presented less of a problem than might have been the case with less well-shaped combustion spaces. There were other bonuses, too: although the hemispherical shape provided the maximum combustion space for the minimum surface area—thereby extracting the maximum power from each charge of fuel—the wider bores did automatically result in there being room for larger valves to be fitted into the roof of the chamber.

So much for the combustion space itself. But what about the valves—was it still strictly necessary to use the old double-camshaft layout? Could not both rows of valves be driven from a single camshaft, for greater simplicity and fewer moving parts? Alfa engineers thought not; with the experience built up over decades of using twin-cam engines, they were still convinced that a separate camshaft for each bank of valves was the ideal layout. First of all, they said there was no cost saving in using a single camshaft. Secondly, switching to a single cam would be a difficult design problem, since the removal of one camshaft would necessitate more complex actuating arrangements to service two rows of valves. Finally, the use of two camshafts made it much easier for them to study problems of timing, such as the importance of valve overlap for running-on problems.

Another view of the basic 1900 bodyshape emphasizes the almost total lack of embellishments. This is a 1900 TI of 1953

The 1900 body was a remarkably efficient shape: in spite of its sleek lines, it contained a boot that provided space which would have seemed unbelievably generous by the standards of the 1930s. This is a series 2 1900 Berlina

But if there were many similarities between the new engine and the classic pre-war Alfa engines, there were also many detail differences. The cylinder block, for example, was cast iron, as was that of the 2500, but the cylinder bores were set at the rather unusual diameter of 82.55 mm. This rather cumbersome measurement was equivalent to 3.25 inches, and the reason for *that* was the shortage of spare parts and components available on the Italian market in the late 1940s. Home-produced pistons were not available, so the engine was designed around Hepolite pistons from England.

Other changes came from the immense reserves of specialized expertise within the Alfa Romeo organization itself. The workers in the Alfa aero-engine department had built up a wealth of experience in aluminium-alloy castings for components like turbine and supercharger blades. All this skill and know-how could not be allowed to go to waste, so as part of the company's self-help rescue operation, these experts were switched to working on the new production car instead.

The immediate result was that aero-engine methods were used to solve development problems arising in the new car engine. The valves were larger than before, so that they allowed larger amounts of fuel and air to pass on each stroke—but the exhaust valves in particular were exposed to larger amounts of hot gases swirling around them, which raised their temperatures uncomfortably high. So the Alfa engineers used the solution they had evolved for the same problem which had arisen in the development of the aeroplane engines: they cast the valve seats in stellite alloy, while the valves themselves had chrome-plated stems with an inner sodium core for easier cooling. The rings fitted to the Hepolite pistons were also chrome-plated, for greater wear resistance, and finished with an angular bevelled cross-section for tighter sealing at the greater speeds and higher compressions at which the new engine would run.

Nor were the aero-engine experts the only people in the Alfa organization with specialized experience. More relevant in some ways was the know-how which had been built up during the pre-war years by the racing department, and they too had worthwhile ideas to contribute to the design—to take one example, the connecting rods were modified at the bottom end to make maintenance easier. In the 2500 and its predecessors, the bottom end of the connecting rod had been split along a line perpendicular to the axis of the connecting rod, so that the big-end bearings could be fitted, removed and replaced. On the 1900, this split was angled at forty-five degrees to the axis of the rod; this effectively narrowed the rod at its lower end, and enabled mechanics to replace the con-rods through the cylinders. The sump was fabricated out of sheet steel, which was not only simpler than the cast sumps used on the earlier cars, but was also appreciably lighter.

This then was the design which Alfa Romeo would rely on to win them a share in the reviving postwar car market. The engine was shorter and wider than the older designs, with plenty of new ideas in the detail design, but relying still on the old Alfa configuration of double overhead cams and hemispherical combustion chambers as being not only what the customers wanted in terms of a link with the past, but also the best way to satisfy the engineers' demands for efficiency at higher engine speeds.

But there were still differing opinions over more basic questions: all the details of the design would apply equally well to a four- or a six-cylinder unit. Which would have the best chances of success? There was much to be said for following the old tradition and staying with the quality market—Alfa's most likely potential customers would *expect* six-cylinder engines and large, well-appointed cars, even if they were turned out by modern mass-produced methods; or so the theory ran. And Satta's team went to the lengths of building a prototype of a six-cylinder version of the design; with a shorter stroke of 92 mm, this gave a total capacity of 2955 cc.

Parts shortages hampered the development of this version in other ways: carburetters were in short supply, so that all six cylinders had to be fed from a double-choke vertical Weber. With 7.5 to 1 compression, the engine developed 120 bhp at 4800 rpm—this peak-power speed was still only slightly higher than the 4600 rpm of the Freccia d'Oro, but the power output per cc was up by a useful ten per cent on the earlier six-cylinder car.

The 6C 3000, as this version of the engine was called, was fitted into a prototype car—a large, spacious, handsomely streamlined four-door saloon, which was a logical development from the larger Alfa models of the late 1930s. This time the bodywork was built up, like the Gazzella, on an integral chassis of welded box-sections weighing a ton and a half complete. This gave the car a useful top speed of 102 mph, and in many ways it was an extremely promising design. But times had moved on: though it could well have found an enthusiastic following among Alfa's old customers, it could never have been sold in sufficient numbers to keep the expanded work force working. The company ran a series of very careful and detailed market surveys to check the six-cylinder car's prospects, and finally it was decided to shelve the project. Only three prototypes were built—and the reluctant action to drop the project was taken on social, political and marketing grounds rather than any engineering objections.

But if the 3-litre car was not the answer to Alfa's need to move towards the mass-market, then what was? Some way had to be found to use Satta's engine design in a more practical way, but there were still formidable problems to be solved. Mass-market sales meant mass-production methods, but Alfa was still chronically short of up-to-date machine tools, with little prospect of being able to buy more. At the same time the company's reputation had been built up in the quality, specialist car business. Jump too quickly into the lower-priced market and the company could be squashed by bigger and more experienced competitors, in addition to losing loyal customers, who would be sharply alienated by any dropping of the old standards on quality and performance and reliability.

The first question to be decided was the size and configuration of the alternative to the 6C 3000. In view of the fact that faster-running modern four-cylinder units were now almost as smooth and efficient as any six, then a switch to four cylinders made sense. Keeping the 6C 3000's dimensions would produce a 1970 cc four—but Satta went a step further and shortened the stroke to 88 mm, cutting the capacity to 1884 cc. Still with a compression ratio of 7.5 to 1, and now using a single-barrel carburetter, the engine's higher speed capability helped to produce a power peak of 90 bhp at 5200 rpm, an improvement of another seventeen per cent on the power per cc of the six-cylinder version.

In terms of the postwar Italian market this was still a large engine; in a country where cars are taxed on engine capacity to the point where at one time more than sixty per cent of Italian-registered cars had engines of 600 cc or less. So a large, or reasonably large, body was called for, though in this case Satta was determined that the mistakes of the past, where increases in power had been wasted by progressively heavier bodies, would be avoided.

The solution was to go one better than the ambitious Gazzella: the 1900, as the new car was identified, was the first Alfa Romeo to use a monocoque body/chassis. Gone at last was the old ladder-frame of girders—gone was its successor, the combination of welded box-sections which could also carry a separate body. In their place was a neat, compact, unobtrusively styled saloon body which incorporated its own chassis in the form of localized stiffening arches and boxes in its construction. It had four doors, a gently curving profile, a short bonnet and a projecting boot with wings faired closely to the body—a far cry from the much more exciting lines of the older 2500s and the Freccia d'Oro.

This was a big departure in styling as well as in engineering. As the purely functional shape of the old 1750s and 2300s had given way to the more extravagant styling and streamlining of the 2500s and 2900s, Alfas had tended to look more and more imposing. Yet now the company was staking its future on a car which looked more like a 1400 Fiat than anything else—a car which was no longer identified with Alfa from its shape and its style. The inside too was Spartan, compared with the opulence of the pre-war Alfa Romeos. Gone were the wooden dashboard, the deep leather seats, the thick carpeting and all the other trappings of luxury—they cost too much and weighed too much for this much more businesslike new Alfa. Only the badge on the front gave a real clue to its identity. The rest of the message, and the car's appeal to its potential customers, would depend on its performance.

Nothing was left to chance in this department. The integral construction undoubtedly helped: though the design was already a clean and simple one, careful detail work in the wind tunnel pared away at the drag coefficient. The weight was cut quite dramatically, the completed car weighing only a ton—just over two-thirds the weight of the Freccia d'Oro. With the 90 bhp power peak of the 1900 engine, this was enough to provide a top speed of 94 mph, a very creditable performance for an otherwise sober-looking saloon.

Speed alone was not enough, however. Handling, too, was of paramount importance. Pre-war Alfa Romeos had evolved from the old semi-elliptic springs front and rear recipe which had satisfied the suspension requirements until the middle 1930s. The final pre-war cars had had independent suspension on front and rear wheels, using progressively more complicated systems. The 2500, for example, used coil springs at the front, with a set of longitudinal torsion bars at the rear.

The problem with independent suspension systems—particularly those at the rear, where the demands of wheel suspension had to co-exist with a need to transmit the engine's power to the road—is that the better they work the more they cost. On these grounds alone, the independent rear suspension fitted to the 2500 was out, as far as its successor was concerned. Something simpler, cheaper and lighter was needed—but what?

Probably the simplest and cheapest independent rear suspension is the swing-axle system, used by Mercedes-Benz and others—and by Alfa themselves on many of their racing cars. But swing-axle suspension produces problems with handling, caused by the large camber changes as the springs deflect under cornering loads. Racing drivers may be able to cope with these, or even turn them to their advantage under certain circumstances, but swing-axles need taming for ordinary road use—as Mercedes did with their revised-geometry low-pivot system, which kept the camber changes on the positive side of the vertical.

Compared with these problems, it was far simpler to use a rigid rear axle instead of a fully independent system. At least this guaranteed the rear wheels were always parallel to one another, at a constant distance apart and usually vertical. But these advantages were only reliable while the wheels were in contact with the road—if the axle were to tramp, or hop, in reacting to bumps or potholes in the road surface, then grip would be lost, and handling would suffer.

There were two ways in which a solid rear axle could be kept more

The classic twin-cam, making its first appearance in a production car in its four-cylinder form: the clean, uncluttered underbonnet installation in the 1900

firmly in contact with the road. One was to reduce the unsprung weight (the weight of the components in between the springs and the road surface) as far as possible, and the other was to tighten up the geometry of the suspension system, so that the axle was only free to move in a specified and controlled way. In a normal rear axle, most of the weight was concentrated in the differential gearbox, and it was the inertia of this moving mass which contributed to axle hop.

So experiments went ahead to strap down the 1900's rear axle and prevent any bad habits from developing. The rear wheels were to be suspended on the same coil springs (each one containing its own damper) as were the front wheels, but originally the axle was located by trailing arms and a transverse Panhard rod. This did not work— there was still enough compliance in the system for the dreaded axle hop to develop, and the Alfa engineers had to think again. The coil springs and trailing arms were retained, but this time the axle's transverse movement was prevented by strapping the differential to the chassis by means of two rods connecting a special mounting on top of the differential box to the sides of the main reinforcement boxes of the chassis undertray.

This was a good idea from two points of view: not only did it have the desired effect in restricting unwanted axle movement, but it also effectively transferred some of the weight of the differential to the chassis, thereby having the effect of reducing the unsprung weight. The front suspension was much simpler, since there was no complication over having to drive the wheels. The wheels were each located by a pair of double wishbones which kept them firmly upright under load. The result of this combination of independently sprung front wheels with a carefully located solid rear axle was a behaviour pattern on every kind of corner or road surface which held no surprises for the driver.

All these things were adding up to a car which apparently still managed to deliver the goods in the same way as pre-war Alfas had done, but in a vastly different package. There were still terrible problems, mainly from parts shortages; the hydraulically operated drum brakes used Girling components, and the clutch depended on supplies from Borg and Beck. But the car was promising material: the engine was able to run at speeds which would have blown many a pre-war unit apart, and was turning out as much power per litre in a standard production saloon as the original fixed-head *supercharged* works 1750s of 1929. . . .

Everything depended on how the customers reacted. Would they be put off by the car's unassuming appearance, Spartan finish and outwardly pedestrian pedigree? Or would the magic of the name create enough interest for people to discover for themselves the real potential offered by a modern engine in a modern chassis? In some ways it seemed as if Alfa had gone overboard to emphasize a total break with tradition: not only was the gearbox controlled from the fashionable but unsporting steering column lever, but the 1900 was the first Alfa Romeo to be designed around left-hand steering as a standard fitting.

The Italian police have long been good customers for Alfa Romeo. This is a police version of the 1900: its reliability, performance and handling were ideal for police work. Note the split windscreen and sun roof

Originally, the 1900 had been aimed at a production target of fifty cars a day, a hopelessly ambitious figure which would have represented an annual output of more than seventeen times the company's best year ever! But machine tools were still in short supply, and there was no chance yet to set up a proper mass-production line. Manpower, however, was not scarce, so that production began with many of the operations which should have been entrusted to machinery being carried out by hand. Body panels were beaten out by hand, until there was money to buy power presses to do the work. Engines were fitted together by hand, and the extra time which these operations took was partly compensated for by the extra care which was taken on a car which held the company's future—but the result was that at the beginning of the 1900's production career, only three cars a day were to emerge from the Portello factory. . . .

These were anxious days for the management and workers alike. The 1900 was to make its first appearance at the Turin exhibition centre in May 1950, but this would be only a brief appearance by one of the two production prototypes before some of the technical press—its first step on to the international stage proper would be at the Paris Show the following autumn, and the car's initial reception was crucial. On the reaction of the press and the customers would depend all the company's hopes for success. Moving down-market was tactically fraught with problems: would the old Alfa loyalists be won over to the new car by its exhilarating performance—and would it find new friends on the merits of its competitive price? Or would old customers notice only the steering column gearchange and the sparse instrumentation, the metal dashboard and the bench seats, the unassuming body style and the keener price, and conclude sadly that things were not what they were? Despite all the plans and all the hard work, the new car had to earn its keep in terms of public acclaim. What could be the curtain-raiser on a new and more successful chapter in the Alfa story could all too easily be the last act in a drama, an epilogue to the great years of pre-war days. For the moment, all was hanging in the balance.

Chapter 2
VARIATIONS
ON THE THEME

After all the preparation, the 1900's final step into the world outside the factory gates was far from dramatic. Rather the opposite, as Alfa Romeo's white hope did its best to back into the limelight. As the world's motoring writers assembled in the old royal city of Turin for the first of the 1950 season of major motor shows, one or two of them were given invitations for a very select event indeed. Delays and difficulties with lack of machinery may have meant that production versions of the 1900 were not available to grace the company's stand in the show proper—but at least one of the prototypes would be present in spirit. Like an uninvited guest on the night of the ball, it literally turned up at the door on the opening day, when those in the know were given a quick preview.

For all that, it was an encouraging beginning. *Autocar* reported on the 'show sensation which was not exhibited', and went on to point out that the 1900 had 'acceleration, speed and handling qualities fully in keeping with the Alfa tradition', and 'when production begins towards the end of this year, the price should be very interesting'.

Towards the end of the year, when the Paris Show opened its doors, the public had its first chance to vote on the 1900's vices and virtues—and the wildly enthusiastic reaction was all that the development team could have hoped for. Even in London, where the customers couldn't buy the car anyway, they had the chance to show how they liked it: although all the rush and uncertainty had left Alfa Romeo too late to book stand space at Earls Court, a generous gesture by Frazer-Nash allowed the Milan company to use half its stand. The proper production version of the 1900 duly showed up to occupy the space, and the *Autocar* show correspondent noted that 'subtle changes in wing lines, radiator grille and bumpers have greatly improved the appearance of the Alfa Romeo 1900 saloon since the prototype was seen in the spring'.

This was heady stuff indeed. It could be that the 1900 was safely on its way to success at last, but even this kind of acclaim was only a means to an end. Real success depended on all these keen would-be customers being able to exchange cash for real cars as soon as humanly possible, and here progress for the time being was still painfully slow. By the end of that hectic year of 1950 only six cars had been finished, though the rate of production was beginning to climb slowly.

By the end of the following year, another 1220 of the basic saloon model had emerged from the factory, and though the car was still hand-assembled to an extent which would have been impracticable without such a shortage of modern machinery, the demand—and the interest—far outstripped the supply. Even in England, where even the most committed enthusiast could only admire from afar, there was enough involvement for *Autocar* to test one of the cars in its homeland. They found it 'undoubtedly a remarkable car', recording a best top-speed run of 105 mph, a standing-start quarter-mile in 21.1 seconds and a 0–60 mph time of 17.1 seconds. Fuel consumption was high by today's standards at 17 mpg when driven hard, but the average figure of 24.6 mpg was well up with its present-day descendants.

The testers were delighted by the car's high-speed acceleration in top gear, which they had seen equalled only rarely by a saloon car of any size, and they found the twin-cam engine very flexible, pulling away happily enough from only 12 mph in top gear. Likewise, they found it difficult to think of another saloon car with better high-speed handling—in particular they found the steering 'superb', with moderate understeer, very little roll and finger-tip lightness of control. They rated the body as comfortable, not only for four people but for as many as six at a pinch!

In terms of reactions like these, Satta's team had got their answers right—but there were features of the car about which the testers were less happy. In the veiled-criticism style of the times, they pointed out that the mechanical noise level was 'somewhat above the average for a

One of the earliest, and most unexpected, variations on the 1900 theme was the 1900 M, a four-wheel-drive Italian jeep which could take tasks like fording a fast-flowing river in its stride

*The 1900 M used a detuned
version of the twin-cam engine
to drive a central gearbox
which was connected in turn to
front and rear differentials,
driving all four wheels*

car in this price category', and that full throttle acceleration produced a 'considerable' roar from the engine. But the *Autocar* men were least happy—as were many otherwise enthusiastic supporters—with the standard of the car's interior finish. There was no rheostat to dim the instrument lighting at night; there was no lining to the glove box so that objects tended to rattle and vibrate in resonance with the speed of the car or the bumpiness of the road; there was no other room for small objects within the car, apart from a small map pocket beside the driving seat. They called for better lateral location than could be provided by the flat bench seat. But in summing up the car they were generous in its praise: although they pointed out that 'it lacks the appearance of luxury associated with the more glamorous pre-war models, and the simplicity of its finish and equipment may cause casual observers to question its price', they went on to say that 'for those who drive fast and far, and who look beyond the superficial to the engineering essentials, it would be difficult to find a combination of speed, stability and fuel economy anywhere else at the price'.

With reactions like these, the 1900 was well on its way to success. And once the model was safely off the floor, in terms of orders and sales, then it was time for the company to take another traditional step—to evolve more sporting versions to cater for the more demanding owners who wanted extra performance for extra money. This had always been sound commercial sense: but with the solid backing of a successful model, developing faster versions of the 1900 to widen its appeal among the sporting fraternity was good public relations as well. At the same time, the essential parts were becoming easier to find, which increased the number of possible options open to the Alfa engineers.

Changes at first were simple enough. In 1951, the first higher performance version of the 1900 made its appearance in the shape of the 1900 TI—the initials stood for Turismo Internazionale, which was the name of a keenly disputed class in Italian racing. This used the same engine as the ordinary saloon, but with the addition of fractionally higher compression pistons—7.75 to 1 instead of 7.5 to 1—and sharper cam profiles to allow for faster running.

But it was the carefully detailed design—as methodical and as painstaking as in Jano's days at Milan—which made the car such a powerful sporting contender. First of all, the breathing had to be improved. Larger valves (41 mm inlet valves instead of 38 mm, and 36.5 mm instead of 34 mm for the exhaust valves) were fitted in the head, and a double-choke carburetter was fitted instead of the single-choke carburetter fitted to the original saloon.

These modest changes were enough to raise the power peak from 90 bhp at 5200 rpm to 100 bhp at 5500 rpm. With the body and running gear largely unchanged, apart from small but important points like stronger linings and springs in the clutch to cope with the extra power, modifications to the cooling system to allow longer bouts of sustained high-speed running, and better-quality gears to deal with higher transmission loads, this power increase was enough to boost the top speed 13 mph to 106 mph from the original saloon.

An unexpected view of a civilian version of the 1900 M, in this case harnessed to a powerful rotary snowplough

Even this modest step forward was good news for owners who liked the 1900 the way it was, but who wanted greater performance. But the other addition to the 1951 range was aimed particularly at those more traditionalist owners who wanted sporting cars to *look* more like sporting cars. As in the old days, the first step was to offer a shorter and more compact chassis—though the 1900 was a modern monocoque design, the floorpan was still rigid enough, when given additional stiffening, to serve as the basis for open or closed bodywork by the independent coachbuilders. Five inches cut from the wheelbase, though the front and rear track dimensions were left alone, was enough to save more than 200 lb when fitted with a neat closed coupé body by Carrozzeria Touring. The convertible cabriolet model, with bodywork by Pininfarina, was slightly heavier, though no heavier than the TI saloon. Since both versions had the uprated TI engine, the top speed varied with the weight: the cabriolet's performance was virtually identical to the TI, and the coupé had a top speed of 113 mph, to go with its undeniably sleek lines.

This was a very shrewd marketing policy on Alfa's part. Though the 1900 had represented a considerable move down-market, it was still priced at the Italian equivalent of £1331, at a time when this would buy a number of other quality saloons—admittedly without the Alfa's sparkling acceleration and roadholding, but with considerably more luxury. But the coupé was priced in a much more expensive bracket, at £1867 complete.

This policy of marketing two very different versions of the same car seemed to pay off. Those more well-heeled enthusiasts who jibbed at the Spartan austerity of the 1900 could buy the same performance in more luxurious surroundings by opting for the Touring or Pininfarina versions—they had elegance and exclusivity without a corresponding drop in speed or handling. And though these more expensive versions sold in smaller numbers than the basic saloons— 353 Sprints sold in 1952, compared with 3107 saloons (standard Berlina and TI versions) in the same year—they were essentially additional sales, rather than alternatives to the basic versions.

More civilian still was this neat little two-door, close-coupled shooting brake/estate car/station wagon version of the basic 1900 M jeep for market gardeners and farmers of 1954

The much-needed competition element was first provided by the exotic Disco Volante prototypes, based on the 1900 for mechanical parts. There were three versions, including an orthodox open two-seater, and this version, with its sharp-edged cross-sectional profile

Another version of the 1900 which appeared late in 1951 in prototype form took the 1900 theme in the opposite direction altogether. This was the 1900 M, an Italian equivalent of the Jeep or Land-Rover, and surely the only military-agricultural workhorse to then sport a twin overhead-cam engine. This wasn't Alfa Romeo's first attempt at this kind of design: before the war, the company had produced a Jeep-like staff-car and army runabout version of the 2500 called the Coloniale. Production had been cut short by wartime conditions, but even so 152 examples had emerged from the factory by 1942, and they found employment all over Italy and—while they lasted—in Mussolini's colonies in North and East Africa.

The 1900 M was a rather more ambitious exercise in engineering terms though. In some ways it was a much tougher and more utilitarian vehicle than the Coloniale—back the engineers went to the

old idea of a welded floor-tray, stiffened by longitudinal and transverse box sections and carrying a stark and simple open body with two front seats and two longitudinal benches at the rear, providing accommodation for six in all. The track was almost an inch narrower than the 1900 saloon, but the wheelbase was a full foot shorter than even the Sprint version. The only family resemblance, on the outside at least, was the set of slits cut to allow air to reach the radiator behind the front bonnet panel—these traced out the familiar shield-shaped pattern of the Alfa radiators fitted to the production cars.

Under the skin, however, the 1900 M had a lot more in common with its passenger-carrying sisters. The engine was almost identical to the basic 1900 unit, with the same single-choke downdraught carburetter and the same valves and valve-gear. Almost the only

This rear view of the Disco Volante shows the sharp-edged ogival cross-section, allegedly intended to improve stability in strong side winds

The closed coupé version of the Disco Volante, again with the ogival cross-section, though without the chrome strip edging

major difference was the use of pistons with flatter crowns, to reduce the compression ratio to 7 to 1. This, in conjunction with revised cam profiles, reduced the usable speed range and brought the power peak down to a still useful 65 bhp at 4400 rpm. The water circuit capacity was reduced slightly from 19.25 pints to 16.5, but the oil capacity was almost doubled, with a deeper sump and the use of supply and recovery pumps to keep the lubrication circuit going.

The engine was harnessed to a four-speed gearbox having slightly lower ratios than the saloon in the intermediate gears—but the output from this gearbox was taken to both axles, driving all four wheels instead of just the rearmost pair, and using limited-slip differential gears at the back to provide extra traction for really hard going.

The weight of the tougher chassis and the extra transmission components pushed the scales round to 2750 lb overall, but even with the detuned engine, the 1900 M was good for a useful 65 mph top speed. The reason for its development in the first place had been an order from the Italian Defence Ministry for an army utility vehicle, and the 2000-vehicle contract provided a useful extra boost for the company at a time when production was still at a relatively low level.

Same shape—but two-tone finish and a lot more chrome . . . The 1900 Super saloon of 1954

There was even a civilian market for this versatile design : suitable kits of parts could be bought to hang on the vehicle or on a separate trailer to turn it into anything from a snowplough to a fire engine, a crop-sprayer to a combine harvester, and another fifty were built and sold to local authorities and private farmers. But perhaps the most unlikely role the 1900 M ever fulfilled was that of racing car—one was entered in the 1952 Mille Miglia, where it came first in the special category for military vehicles. Perhaps, though, given its pedigree and the kind of opposition it was likely to meet in its category, the result wasn't so unlikely after all!

But racing of a more serious and intensive kind was soon to be on the agenda for the other 1900 models as well. These early years of the nineteen-fifties were seeing the final retirement of the company from Grand Prix racing. The brilliant but elderly Alfettas, using the straight-eight engine which had been designed as one half of the pre-war 3-litre Grand Prix V16, had beaten everything the racing world could pit against them. But after four successful seasons, they had reached the limit of their development; running with higher and higher boost pressures for higher and higher engine speeds, they were

Right
Another 1900 Super with the same basic styling but single colour finish. This time it's 1958

Below
More 1900 for your money—a 1958 limousine version of the 1900 Super with a lengthened wheelbase and a stretched centre section to provide room for two extra folding seats behind a glass partition

now topping 11,000 rpm and swallowing a gallon of high-octane spirit for every mile and a half of track. Not only did the complex multi-cylinder engines have to be taken apart and rebuilt after every race, but they were literally strapped together around cracks in the cylinder blocks and crankcases. And what was perhaps more important, the racing rules had opened up an entirely new avenue which seemed to offer new promises to their opponents. With the option of an unblown engine of three times the capacity, Ferrari was approaching competitive speeds and power outputs with a simpler and less highly stressed engine still at the beginning of its development. If Alfa Romeo were to maintain their ascendancy, they would have to start all over again with a totally new design, and accept the inevitable defeats until they could catch up in turn with Ferrari's achievements.

Better by far, they decided, to bow out gracefully at the moment of triumph. So the close of the 1951 season saw the end of Alfa's domination of Grand Prix racing after their second consecutive year as World Champions. For a while, the memory of their solid achievements would carry the message to the buying public that Alfas, all Alfas, were cars to be respected by sporting-minded drivers. But this was a wasting asset—and lack of a racing effort would mean a cutting off of the vital flow of engineering know-how and information needed to keep the sharp performance edge of the production cars honed to perfection.

So Grand Prix racing was, for the time being at least, too complex and too expensive. Before the war, the obvious course had been to turn to racing the production cars instead. So far the very different postwar cars had gone a long way towards replacing their illustrious forebears in the showrooms and in the affections of loyal Alfa fans all over the country. Could they now go a step further and replace them in the even more 'cut-and-thrust' arena of the competition world itself?

The first tentative steps had been taken in 1951, with what was called a 'Raid'. This was a long-distance run over the wastes of the Sahara. The car was a production 1900 saloon driven by Bonzi and Lualdi, who took it all the way from Milan down through Italy, by ship to Tripoli on the North African coast, and then down through the desert (pausing on the way to be photographed passing through Mussolini's old triumphal arch near El Agheila, which the Eighth Army had christened 'Marble Arch') and over the mountains of Ethiopia to Mogadishu on the Indian Ocean coast of Somalia.

In the following year, the 1900 was entered in more competitive events: Sanesi drove a 1900 TI in the Stella Alpina rally, but the most impressive result of the year was his drive in the Mille Miglia in a Touring-bodied 1900 Sprint, when he finished third in his class.

But by this time, something more exciting still was brewing in the Alfa Romeo competition department. The 1900 engine seemed to offer a good basis for an out-and-out sports-racing car, and Gioacchino Colombo wanted to produce a car which could take over from the Alfetta as the company's competition standard-bearer. So

The shorter-wheelbase 1900
Super Sprint variant of 1955,
this time with neat coupé
bodywork by Boano which
all but disguises the origins of
the car

*Another Boano design: the
1955 limited-production
Primavera semi-coupé on the
1900 Super saloon*

the C52 was born—a car which would always be better known as the Disco Volante, or Flying Saucer.

The first step was to increase the engine output, to allow the car to compete effectively in the 2-litre class. The bores were widened to the more convenient diameter of 85 mm, providing a capacity of 1997.4 cc. The compression ratio was raised to 8.73 to 1, and the engine was fed through two horizontal double-choke carburetters. Oddly, in view of the intended increase of power, the valves were actually slightly smaller than those used on the Sprint, but the use of racing camshafts and other detail alterations raised the peak power from 100 bhp to 158 bhp at the much higher engine speed of 6500 rpm. This vastly more effective power unit was fitted into a specially designed tubular space frame which carried a sleek sports body. Fitted with front and rear suspension systems similar in layout to the ordinary production car—though with different settings—the whole vehicle weighed a mere 1600 lb, or just under three-quarters the weight of the Sprint, with over fifty per cent more power.

This prescription meant a highly competitive car in terms of the figures for acceleration alone. But the unusual features of the Disco Volante centred on the bodywork: three prototypes of the car were built, and each one had a different body shape. What they had in common was a carefully shaped undertray, intended to cut down

Touring's version of the Super Sprint—a remarkably dateless design of the early 1950s

drag and turbulence in the airstream flowing below the car. This was a curved, convex shape, which was as close as possible to a mirror image of the upper part of the car, with its low bonnet line and low wings carefully faired into the sides.

In the case of two of the cars—one open two-seater and a closed coupé—the upper body met the undertray in a cross-sectional shape which came to a sharp point, rather like a Gothic arch laid on its side. This produced a very obvious sharp-edged line running right round the car's body along the axis of symmetry, about five inches above the wheel centres. Apart from the styling, which accounted in some degree for the car's unusual name, the reasoning for this ogival cross-section was obscure. The official explanation was that it provided the car with a highly aerodynamic profile even in conditions of strong cross-winds, but this seems highly doubtful. The third car, which was intended officially as a hillclimb version of the design, was built with ordinary rounded-off side panels, and there is evidence that this was certainly no less successful than the other two versions.

Clearly aerodynamics *did* have a high priority in the design of the Disco Volante, however. The smooth body shape was only spoiled by openings for the lower halves of the wheels, and by farings for the wheel-arches and for the headrests for driver and passenger. The whole body was inclined downwards at the front, in an attempt to ensure greater stability and better roadholding. All this patient, detailed care and the combination of power in plenty, light bodywork and efficient streamlining, made for a car which could not only boast a top speed of more than 135 mph, but could well beat its opponents on handling as well.

The Disco Volante coupé's first public appearance was at the International Motor Sport Show, held in New York in the spring of 1953. But alas for all the high hopes which the company and the fans held for the car: though careful wind-tunnel tests had been used to refine the body design for minimum drag, very little was known at the time about the problems of lift, and in some ways the clean profile of the Disco Volante was proving rather *too* efficient. The car's shape

Farina's classic 1900 coupé: only the front end of the car reveals the production model on which it was based

was channelling large volumes of air below it, and because of the body's nose-down attitude and the relative absence of turbulence below the car, this high-speed airstream was causing the rear end of the car to lift—not enough to lift the wheels clear of the ground, but just enough to reduce their grip to the point where the car's roadholding suffered.

It was this, coupled with a succession of small problems, which meant that the Disco Volante's theoretical performance remained a matter of theory rather than practice, and which finally stopped the project from proceeding any further. The Disco Volante remained a curiosity in the Alfa story, and the only time the name appeared in the record books was due to confusion with a different model altogether.

This was the Disco Volante's cousin, which had descended from the big 6C 3000 prototype originally developed as an alternative to the four-cylinder 1900. When the idea of producing the six was dropped, the engine was given higher compression and three horizontal double-choke carburetters to boost its power peak from 120 bhp at 4800 rpm to 168 bhp at 6000 rpm, and then it was fitted into one of the competition coupés which had been built earlier on modified 6C 2500 chassis. The result was the 6C 3000 C50, which was entered in the Mille Miglia of 1950 without success.

But at the time of the Disco Volante's introduction, this project too had taken another step forward. The 3-litre six was bored and stroked to 87 mm bores and a 98 mm stroke to take its capacity to 3495 cc. With 8.2 to 1 compression and six separate single-choke carburetters, the bigger engine turned out a creditable 246 bhp at 6500 rpm, and it was fitted into a tubular space-frame similar to that of the Disco Volante but with a central box section and outriggers to carry the front and rear suspension mountings, with an inch and a quarter more in the wheelbase and three inches wider track. The bodywork was again similar in its treatment—though larger and without the sharp-edged flanks which gave the smaller car its name—to the Disco Volante's, and the top speed was higher at 155 mph.

Five of these cars were built, four coupés and an open two-seater, followed by another open car with a different version of the engine in a chassis shortened by two inches. This was the 6C 3000 PR (for passo ridotto, or reduced wheelbase); instead of the original 3-litre six—which had the same unusual bore dimensions as the 1900 to cater for the British engine components—this now retained the wider 87 mm bores of the 3.5-litre unit, but with the crankshaft throws reduced to shorten the stroke to 83 mm and bring the capacity to 2943 cc, or in other words within the 3-litre capacity limit scheduled for the 1954 sports-car formula.

In spite of the reduction in capacity, this engine was actually more powerful than the longer-stroke 3.5-litre unit, delivering 260 bhp at a higher speed of 7000 rpm. The car's top speed was higher too, at just over 160 mph, but once again it was to be a disappointment. It was entered for Sanesi to drive in the Supercortemaggiore Grand Prix at Monza on 27 June 1954, but during practice three days before the race, Sanesi slid off the track at the Ascari curve and the car crashed and burst into flames. Sanesi suffered severe burns, and the car was a total wreck.

By this time, however, the bigger cars—still, confusingly, identified as 6C 3000 CMs, in spite of their 3.5-litre engines—had also passed into history. But not before they had turned up for the 1953 Mille Miglia in strength: three coupés for drivers Fangio, Sanesi and Kling, backed up by Zehender in the open Disco Volante hillclimb car. The small car, still plagued by the recurrent handling and reliability problems which eventually killed the project, did not last long. But the big cars had their difficulties too: Sanesi dropped out with engine trouble after leading the race at Ravenna. Kling took over the lead until *he* dropped out with transmission failure, and then it was all up to Fangio.

When the steering failed on the last of the big Alfas, it seemed as if the company's efforts were to be totally blighted—but in an extraordinary epic of skill and endurance, Fangio refused to give up the race. Although the left-hand front wheel was not contributing to the steering at all, it did at least behave itself properly when the car was going straight and level. But on each corner he had to haul the car round by a combination of brute force and the influence of the right-hand wheel alone. It imposed a fearful strain on the steering, the suspension, the tyres and above all on the driver. It cut down his average speed, despite all his unequalled driving skill, and it seemed that if the car would hold together to the end, he must surely finish last. But only Marzotto in a Ferrari succeeded in passing him before the endless succession of mountain hairpins was past, and the Alfa was able to make better speed on the flat, straight stretches to the finish. On this kind of going, even with half his steering out of action, there was no one alive who could catch Fangio, and to everyone's amazement he came pounding home in second place.

This was the highspot of the six-cylinder's competition career. Three cars turned up for the Le Mans 24-hour race later in the season, and once again they performed well enough to raise everyone's hopes. But once again time began to tell: Fangio's car dropped out with a burned-out piston, and Sanesi (having set fastest lap) finally retired when in third place behind a C-type Jaguar and a Ferrari after his De Dion rear suspension collapsed. Not long afterwards the last of the Alfas, driven by Kling and Riess, retired with transmission failure having taken over that promising third place at the race's halfway point.

The only outright victory to the car's credit was the first Supercortemaggiore Grand Prix, to be held at Merano in the South Tyrol, where Fangio took first place in the open 3.5-litre car after watching the opposition—for once—fall to pieces instead. After that, the cars were retired to give way to other, more promising projects on

Another Touring 1900 Super Sprint coupé, which manages to look a much bigger car altogether than its stablemate

the competition front; but not before they had played their part in compounding confusion over exactly what was and what was not a Disco Volante.

According to Alfa historian Luigi Fusi, whose detailed pedigree of every type of Alfa ever built is the Alfisti's Bible, only the 2-litre cars with the sharp-sided bodywork were officially called the Disco Volante. Certainly this makes sense: the peculiar bodywork could just about justify the title of Flying Saucer from some angles, but there was nothing about the shape of the other cars to make the name appropriate for them. Yet even now, Alfa's own engineers refer to the larger cars as Disco Volantes, and the *Autocar* write-up at the time of their introduction specifically mentions that 'four [of the cars] have 3-litre six-cylinder engines and two are slightly smaller models, identical in general outline but shorter in the wheelbase and fitted with a special version of the Alfa Romeo 1900 2-litre engine'.

Farina's cabriolet 1900: almost the same as its closed coupé equivalent with a neat folding hood, this car was a clear ancestor of Farina's later Spider versions of the Giulietta and Giulia Alfa Romeos

B·2612

Though several of the facts were wrong, perhaps the confusion is understandable: with cars so basically similar being introduced at the same time as part of the same competition programme, it was almost inevitable that the name should come to be applied to all the different variants.

With the demise of the Disco Volantes, something else was needed to rescue the company's competition programme and avoid it sinking totally without trace. As so often before in the Alfa story, it was up to the private owners to keep on delivering the results with their assortment of hotted-up production cars. Fortunately, from 1954 onwards, they had more promising material to rely on, with the improved 1900 Super models. These were still very similar to their predecessors, except that Italian-made parts were now more plentiful, and the awkward 82.55 mm bore measurement could now be replaced by wider bores measuring 84.5 mm, just a fraction narrower than the 2-litre Disco Volante unit. With the stroke left unchanged at 88 mm, this added up to a capacity of 1975 cc. In the case of the ordinary saloon, this made no difference to the power peak, but the

One which has dated—fortunately—is Boneschi's messy and over-fussy spider of 1953

Much nicer altogether is another Boneschi design: a semi-coupé rather reminiscent of Boano's Primavera version of the 1900

Two famous figures from Alfa's past, with a 1900 Super Sprint: on the left Nuvolari's co-driver from his epic 1930 Mille Miglia win, Gianbattista Guidotti, on the right Alberto Ascari, racing driver of the 1950s and son of Antonio Ascari, champion Alfa driver of the 1920s

improvement in low-speed torque made the car more flexible to drive and raised the top speed by 6 mph in spite of an increase in weight of 100 lb. The styling was modernized too, with a chrome strip along the waistline of the car from headlamp to tail-light, together with chrome along the doorsills and window surrounds.

But the real improvements came in the sporting versions. The TI engine went up from a 100 bhp power peak to 115 bhp at the same 5500 rpm, thanks to higher 8 to 1 compression and two double-choke downdraught carburetters. This change was the outcome of detailed work by Alfa's development engineers, with the intention of avoiding all compromises in the supply of fuel to the engine's four cylinders. Engineer Garcea, one of Satta's team responsible for the engine design, recalls proudly that this was the first production car to have one carburetter barrel for each cylinder—not only did this avoid irregularity and running-on problems on tickover, but even more importantly it eliminated cross-flow problems in high-speed running. At the beginning of the inlet stroke, the pressure is atmospheric, so that some of the fuel–air mixture could be lost in the pipework—but with an individual barrel and butterfly valve, then each cylinder received all the fuel–air charge due to it at the right time

A completely cutaway open top version of the 1900 produced in 1954 as a military staff car—but no large-scale production resulted from the idea

with the least possible loss. Not only was this more efficient, but it allowed sharper cam profiles and faster running, all of which conspired to raise the power delivery that much further. To balance the other side of the timing equation, the exhaust pipework was arranged with individual exhaust ducts from each cylinder, which allowed the engineers to tune each duct individually so that the resonant pulses occurred at the right time to suck the exhaust gases out of the cylinder at the moment the exhaust valve opened.

The result of all this was a car which went better than ever before. Though the interior was slightly less crude than on the original 1900 range—a change which was reflected in a 100 lb increase in weight— the extra power, speed and flexibility of the engine pushed the top speed of the car to 112 mph. With a restyled dashboard having hooded instruments to reduce distracting reflections in the dials, and fractionally larger luggage space and rear window area, the car was also blessed with mechanical improvements which were intended to maintain reliability even with the higher speeds and stresses inseparable from the higher power output. For example, the gearbox was fitted with tougher-specification gearwheels, the prop-shaft joints were strengthened, the clutch linings and springs were replaced

Another view of the Farina cabriolet 1900, outside the Turin workshops where the bodies were designed and built

A racy looking coupé on the 1900 chassis—Alfa records don't show who was responsible for this design, but it could well have been Boano . . .

An interesting design on the 1900 Super Sprint chassis by Ghia—the shape was to turn up again on another more sporting Alfa special by Conrero (see page 143)

*Zagato's version of the Super
Sprint was another design
which was to have
distinguished descendants—its
shape was an odd combination
of the 1900 and later racing
Alfas like the Giulietta SZ
and the Giulia GTZ*

by heavier-duty equivalents, and the front brakes were improved.
Not only were larger 12-inch drums fitted, but the cooling was
improved by ducting the airstream over a set of fins mounted on the
outer radius of the brake drum, which then deflect the air out through
a set of holes in the wheel-discs.

For Alfa's sporting customers, this was really good news. While the
Disco Volante and 3.5-litre sports car programmes had been finally
falling to pieces all around the circuits, the TI had behaved itself well,
winning its class at the Tour of Sicily in 1953. The new TI Super was
to do even better, in events ranging from the Tour de France—where
the car came first in the Turismo category in 1954—to the Carrera
Messicana and the eighth Stella Alpina, where the Super Sprint
versions of Sanesi and Crespi finished third and first overall. The Tour
of Sicily was won outright by another TI in 1954, the same year
which saw a TI win its class in the Mille Miglia.

All this was reflected on the production front too. With the factory
rebuilding and re-equipment programmes still continuing, Alfa were
now producing the cars more efficiently, with less of the work done
by hand and more by machinery. This series of savings allowed them
to drop the prices of these new, more powerful and slightly more
luxurious cars by sixteen per cent, which, added to their increasing
sporting reputation, made for brisk sales. During 1954, the last of the
old 1900 range—948 cars in all three main variations—left the factory,
to be followed by another 2807 of the Super range before the year was
out. This was actually a drop from the high-spot of 1953, which saw a
grand total of 5411 cars—by far Alfa's most successful year yet—
produced and sold. These included 3115 of the saloons (Berlinas and
TIs), 353 Sprints, ninety-one cabriolets and five of the military
1900 M. Partly, the fall in sales during 1954 was due to the
reorganization for the Super models, but it was mainly due to
something much more important altogether. For some time now it
had become increasingly obvious to the Alfa management that their

bold step in moving down-market with the introduction of the 1900 was no longer bold enough. Increasing public awareness of Alfa Romeo's sporting qualities—thanks in part to the domination of the Grand Prix Alfettas in the late 1940s and early 1950s, but mainly due to the more recent successes gained by the production cars—had created an enthusiastic following among customers in the lower price bands, now being offered an increasing choice by new designs from makers such as Fiat. If Alfa could take another step forward into this still lower-cost, high-volume market without losing the standards of reliability and performance which had brought them this far in commercial safety, then a bigger buying public altogether was there for the taking.

This meant totally new models, designed for more genuine mass-production from the start than the 1900 had been, and no mere face-lift on the existing design. For the time being though, the 1900s would have to carry on: even when this new market was supplied, there would still be the loyal and better-off customers, who preferred a relatively large car and the choice of independent coachwork which was still provided by the different 1900 models and the independent specialist designers. Already a plethora of different 1900-based designs had emerged from all kinds of workshops: some, like the elegant Super Sprint hardtop coupé, or the Pininfarina cabriolet, could stand

One of Bertone's BAT series (see page 96 for the confusion over the numbering of these prototypes), with its exotic but aerodynamic sweeps of metal to channel the airflow over the car to the best advantage

the test of time well. Another Farina design for a fastback closed 2-plus-2 coupé was a classic design, foreshadowing the later Aston Martin DB3 and DB4 designs in its combination of speed and elegance in a single balanced shape.

Others were less happy: perhaps the ugliest, to present-day eyes at least, was a flamboyant open two-seater by Boneschi with an oval radiator grille flanked by intakes like the mouths of jet engines which contained the headlamps, angular wings faired into the body and huge tail fins reminiscent of American designs of the later 1950s. But other versions were to look forward in happier ways—Zagato, in particular, had produced a very interesting closed coupé on the 1900 theme. This had a body frame made up from small-bore square-section tubing in the usual Zagato manner, which carried all the stresses, leaving the body panelling to be as thin, as light and as carefully shaped from an aerodynamic standpoint as possible. The lines were shaped to keep wind resistance to a minimum, fitting as closely as possible around the shapes of the engine, the wheels and the occupants. The front of the car was swept down to bumper level, with separate fairings to cover the engine and each of the wheel-arches. The steeply raked screen led back to a low-roofed passenger compartment and then a sharply sloping fastback tail. The whole body made a compact, aggressive, functional package, and was to

A later version of the BAT (Berlina Aerodinamic Tecnica) with higher tailfins and a deep central fin, on the Bertone stand at the 1954 Turin Show

found a line of Zagato-bodied Alfas that would lead to some very interesting cars indeed.

The Zagato coupé made no impact on the commercial front: but another Boneschi design produced in 1952 was a direct precursor of an unusual and successful 1900 variant three years later. This was a low-roofed, four-seat, two-door closed coupé with semi-pillarless construction and restrained, rudimentary tail fins. In 1955, this theme was repeated with a Boano design having very slightly revised contours around the rear quarters; finished in the then very popular two-tone style, this version was christened the 1900 Primavera, or Springtime, and in all 300 examples of this version were sold between 1955 and 1957.

There were also other, more utilitarian variations on the 1900 theme: one was a four-door, four-seat open-top car as a prototype for a military staff car, a rather more civilized alternative to the go-anywhere 1900 M. There was also, eventually, a long-long-wheelbase version of the 1900, which carried truly imposing limousine bodywork. Considering that the car was stretched by the fitting of an extra window and centre section of bodywork, it looked surprisingly neat and well balanced. Finally, there was the first model in what was to become another postwar Alfa tradition: a special 1900 developed for the Italian police patrolmen with a tuned engine, extra spotlights, radio equipment, opening roof and the characteristic all-black finish.

But if some versions of the 1900 were ordinary working cars, one other went to the opposite extreme. This was a Bertone design, tagged appropriately enough the BAT, as it would have looked completely at home in any episode in the Batman series. In fact this extraordinary finned monster of a car was devised with an entirely serious purpose in mind: the initials stood for Berlina Aerodinamica Tecnica, and it was intended to investigate ways of improving the roadholding of high-speed cars by using the airstream itself to impose pressure in the right places.

This was a problem very close to Alfa's heart. In one way, the excellent streamlining of the Disco Volante had been the car's undoing. Makers of really well streamlined cars were finding that the better the streamlining, the greater the tendency for the centre of pressure of the airstream over the car to move farther and farther forward. This not only reduced the grip exerted by the rear wheels on the road, but when this centre of pressure neared and finally passed the centre of gravity of the car, it had a disastrous effect on its stability. These were exactly the difficulties from which the Disco Volante had suffered, and clearly the same problems would impede the development of other streamlined racing cars if some way were not devised of reversing this tendency.

Bertone's idea was to shape the car so that the use of channels and fins could induce the airflow to shift its centre of pressure farther back towards the tail of the car, without paying the penalty of increased turbulence and drag. He produced a series of prototypes which came closer and closer to this ideal, culminating in the summer of 1953 with

Above
*The 1900 in competition:
Sanesi driving a 1900 T1 in
the 1954 Carrera Mexicana,
and giving an American
Lincoln a run for its money*

Left
*Sanesi's team-mate Corini in
the same event*

the unveiling of BAT 5 (if you believe *Autocar*) or BAT 7 (if you believe Alfa archivist Luigi Fusi). Whatever the number, its relevance here is that the car was based on the Alfa Romeo 1900 Sprint— deliberately, according to Bertone, because the performance of the same mechanical package in a variety of other body styles could be studied and used as a yardstick against which the efficiency of the BAT body shape could be measured accurately.

The engine, chassis, transmission and suspension of the car were all standard 1900 Sprint parts—but there any similarity with the production car came sharply to an end. The bonnet line sloped downwards from the base of the steeply raked windscreen forwards, ending in two wide air intakes for the front wheels, inboard of the rounded front valances which covered the upper halves of the wheels

Corini and Artesoni being flagged home in their 1900 TI in the 1954 Mille Miglia, where they won their class

to reduce drag-inducing turbulence. This cooling airstream escaped through narrower vents behind the wheels.

Behind the deeply curved windscreen was a reasonably orthodox passenger compartment, except that the rear screen panel was swept right back to the extreme tail of the car, so that the plan view of the cabin from above was rather like a teardrop, with the rounded windscreen tailing back to the tail of the car. The object of this was to keep the airflow from separating from the body of the car as far as possible, again with the object of keeping drag to the minimum.

Directional stability was further increased by the two dorsal fins, one on each side of the car. These began to rise from the points level with the front of the windscreen until they reached their maximum height at the rear end of the car, at which point they were higher than

Corini and Artesoni again:
this time on the way to
winning their class in the 1954
Tour of Sicily

Line astern for some very handsome 1900s—the time and place are unknown

Left
*A Swedish-registered 1900
TI complete with fashionable
bug-deflector on the bonnet,
running at Silverstone in a
production touring car race in
1956*

Below
*One of the most interesting
and attractive of all the might-
have-beens in Alfa history:
the elegant 2000 Sportiva
racing sports car of 1954*

the rear end of the passenger cabin; they carried slots to equalize the air pressure on their inner and outer surfaces, and by curving the fins inwards at the top, this created extra downward pressure to keep the airflow in contact with the car's body and eliminate the tendency to rear-end lift which had plagued cars like the Disco Volante.

Was it successful? Problems like the lack of headroom, the visibility and the difficulty of convincing the buying public that good aerodynamics were as worth while as good aesthetics, would be bound to limit the BAT's usefulness in the commercial sense. But some of the ideas, notably the use of tailfins, were to find their way into competition cars, where ensuring straight-line stability at higher and higher speeds was becoming more and more of a problem. The other difficulty—the tendency towards rear-end lift—would follow a different path with rear-engined racing cars, the adoption of spoilers and aerofoils, and the development of different design ideas with the same objective in mind. All the same, Bertone's BAT was one of the most interesting and unusual of all the one-off Alfa 1900 variants, and it played a crucial role in competition car development by exploring some totally new ideas.

By the middle of the nineteen-fifties, the 1900 series was nearing the end of its long and varied career, though the basic design is still with us, of course, in half of Alfa's current range. The model itself would soldier on until 1959 in basically unchanged form, selling in smaller and smaller numbers alongside newer and more popular

Another Zagato body on the 1900 Super Sprint—a convertible—pictured in the paddock at Le Mans in 1956

Alfas. But there was still one more opportunity left for the 1900 on the sporting front—a final chance to snatch back some of the hopes so cruelly lost over the Disco Volante disappointment.

This was a much more practical project, an idea much more solidly rooted in real commercial commonsense than its predecessor had been. The intention was to develop a more genuine sports-racing car by producing a series of one hundred cars to supply the factory racing team and enough private owners to satisfy homologation requirements. Two versions would be offered: an out-and-out sports racing car, and a luxurious road-going coupé version, to satisfy keen drivers of both touring and sporting persuasions.

The heart of the new car, the 2000 Sportiva, was to be the 2-litre version of the 1900 engine, as developed for the Disco Volante but with the cast-iron cylinder block of the production 1900s rather than the light alloy block of the other competition cars. Compression ratio was increased from the 8.73 to 1 of the Disco Volante to 9 to 1, and coil ignition was fitted instead of magneto ignition. Another change was in the rear suspension: instead of the carefully located rear axle of the production cars (and the DV), the Sportiva was fitted with a De Dion axle to carry the back wheels.

The cars were built up around a space frame of square-section tubes, large tubes being used for the longerons and main cross members and smaller-section tubes for the lattice which supported the body panels. The wheelbase was an inch shorter than the DV, but

Even now, the Sportiva's sleek Bertone lines seem modern and aggressive: no mean feat on a car more than twenty years old

the track was widened by an inch and a half at the front and a full four inches at the back. The weight was up, compared with the DV—the Sportiva weighed just over 2000 lb in roadgoing trim, compared with the 1600 lb of the earlier car—yet, although the higher compression engine of the Sportiva delivered less power (138 bhp instead of 158 bhp), the flatter torque curve and the use of a five-speed gearbox helped to keep the top speed the same, at 136 mph.

The racing version was a simply shaped, bare two-seater body, with flat sides and a tail rounded down to a sharply curved rear end, and a low wrap-round screen. The road-going closed coupé, on the other hand, was a much more elegant creation with steeply raked doors, curved window panels and a long fastback, which was a more restrained version of the shape adopted in the Bertone BAT car.

Both versions were extremely attractive and promising cars. But once again the Sportiva was to be another project which never lived up to its expectations—in this case, it was never even allowed to turn a wheel in earnest. Although all the chassis for the series had been built, and although several cars had been built (two of the road-going coupés, according to engineer Garcea; two coupés and two racing cars, according to Fusi), the project was finally rejected as being unprofitable. It was a sign of how uncertain Alfa's management were at the time over what their priorities should be. Here was a cherished idea of the design and development department being axed after most of the work had been done, on the grounds of cost and profitability—

A battered but purposeful racing version of the Sportiva filling up at the factory during tests in 1956: note the hurried repair at the bottom of the door sill

two factors which should have been investigated right at the beginning. Perhaps the reason lay in poor interdepartmental communications—or possibly the directors wanted to concentrate all their resources on the new production models which were already in the development pipeline.

Whatever the reasons, the Sportiva was condemned to a page or two in the history books, and a space for one of the coupés in the Alfa museum collection. With their departure, the competition record of the 1900 would have to rely entirely on the exploits of the production cars. Fortunately for the company, and for the Alfa supporters, they rose to the occasion magnificently. One quotation from *Autocar*, describing a race in Belgium involving an Alfa Romeo with, in their words 'very little special equipment' and driven by Pierre Stasse and Oliver Gendebien, could stand for any of the results achieved by the varied and ubiquitous band of Alfa saloons and coupés which appeared on start-lines and grids of every possible event throughout Europe:

'But out in front was that Alfa Romeo, simply tearing round, engine as sweet as it could be, suspension a model no matter what the bends. If ever a car and driver looked a winner, these two did. And they were.'

Chapter 3
ROMEO E GIULIETTA

The shape of things to come, at least as far as Alfa Romeo was concerned, was first revealed to the public at the Turin Show in April 1955, with the appearance of an entirely new model. This was the Giulietta—a neat play on the old Romeo name and the second half of a combination almost as familiar as eggs and bacon or fish and chips.

But one of the questions put by the original Romeo was 'What's in a name?', and in truth there was a great deal more to the Giulietta than a new title. This was no mere exercise in cosmetic restyling, a partially disguised replacement for the 1900. Apart from the fact that the 1900 had another four years to serve, the Giulietta was breaking entirely new ground. It was, in its way, every bit as brave a step forward as the 1900 itself had been.

The 1900 had been a reaction to a new postwar world and a new set of requirements: the first Alfa to enter the mass-production market, designed as a means of keeping a large and skilled work force busy as much as anything else. Only because the design team had lost none of its cunning did it turn out as good a car as it undoubtedly was. But because providing work was the first objective, at a time when machine tools were expensive and in short supply, it was still only a compromise between the old pre-war cars and the new generation of vehicles which would carry the company's name into the sixties, seventies and eighties. In terms of the other cars available from competing companies like Fiat, for example, it was still expensive, produced in small numbers and with a much higher hand-built content.

All these factors limited the success of the 1900, in numbers at least. It was never available in Britain or North America, and most of its sales were at home in Italy. But by the nineteen-fifties, conditions were beginning to change. The skilled work force was still there, but economic improvements, the rebuilding of industries devastated by war and, most important of all, massive American aid under the Marshall Plan, meant that they now had the machinery to back up the efforts of the men on the production line.

So the Alfa Romeo work force now had the capacity to produce many more cars from the same plant. Unfortunately, expanding production of the 1900 series would not make use of this extra capacity; selling the top-of-the-range versions on the UK market, for example, would involve paying taxes and import duties which would have put the car on the same price level as the Aston Martin DB2! Instead, the company needed a still cheaper and easier car to make in larger numbers at a lower price to expand into the wider market, where the Alfa virtues of performance and handling were still very definitely in short supply.

This was the specification for the Giulietta: it had to be easy to make and easy to sell. Easy to make meant a newer, simpler, monocoque body-chassis which exploited the experience the company had gained with the 1900 over five years. The Giulietta was shorter by ten inches in the wheelbase than the 1900, and narrower in track by an inch and a half at the front and two inches at the back. Its more rounded contours concealed a more efficient use of space which allowed room for four passengers—or five at a pinch—within the smaller body dimensions. Other details like the narrower window pillars and the larger glass area showed how much the state of the engineering art had advanced since the first monocoque designs, as did the weight of the car. The standard Giulietta saloon turned the scales at only 2000 lb complete, compared with the 2450 lb of the 1900 equivalent.

The body beautiful: the Giulietta, in this case a TI, still shows a strong resemblance to its 1900 parent

This is where the other half of the Giulietta prescription came in. The Italian market was dominated by the Government taxation system, which was based on a complex capacity measurement; the upshot was that a car with a smaller engine than the 1900 would be cheaper to tax and therefore a much more attractive marketing proposition. The original 1900 saloon had an engine which delivered 90 bhp from almost 2 litres. The Giulietta saloon would cash in on its smaller size and lighter weight by using a smaller and therefore cheaper version of the classic twin-cam design.

The shape and configuration of the engine was basically the same as the original design. But instead of the cast-iron block of the 1900, the Giulietta engine was able to save more weight by exploiting the company's aeronautical experience in casting precise and complex components by reverting to light alloy for the block, with steel liners for the cylinders. The old traditional method of valve adjustment, used on Alfa Romeo engines from pre-war days—a threaded

Like the 1900, the Giulietta range was to include a long wheelbase stretched-body limousine version with a pair of extra folding seats

adjustment on the cam followers—had given way to the use of different-sized shims in the later series of 1900 Supers from 1953 onwards, and this new method was to be continued on the Giulietta.

There were other changes too: most important was the physical reduction in size, with the bores narrowed to 74 mm and the stroke shortened to 75 mm. Not only did this cut the capacity to 1290 cc—a worthwhile drop from the taxation point of view—but it also gave a more up-to-date bore-to-stroke ratio than the 1900 had had. The narrower bores gave less room for valves, but in any case smaller valves were perfectly adequate. Instead of the 38 mm inlet valves and 34 mm exhaust valves of the 1900, the Giulietta's valves measured 31 mm and 28 mm respectively. This smaller size of valve opening allowed a change in the combustion chamber shape for more efficient burning of the fuel, too: the valves were brought slightly nearer to the vertical so that the angle between the two rows was now eighty degrees instead of a full right angle.

The compression ratio, for the saloon version, was left unchanged at 7.5 to 1—so was the carburation, with one single-choke vertical carburetter. The peak power, which was delivered at the same 5500 rpm as the 1900 Berlina engine, was only 53 bhp, representing a power-per-cubic-centimetre ratio of only eighty-seven per cent that of the 1900. But there was one important factor—with the lighter body, this was still enough to give the Giulietta a useful top speed of 87 mph, and this was an engine at the beginning of its development. The shorter stroke would allow faster engine speeds, and with more sophisticated carburation and higher compression ratios, the relatively understressed Giulietta Berlina unit could be turned into a much more powerful and competitive motor altogether.

*Estate-car version of the
Giulietta: a skilful blending of
lines to provide more space*

In fact the Berlina was not the first version of the Giulietta to make
its bow: that honour belonged to the already more interesting—for
sporting-minded drivers at least—variant called the Giulietta Sprint.
Like the 1900 Sprint, this was a lighter, special-bodied variant of the
basic production saloon, though in this case the dimensions of the
body were identical. The body shape itself was an elegant Bertone
two-plus-two closed coupé, the first appearance of a design which
was to serve Alfa Romeo well for another twenty years in succeeding
models.

But the interesting part of the Sprint was the set of power and
performance figures it possessed. Not only was the car lighter than the
standard saloon by a useful 77 lb, but the engine was a good deal more
powerful. With 8.5 to 1 compression and a double-choke Weber
carburetter, the engine turned out a much more useful 80 bhp at
6300 rpm. In the lighter body of the Sprint coupé, this was dynamite:
using the same four-speed gearbox with the same ratios as the saloon,
it allowed a top speed of 103 mph. The suspension was the same
system as had been developed for the 1900, and was well able to cope
with the new car's performance. But the most vital figure of all was
none of these: it was the price. The sleek, fast, agile coupé could be
bought in Italy for £1000—or just fifty-four per cent of the two-
seater Touring-bodied 1900 Super Sprint coupé of only fractionally
better performance!

For the Alfa customers—especially for those who wanted to be

Alfa customers in fact as well as in spirit, but who previously couldn't raise the entry fee—this was powerful medicine indeed. And the extra capacity promised by the new machinery on the assembly line would soon be needed as the orders came flooding in. During 1954 only a dozen Sprints were built, but in the following year 1415 were turned out of the Portello works, with more than 2000 following in 1956—and this was just the sporting version! The Giulietta saloon, which entered the lists after the coupé had made the name famous, was an even better proposition on the grounds of price at £793 complete on the Italian market.

What coupé customers had for their extra money was a sleek Bertone body; saloon buyers had to be content with the more pedestrian factory design. According to Alfa engineers, styling came just about bottom on their priority list. Market research investigations had shown them that most buyers bought on the feel and performance of the car, and that usually a short test drive was far more likely to end in a sale than any amount of sophisticated body design. So the Giulietta saloon had a deliberately simple line: one reason why the design still looks surprisingly modern, more than twenty years after its first appearance. In another respect too, the Alfa engineers wrought better than they knew. Although Engineer Edo Mazoni, who was working in the Experimental Department at the time, insists that wind-tunnel testing played no part in evolving the Giulietta body, he admits that it had a very good aerodynamic performance,

Sporting Giulietta: the Bertone design for the Giulietta Sprint Veloce was an immediate success with buyers who wanted a car which looked as speedy as it was

The basic Sprint version of the same design, with a slightly less powerful engine—just in view is the revised dash with its large and legible circular instruments

which he puts down to Alfa's aeronautical experience and know-how. But styling, he says, meant the badge which the car wore on its bonnet—the fact that the body reminded him of the contemporary Fiat 1400 mattered not at all, provided the performance was there.

With the Giulietta saloon having to wait until April of 1955 to make its appearance, there were only eight months of that first year for buyers to make their feelings felt. Yet in those eight months they bought 1430 cars, a total which was to be dwarfed in 1956 by 6348 Berlinas, and in 1957 by 8939 of the saloon cars—almost three times the total of 1900 saloons sold in the model's best-ever years of 1952 and 1953.

In the meantime, the Giulietta's appeal was to be widened by open sports models and by engine improvements, and the company's range would be buttressed at the top end by the last production variants of the long-lived 1900 series.

First of these additions to the line was the open two-seat sports Spider, which followed the saloon on to the market in the summer of 1955. For many Alfa enthusiasts of the fifties and sixties, this was the model which symbolized the make more than any other. It was everything which an Italian sports car ought to be: the Pininfarina bodywork was neat and functional and, in the eyes of many, positively beautiful. The front end of the car followed essentially the same lines as the Berlina and the Sprint, establishing a strong family resemblance between the three basic variations on the Giulietta theme. In the case of the Spider though, the windscreen pillars were much thinner, and they carrried quarter-lights, which the coupé and the saloon did not have. It also had the comfort and convenience of wind-up windows, at a time when most sports car owners had to put up with flapping side-screens, which all too often let in the draughts but kept out the visibility.

The wide doors led back to a completely new tail, with a flat-topped, slightly squared-off profile which combined happily with the standard front-end treatment to produce an extremely attractive shape. Unlike many sports cars, the Giulietta Spider looked almost as good with the hood in place as it did with the hood folded—and one optional extra soon offered to Spider owners was a removable hardtop which contributed to the car's looks by reproducing in glass and metal the simple, balanced shape of the fabric and Perspex hood.

But the car's trump card was its performance. There had been pretty sports cars before, which had disappointed by a lack of performance. Fortunately, the Spider's body, thanks to identical track measurements but a wheelbase fully five inches shorter than the Sprint and the Berlina, was fully 45 lb lighter than the by no means overweight coupé, and it shared with that version the same beefy 80 bhp variant of the Giulietta engine. Top speed was identical at 103 mph, and the price was only fractionally higher at £1095 on the Italian market. Though this would be bound to sell in smaller numbers than the other two versions—if for no other reasons than that it had but two seats—the forecasts were wrong, and for many years it was a very close rival indeed to the Bertone Sprint coupé. For racing, it was ideal—a simple windscreen removal left a body which was almost as good as a purpose-built sports-racing car from the aerodynamic and weight considerations.

In other ways, the Spider led the way for improvements to the rest of the range. Today's Alfa enthusiasts may be surprised to know how unsporting some of the details of these early cars still were: the speedometer of the Giulietta was a horizontal strip rather than a circular dial, and the four-speed gearbox was still controlled by a column-mounted lever with its long and clumsy linkages. Though this was now becoming less fashionable even for closed cars, it was definitely out of place on an open sports car, and the Spider was blessed with the longish but still beautifully precise floor-mounted direct-linkage lever which was to become an Alfa hallmark in later years. Circular instruments were fitted as standard—three matching dials containing speedometer, rev counter and a combined gauge for oil, fuel and water—and the open top made the less than luxurious appointments of the saloon—with its rubber mats rather than pile carpets—seem more logical in this context.

The reaction of the motoring press was ecstatic. Four years later, Giulietta Spiders were still only made in left-hand-drive form, and were rare indeed in Britain and the United States. *Autocar* managed to test a privately owned example, and they professed themselves delighted with its relatively enormous cockpit and its delicate lines. They were agreeably surprised by its flexibility: 'In traffic it will potter, snatch-free, in top gear at under 20 mph, and pull away without signs of distress. This speed represents no more than 1100 rpm.' They found the bodywork entirely free of flexing, and the steering was free from shock or vibrations. This they put down to good design, 'because the kerb weight of the car is only a moderate 16.25 cwt'.

The engine they found to be 'completely smooth', and they encountered difficulty in staying below the 6000 rpm limit because 'the engine gives no indication of the high speed and would, apparently, be happy to turn faster still'. They summed the car up in terms which would not sound out of place coming from the most dyed-in-the-wool Alfa fanatic: 'There is no more desirable small sports car; it sets standards of performance, handling and refinement that very few others can match.'

Praise indeed. And enough keen drivers shared *Autocar*'s estimation of the Spider's virtues to add up to a total of 14,300 vehicles in just eight years. Its only real competition came from a more powerful version of itself—the Spider Veloce—which was introduced in 1956. This had

a higher-compression 9.1 to 1 version of the engine, with two double-choke carburetters delivering 90 bhp at 6500 rpm, which pushed the top speed up to 112 mph. It was, however, intended mainly for competition driving, a car to keep the loyal band of amateur racing men who backed up the factory efforts so effectively (and in many seasons virtually replaced them altogether). It was more expensive, at £1282—though this was actually less than the basic 1900 saloon four years before!—and therefore it sold in smaller numbers, with 2796 Spider Veloces sold by 1962.

The Spider Veloce had a stablemate—the Sprint Veloce. This was, as the name implied, a similarly competition-oriented version of the Bertone-bodied Sprint coupé, with the higher-compression 90 bhp engine and the same top speed and slightly higher price. As befitted its competition intentions, this version of the coupé was the first to follow the Spider in forsaking the steering-column gearlever for the infinitely superior floor-mounted change. A total of 3058 Sprint Veloces would appear by 1962, adding another valuable bonus to the overall Giulietta production total of 177,690 cars during the model's ten-year career.

Competition enthusiasts had an even bigger surprise in store however, from the Alfa experimental department. This was another experimental version, aimed at sports-car racing proper rather than

Another Giulietta open-top— this time a variation by Bertone on the Sprint chassis, which did not go into production. Oddly, the design had something in common with the later Duetto, but that was by Pininfarina . . .

the production-based classes: in this case, the company was aiming at the 1.5-litre sports car formula current in 1955. The car was the Tipo 750 Competizione, and this time it was a joint project between Carlo Abarth, who built the welded steel body-frame, and the sleek open two-seater shell designed and built by Boano. It was a much more elegant racer than the 2000, owing its rear end shape to the Spider and with the front end a lower and more functional version of the Giulietta in its shape.

Alfa Romeo's part in all this was to supply the mechanical components: the intention was to explore production with fifty or so cars, to be sold to private owners who would then race the cars for the factory, with back-up from the company. The car was five inches shorter again than the Spider, with fractionally narrower track front and rear, but the wheels were hung on Giulietta suspension units. The engine was a mixture of the Giulietta design, with variations: though it had the Giulietta's light alloy block with steel cylinder liners, its combination of 76 mm bores and an 82 mm stroke went right back to the proportions of the original 1900 unit. Its valves were set at right angles to one another, rather than the eighty-degree angle of the Giulietta, and intermediate-size valves were fitted—35 mm inlet valves and 31 mm exhaust valves.

To increase the power, the compression ratio was increased to a

An even rarer Bertone design on the Giulietta—a design sketch for a single-seat competition prototype, drawn in 1955

6486

round 10 to 1. The capacity measured 1487.972 cc (!) and the engine was fed by two double-choke carburetters. It produced a staggering 145 bhp (almost 100 bhp per litre), which was fed to the rear wheels through a five-speed gearbox, controlled by a floor lever. With a body weight of only just over 1500 lb, the car had a top speed of 136 mph, which was the same as the bigger 2000 sports prototype of two years before.

In many ways, the Tipo 750 was the most promising of all the specialized racing Alfa Romeos to be developed since the war—but it progressed no further than most of the others. During the course of its development, the Giulietta programme was gathering momentum, and when the first two prototypes were complete, the Technical Department was working at full stretch. So important was the introduction of newer, more powerful versions of the Giulietta, that the 750 project had to take a back seat. Worse than that, it was eventually to be left behind altogether, as all the company's efforts

Harry Schell's Giulietta Sprint queuing up behind a gullwing Mercedes 300 SL and a Porsche during the 1956 Tour de France

Left
*Harry Schell's car later in the
same event*

Styling reduced to a minimum on the Alfa 750 Competizione prototype, with twin wrap-round screens, and the Alfa radiator grille reduced to a bare metal outline

went into the production models. The two cars which were finished were never entered in a race—the others were cancelled, and another promising idea stopped as suddenly as if it had been driven head-on into a concrete wall.

Yet, in a way, the decision was to prove to have been the correct one. For the next assignment for the specialists of the Technical Department was to be the most successful Giulietta of all: the Giulietta TI. Although comparison with the 1900 range suggested that this hotter version of the basic saloon was probably inevitable, the Giulietta TI was to be much more successful than the 1900 TI. What should have been a compromise between opposing ideals—the room and convenience of the saloon with the performance of the sports car—turned out to be such a pleasing combination that many buyers preferred it to any other version. Even though the company engineers may not have taken much trouble over the body styling, it still looked sporting enough to live up to the increased performance provided by the more sporting engine—and, as always, the suspension and chassis required no modification to provide ride and handling up to sporting standards.

With material like this to build on, most of the work facing the Alfa engineers was in the car's engine room. With 8.5 to 1

compression and a double-choke carburetter, the 53 bhp of the ordinary saloon was raised to 65 bhp, enough to propel the car at a top speed of 93 mph. In keeping with its character, the car inherited more instruments: an oil temperature gauge and a circular tachometer to back up the speedometer, which was still a horizontal ribbon-type instrument. There were still other distinctly non-sporting touches, like the steering column gearchange and the bench seat in front as well as in the rear.

Yet there were few cars which could offer the same combination of performance and utility at the price. The TI sold in Italy for £878 when it first appeared—and it sold and sold and sold. Introduced at Monza on 2 September 1957 to the motoring press, and to the public at the Frankfurt Show later the same month, the TI hit the market with the impact of a hammer blow. In less than three months, 1268 TIs were sold. In its first full year of production, 1958, 9948 TIs were sold, and 10,599 during 1959. In its best year, 1961, almost 20,000 Giulietta TIs were sold, making it by far the most popular Alfa of all. By 1965, the Giulietta TI had accounted for 89,408 of all the Giuliettas made—more TIs, in other words, than all the other Giulietta variants put together.

What was it really like, this wolf-in-sheep's bodywork which hit

Even the pretty little Spider came in for some pretty gruelling treatment, like this one in the 1957 Liège-Rome-Liège . . .

the sales jackpot for Portello? *Autocar* tested a first-series TI in 1961; by this time, the factory was turning out right-hand-drive versions for the British market (though buyers of other Alfas still had to go to specialists like Rudds of Worthing, who would convert a left-hand-drive production car for between £175 and £275, depending on the model), which were also blessed with the floor gearlever as used on the Spider.

The testers found several snags. In particular, they found the front seat uncomfortable: 'The seat cushion, with a length of seventeen inches, is extremely short; this, combined with a pronounced roll on the leading edge, which pressed into the back of the thighs rather than lending support behind the knees, caused discomfort on long journeys.' Internal fittings, they said 'were good without being outstanding in the car's price class'. The three indirect gear ratios were more 'widely spaced than on the average British car' and anyone taller than 5 ft 9 in 'would find that the screen top rail limits forward vision'. Oddly, they found the back seat more comfortable than the front, though if a tall driver set the front seat back to the limits of its travel, 'knee-room for the rear-seat passengers is severely restricted, despite deep recesses in the seatbacks'.

To set against these complaints, they were particularly struck by the smoothness of the engine ('Throughout its wide range there was

Alfas by the score . . . a 1958 view of the assembly line at the old Portello factory with Spiders and Sprints in profusion

never a trace of roughness, although it became noticeably noisier at speeds above 5000 rpm, mostly through increased air intake roar') and the starting, which was 'instantaneous, hot or cold'. They found that taking a long right-hand bend fast caused temporary fuel starvation, and the engine cut out on a 1 in 4 hill—in almost all other circumstances, they found the performance excellent. In particular, like many other Alfa drivers since, they were entranced by 'the delicacy and precision of the steering'. With only 2.5 turns from lock to lock it was very quick, 'light at low speeds and when cornering fast, with no impression of springiness in the linkage'.

There was another characteristic of the Giulietta which was to become an Alfa tradition, like the light and lively steering. Because of the shorter wheelbase, the designers had had to go for extra height to fit the passengers in, which meant a fairly high centre of gravity. The practical effect of this on the driver was a noticeable body roll when cornering, though once he became accustomed to this, the suspension coped well, so that the ultimate cornering power of the car was as high as ever. The *Autocar* test team found this body roll was more obvious if 'a fast corner is taken late and hard, rather than attacked early and smoothly'. But they agreed that 'once the driver had assimilated the cornering technique, he usually drove much faster than in other cars of similar class or performance'.

Spider bodies, fresh from the Farina workshops, being wheeled from stage to stage at Portello before being fitted with their own suspension and running gear

Perhaps a clue to the Giulietta TI's success lies in the magazine's summing up of the car: 'few of its competitors in world markets can match it for performance, safety in handling, and running economy.' But another powerful factor in its favour was its brilliant sporting record: when the TI first appeared, the under-1300 cc racing class (another factor in deciding the precise capacity of the car had been the racing classifications) had been dominated in Europe by the Sprint Veloces in the hands of private owners for two years. And the TI was soon to join in: in what everyone agreed was just about the toughest of the Alpine rallies, in 1958, only twenty-five cars managed to finish out of fifty-eight starters. The first three of those finishers were Alfa Giuliettas, winning the team prize and three of the seven Alpine Cups. The overall winner was a French-entered Sprint, but second and third were French and German-entered TIs respectively.

The TI took to rallying like a duck to water: its high body shape actually helped here, since the ground clearance was good enough to take horrible road surfaces in its stride. Mesdames Aumas and Wagner won the Ladies' prize in the Tour of Corsica in 1958 in a TI. In 1959 another TI won the Lyons-Charbonnières rally, running in the standard and modified touring car class, and in 1960 Oreiller and De Lageneste won the Geneva Rally in a TI, with another Giulietta in third place overall. In event after event, for season after season, the TIs joined the earlier, more specifically competition-aimed Veloce models in building up a near-total Alfa domination in several classes of production-car-based racing and rallying.

In 1961 the TI was improved in two ways: mechanically, with a more highly tuned engine delivering 74 bhp at 6200 rpm, and commercially, with a seventeen per cent price cut. In Italy, the TI now sold for an astonishing £731, which was value for money in anyone's language. Even in Britain, the right-hand-drive, floor-change version sold for a basic £1125, though the addition of British taxes brought the total to a still attractive price total of £1641. With figures like these, it was hardly surprising that the TI became the mainstay of Alfa Romeo production.

Yet for many of the TI's most successful years, its predecessor was still in business, though in a different guise. The 1900 still had a following among those who were willing to pay for a bigger and more powerful Alfa than the Giulietta, and though the model formally came to an end in 1959, it had already found a new role. The last of the genuine 1900s had been half a dozen 1900 Super saloons— but the year before they rolled out of the workshops, another car called the 2000 Berlina had appeared to replace it. This was more than a development of the 1900—it *was* a 1900 in all but name and shape. True, the chassis was bigger by almost four inches in the wheelbase, three inches in the front track and two at the back, but the engine was exactly the same in its design and dimensions as the 1900 Super power unit—84.5 mm in the bores and 88 mm in the stroke, 1975 cc in total capacity. The body shape can be described as a 'square-rigged' 1900 Berlina. It was, if you like, to be a stepping stone between the 1900 and the forthcoming Giulia saloon. The 2000 Berlina pioneered the

A Swedish-registered Giulietta TI leans into a corner in typical Alfa style on the 1960 Monte Carlo Rally

1961, and the number-plate is French . . . but the car, the event and the background can stand for successes innumerable for the Giuliettas all over Europe during the 1950s and early 1960s.

The old 1900 in its final guise: the imposing, square-rigged 2000 Berlina of 1961 was the largest production four-cylinder Alfa

shape of the 2600 six-cylinder which succeeded it.

There were some detail changes, to make the engine more suitable for its newer and bigger burden—the compression ratio went up to 8.25 to 1, and a double-choke carburetter was fitted, yet the power peak was only 105 bhp at 5300 rpm, lower than the 8 to 1 compression version used in the 1900 Super Sprint. This was because the engine had been retuned to give more power lower down the speed range, to improve its overall flexibility. Another step in the same direction was taken with the fixing of a five-speed gearbox, though the gearlever was still mounted firmly on the steering column rather than even more firmly on the floor.

Suspension was exactly as before—on the 1900s and on the Giuliettas, for that matter—with coil springs and double wishbones at the front and the rigid rear axle with its locating triangle at the back. The price was only fractionally higher than the 1900 Super Berlina—but the sales figures reflected the way the market had changed, and the increasing preoccupation with the Giulietta. The old 1900 Berlinas and Super Berlinas had sold an average of 2000 cars a year over eight years. Between 1958 and 1961, only 2804 2000 Berlinas were made; compared with the booming sales of the other models, this was merely a small but useful additional bonus.

Yet it was enough to support two other variants, like the other postwar Alfa saloons had done: a Spider open sports car and, eventually, a Bertone-bodied Sprint coupé. The Spider appeared in the same year as the Berlina, using a wheelbase nine inches shorter but with identical track measurements to carry a large and handsome body, this time by Carrozzeria Touring, but which bore more than a

passing family resemblance to the neat little Pininfarina body on the Giulietta Spider. Some of the extra room provided by the car's larger dimensions went on providing an unusual luxury in this type of car: two extra occasional seats behind the front pair. Even so, the Spider weighed 400 lb less than the saloon's massive 3000 lb, and it was provided with a more powerful version of the 2000 engine.

This time the engine had the higher compression ratio of 8.5 to 1, and the same power output as the old 1900 Super Sprint engine. But blessed with its wider power band and the five-speed gearbox—this time controlled by a floor lever—it gave the car a useful top speed of 109 mph. Though the Spider was more expensive than the saloon at £1556 on the Italian market compared with £1494, it seemed to fill a more obvious gap in the range, and it actually outsold its more pedestrian but roomy stablemate—3443 Spiders were made by 1961.

The Paris Motor Show in October 1958—and the 2000 Spider makes its debut on the Alfa stand

By the time the last Berlinas and Spiders rolled out of the Portello factory, they had been joined by the missing member of the trio: the 2000 Sprint. This appeared at the end of 1960, with a supremely beautiful Bertone body which was, in fact, a stretched and enlarged version of his Giulietta Sprint body, but which seemed to many people better suited to the 2000's larger measurements. The front end was fitted with the newly fashionable set of quadruple headlamps, arranged in pairs on either side of the familiar shield-shaped Alfa radiator.

The Sprint had a wheelbase three inches longer than the Spider, but was only 45 lb heavier. With the same more powerful 115 bhp version of the engine (like all the 2000 engines, this had changed the valve adjustment to the shims used on the Giulietta power units) and the same five-speed floor-change transmission, the Sprint shared the same exhilarating performance. But because of its later start, only 700 were made by 1962.

In competition and commercial terms, these cars were very much a sideline. But it was almost as if the company could not bear to sever the final link with its past. If the modern, mass-market cars like the

The sleek 2000 Spider, fitted here with the optional steel hardtop, was in every way a much bigger car than the Giulietta—and when it switched to a six-cylinder version of the twin-cam engine, which measured 2.6 litres, it became a very attractive proposition indeed

Giulietta represented the future, then so be it: but the very existence
of cars like the 2000s also served to show the world that the old hands
had lost none of their cunning and that those who still could afford to
buy bigger, faster, more luxurious Alfas would still be looked after. In
a way, this process had a touch of supreme irony about it. The 1900
had been the first step towards the new cars which had replaced the
old super-luxury models: yet Spartan youth had given way to
comfortable middle-age. The last of the 1900s, like children growing
up to resemble their parents, had come to have more in common with
their ancestors than with their smaller sisters in the company's range.

The Berlina and the Spider ceased production in 1961, and the
Sprint a year later. This was the end of the 1900 story in one sense,
though the models had lasted almost as long as the Giulietta range
itself. But, in another, it gave way almost immediately to a
reincarnation of the same philosophy. In 1962, almost as soon as the
last 2000 Sprint had been delivered, production began of three new
models at the top end of the range: the 2600 Berlina, the 2600 Spider
and the 2600 Sprint.

From outside, these cars were identical with those they had

replaced: the Berlina had the same squared-off, three-box profile as the 2000 saloon (similar also to the Farina designs for the British Motor Corporation a few years earlier, and for the Peugeot 404), the Spider the same Touring body—which looked like the Pininfarina Giulietta Spider stretched and inflated—the Sprint the same lovely Bertone coupé shell. (Later there was also to be a 2600 SZ of which 105 were produced between 1965 and 1967. This resembled the Giulietta SZ in shape but with everything simply bigger, although this should not imply anything less than a graceful car.) But even in their mechanical designs, they shared much with the cars they replaced: the old 1900 engine had finally gone, but put in its place was virtually the same unit with two extra cylinders added. The cylinders were linered down to 83 mm bores instead of 84.5, and the stroke shortened from 88 mm to 79.6, to give a better bore-stroke ratio and an engine capable of higher speeds and greater efficiency. Smaller combustion chambers meant valves smaller by a single millimetre in diameter, and this time the block was in aluminium alloy, like the Giulietta engine.

Otherwise the prescription was the same as before: five-speed gearboxes, with floor levers for the Sprint and Spider and a column change for the Berlina. The weight was slightly increased, thanks mainly to the larger engine, but the increase in power more than made up for it. The saloon now had 130 bhp at 5900 rpm to call upon: enough to lift its speed to the same as the 2000 Sprints and Spiders. The sports models on the other hand now had 9 to 1 compression instead of the 8.5 to 1 of the Berlina—with three double-choke carburetters instead of the single unit fitted to the saloon, they had one barrel per cylinder and a power peak of 145 bhp. This lifted their top speed to 124 mph, and in order to provide stopping power to match this speed, the front wheels were fitted with disc brakes rather than the familiar drums. The following year, further improvements were made in the braking department, with disc brakes and servo assistance on all four wheels.

So, with six cylinders and 2584 cc, the 1900 engine design reached its largest size and its greatest power output. It was a striking tribute to the efficiency and the basic soundness of the original configuration that different versions of it were now powering six-seater limousines and tiny sports cars with almost identical performances—one with a 2.5-litre six, the other with a 1300 cc four! But handsome as the big sixes were, there was no doubt that for Alfa Romeo, and for the next fifteen years at least, the future lay with the fours—a future which would dwarf even the noble achievements already to the company's credit on its postwar record.

Chapter 4
THE BODY BEAUTIFUL

In following the 1900 story through to its final conclusion, we left the Giulietta at the pinnacle of its success, with the brilliant TI making an enviable name for itself on the track and in the showrooms. But during these years which saw the 2000s mature and give way to the six-cylinder cars, much had been happening to the Giuliettas too. During the later fifties and the beginning of the sixties, the staple models went on selling well, and the sports versions went on winning races with what must have seemed—to their opponents, at least—depressing regularity. Meanwhile, the real changes were going on in workshops and on test tracks, laying the foundation for even greater competition successes to come.

First of these was another Bertone variation on the Giulietta—a sort of Super Sprint, though in this case its SS initials stood for Sprint Speciale, and to many collectors one of the most desirable Alfas of all time. Essentially the car was a refined and restyled version of the existing Sprint, and there was a distinct resemblance between the two. But the SS was sleeker, lower, leaner, and very much the prettier of the two cars.

The idea was to take the undertray of the shorter wheelbase Giulietta Sprint and reshape the body to produce a cleaner aerodynamic profile with considerably less drag and a real saving in weight due to the use of aluminium alloy panelling and more Spartan appointments. The weight saving was largely illusory—but the aerodynamics made a real difference to the performance, using a high-compression 9.7 to 1 version of the Giulietta engine, with twin double-choke carburetters developing 100 bhp at 6500 rpm, the car was resoundingly fast—124 mph top speed, the same as the 2.5-litre six-cylinder 2600 Sprint of five years later!

On top of everything else, the Sprint Speciale was cheaper than its top-of-the-range performance rival—but with only two seats and minimal luggage room it was less practical as day-to-day transport. It was almost too pretty to race, though some were used for competition following its introduction in 1957; but in a year noted for some particularly vile designs from other manufacturers, the Giulietta SS remains a rarity. Because they were built from Alfa components in Bertone's small workshops, the production rate was bound to be small. In five years, up to the end of Giulietta production, only 1366 Sprint Speciales were made, though the model would soon surface again in a new guise altogether.

Fewer still were made of the less beautiful but more radical variation on the Giulietta Sprint; only 200 Sprint Zagatos were ever made, but the SZ carried an influence on racing far beyond its

numbers. This was a car which was intended purely and simply for racing: and because of Zagato's system of dispensing with normal body/chassis design as far as possible, and replacing it with a hybrid of the original undertray and a close-mesh, small-bore space frame to carry super-thin alloy panelling, the weight savings which had eluded Bertone in the Sprint Speciale were achieved in the SZ. The original version weighed just 1720 lb complete, a full 180 lb less than the SS. Granted, top speed was influenced as much by aerodynamics as anything else, and even though the SZ lacked the lovely curves of the SS, its squat, tubby shape with the rounded-off nose and tail, low roofline and almost circular cross-section was free of any drag-inducing features, so that it was good for the same 124 mph top speed. What the weight reduction achieved was a much shorter time for the SZ to reach that speed, and this was of paramount importance in racing. With the Giulietta's already good roadholding, the extra performance made a formidable contender indeed.

The best possible racing car still needed the right people to drive it and maintain it—and the SZ was edging into a much more specialized area than the production-based saloons and sports cars had done. The old loose arrangements whereby the factory had given a little assistance (mainly in spare parts and advice) and a great deal of encouragement to the private entrants would have to give way to an altogether more comprehensive and more professional back-up programme. On the other hand, the factory had already started several racing projects and dropped them when they were beginning to show promise, largely because its own technical department was needed for work on the production cars which earned the company's income. What hope had they now for backing up an entirely new racing effort?

The answer was to set up an entirely separate organization, factory-sponsored and factory-backed, but entirely free of involvement with the production cars. In the past, this kind of work had been done by individual specialists with works blessing: like Fachetti, or like Virgile Conrero, who would build special cars, relying on works advice and instructions, and a supply of the right parts. For example, in 1953 Conrero had built an Alfa-based special for Robert Fehlmann, a Swiss racing driver, which had combined parts from Alfa Romeo, Lancia and Fiat to produce a very individual racing coupé.

The tubular frame and the body were designed by Ghia for the Alfa Super Sprint—but Conrero used front suspension from the Fiat 1400 and rear suspension from the Lancia Aurelia rather than the standard Alfa components. The engine was a normal Sprint unit, but fitted with no less than four separate Dell'Orto carburetters and higher compression, it produced a power peak of 130 bhp at 6400 rpm, enough to push the light (1760 lb) car to a top speed of 140 mph. Fehlmann entered the car in the 1953 Mille Miglia only weeks after it was completed and—hardly suprisingly—it didn't get anywhere. But the performance of this hybrid showed how much other would-be racing Alfas could be improved in the right hands.

Left
An unusual view of the lovely Bertone-designed Giulietta Sprint Speciale, with some of its admirers, on the Alfa stand at the 1961 Paris Motor Show

The beauty of the Giulietta SS concealed a shape which was in fact highly aerodynamic, as this side view of the car shows to advantage

But the Giulietta SS had its part to play in the Alfa competition story too: this French-owned car is running in the 1961 Alpine Rally

In the case of the SZ, the initial work was done by the factory's own test department. First of all, they put the Zagato body design through detailed aerodynamic testing. They found turbulence, particularly at the rear end, which was cured by adopting a slightly longer nose and a tail which was not only longer than its predecessor but which ended in a sharply cut-off flat end panel according to the teachings of Professor Kamm. The weight was further pared down by another 30 lb, and the first of the revised SZs was put through a detailed test session on a section of finished but unopened autostrada.

The results were electrifying: the carefully tuned engine was notched up to a power peak of 110 bhp, and the car was timed at 219 kph—136 mph from 1300 cc, which seemed all but unbelievable. Even so, two days' more work, and the car was topping the 150 mark. Fitted with disc brakes at the front, the last thirty cars of the batch of

200 were turned out to the revised standard, and very successful they were in the hands of private owners all over Europe.

Alongside specialized cars like these, the ordinary production-based Alfas were still doing well, however. Conrero had built up a prosperous trade in tuning and supplying conversion parts like specialized racing camshafts to suit the very ambitious plans of owners who wanted that little extra. The strength and flexibility of the Giulietta engine—in 1959 the engines were strengthened through detailed alterations like fractional increases in length of crankcase and crankshaft, deeper cylinder head castings, longer valves and valve guides and tougher bearings and connecting rods—made them ideal candidates for careful boring-out surgery to provide the extra cc needed for the cars to do well in the 1500 cc competition classes.

This idea worked overseas, too: in South Africa, Alfa specialist Sid

Zagato's treatment on the Giulietta, the Giulietta SZ, was altogether more functional and less exotic: but it was spectacularly fast and agile, and a formidable racing combination

Right
*A Giulietta Sprint Zagato
passing the start–finish line at
Stazione di Cerda in the 1962
Targa Florio*

Van der Vyver bored out Giulietta engines to 79.5 mm, to increase the capacity to 1490 cc. The rest of the prescription involved improving the breathing with wider valve ports and 33 mm inlet valves, and minimizing the unnecessary workload by cutting off the fan blades and fitting lightened flywheels. The finished engine was then fitted into a Lotus or Cooper Grand Prix chassis, where the combination worked well enough to win a steady stream of customers.

Just how much work was involved for an owner in increasing the size and power of the engine was shown by an *Autocar* road-test of a British Giulietta Sprint Veloce in 1961. Belonging to Jack Mount of Surbiton, the car was a standard 1957 model which had been bored out to 79 mm and fitted with new cylinder liners. This process sounds simple enough; but not only did it involve ordering special pistons from Italy, which also had higher crowns to increase the compression ratio to 10 to 1, but since the wider cylinder bores now cut into the cooling water passages, these had to be revised and welded up afresh. This caused further problems with head distortion, which threw the camshaft bearings out of alignment—so *these* had to be rebored as well, and then the journals on the camshafts built up to fit the wider-bore bearings by electro-plating.

The bigger engine needed bigger valves—but bigger valves were too big for the recesses machined in the piston crowns, so these too had to be enlarged. With standard camshafts, but with reduced valve clearances to prolong the valve openings, the power peak was approaching 130 bhp at 6500 rpm after six weeks of detailed work and a lot of specialized parts. But all the work had been confined to the top end of the engine—and since the Giulietta power unit was descended from the larger and beefier 1900 engine, its five-bearing crankshaft was well able to cope with the increased loads needed to push the car to a top speed of 120 mph!

When the private customers started to improve on the factory product to such effect, it was time for Alfa to do the job themselves. Not only was there increasing interest in the up to 1600 cc competition class, but with the replacement of the four-cylinder 2000s with the 2600 sixes, the gap between the Giuliettas and the big cars was now rather too wide. What was needed was another model to help bridge the gap, to offer competition customers a new class of racing into which they could carry the Alfa flag, and above all to do a job properly which was beyond the skill or resources of many privateers, without risking unreliability and breakdowns which would rebound on the marque's own reputation.

By the early sixties, the time was becoming ripe for a new model to do all these things. The Giulietta had broken all records for Alfa Romeo production; the 1959 production of 21,332 cars, itself a company record, had been succeeded by 33,606 cars in 1960 and 35,711 in 1961. But demand was beginning to tail off, and market research surveys showed that public interest was centred on a larger and more powerful series of models.

But if the production was higher, then so were the stakes.

Expensive machinery and extra workers had to be kept fully occupied, so that the replacement had to be up to the job. It was no use simply aiming for sales at the 1900 level: the Giulietta's successor had to improve even on these record sales. Yet stepping up production still more demanded more space—and Portello was by now bursting at the seams. If the new models did well, then a move to new premises, with more room to expand, would be an obvious step. But if production fell from the heady levels set by the Giulietta, then costs would have to be cut.

There was one other question to be borne in mind. If shifting back up-market was successful, would this leave another gap below the company range? Another result of the market research surveys had been that the small-car market was in a ferment, following the introduction of Alec Issigonis's brilliant mini-cars. Though their design background was entirely different, they had many of the attractions for keen young drivers which Alfa had always aimed to provide. They were already making a name for themselves in the smallest classes on the racing circuits, and they had a vital part of the

A later version of the Zagato Giulietta SZ, with a more aerodynamic stretched tail—a clear halfway stage between the SZ original and the later and even more successful Giulia GTZ

The Conrero special 'Supersonica' on the 1900 with Ghia bodywork—the car was entered in the 1953 Mille Miglia, where it was driven by Fehlmann and Vuille, but without success

market almost to themselves. Already Alfa's closer competitors were queuing up to enter this same arena—could Alfa Romeo afford to ignore it entirely?

This course, too, was fraught with problems. With the larger Giulietta replacements on the stocks, any ideas of developing an entirely new design were out of the question for some time. The only alternative would be to use the trusty twin-cam to power a radically new mini-Giulietta, and that was a possibility which bristled with difficulties from the very beginning; stretching the engine had worked well enough, but could it be shrunk to the size required? After seven years with sales in the magic five-figure bracket, Alfa Romeo had reached another cross-roads. With the much more competitive market of the 1960s, their earlier experience would be of little use to guide them; but the answers to the company's various problems had to be right first time for its new-found prosperity to continue.

Left
*A classic Alfa—the plain,
unadorned Giulietta Berlina—
in a classic Alfa colour, that
slightly faded Italian racing red
which fades to a near orange
hue*

Below
*The Giulia, in its smaller
version—the Giulia 1300—
with the same square-rigged
body as its larger sisters, but
single headlamps*

Above
Could have been mine—the colour's right, but the Kamm squared-off tail identify this as a 1750 or 2000 Spider rather than a Duetto

Right
Pininfarina's wedge-shaped Alfetta Spider, with its unobtrusive roll bar and removable top panel could well form the basis for a new open-top Alfa

Far right
A 1900 coupé working hard for its living—high in the Sicilian mountains during a Targa Florio of the 1960s

Above
A Tubolare on the track, at Spa in early 1965—by this time the cars were losing their competitive edge, and the main role in racing was passing to their successors, the TZ2s

Left
Another Targa—and another Alfa. The bulbous little Giulietta SZ, in spite of looking functional rather than exciting, was to pave the way for the Alfa works team's return to racing

Far left
Organized chaos in the pits before the start of yet another Targa Florio in the middle 1960s—in the foreground the sleek lines of an Alfa Tubolare, the Zagato-bodied GTZ

Right
Another GTA, daintily lifting a wheel to take a bend at the Nürburgring in a European Saloon Car Championship event

Below
High on the Col de Turini in the 1973 Monte Carlo Rally, Gerard Larrousse and Christian Delferrier on their way to overall victory in Group One, driving an Alfa 2000 GTV

Below
An Alfetta GT, pictured in another of Alfa's happy hunting grounds of recent years, in the 1978 San Remo Rally

Chapter 5
THE GIULIETTA'S
BIGGER SISTER

In one way, the task facing Alfa Romeo at the beginning of the 1960s was a great deal easier than the one they had faced in the middle 1940s. The 1900 had been a car they had had to start from scratch—now, at least, they had the solid success of the Giulietta to build on. The engine, the transmission, the chassis and the suspension, all had been well proven on the road and on the track. All that remained to be decided was the packaging of the new model: if it was to be bigger and more powerful than the Giulietta, then how much bigger and more powerful should it be? What should it be called? What would it look like? What kind of a range of models would be offered—and what kind of a reputation would they succeed in building up for themselves?

One of the questions was settled very early on: the name of the new car. If calling its predecessor the Giulietta had been an obvious enough idea, given the association with the name of Romeo, then the name for its bigger sister followed logically too. Giulietta meant 'little Giulia' in Italian, so what more appropriate name for the larger car than Giulia?

This family resemblance extended to much of the car's engineering: but in some cases the looks would be quite different. In the relatively new and small-production versions like the Spider and the Sprint, the Giulia versions would be outwardly similar to the Giulietta equivalents. But the basic saloon models needed updating in styling, a new body shape to underline the fact that this was the basis of a new range, and not simply another version of the existing one. Normally, a decision like this would be left to the body designers, but in this case Satta himself took a hand. Whatever the fashion, whatever the trends, he knew *exactly* how he wanted the Giulia to look, and no objections would be allowed to stand in his way.

It all went back to another experimental prototype, but one which had been moving in the opposite direction from the successful Giulietta range. Conscious of the ever-widening appeal of the ultra-small-car market, Satta and his team had looked at a smaller version of the Giulietta engine to power a miniature and unorthodox Alfa Romeo, to win the company a stake in the business which was being monopolized in Europe by Alec Issigonis's Mini. In 1959, the year which had seen the appearance of the front-wheel-drive, transverse-engine, rubber-suspension British cars, the Alfa engineers had drawn up plans for a new Alfa which was strikingly similar in many of its ideas.

Far left
The 1979 Elba Rally, and an Alfetta GT against the background which has become so appropriate for these highly sporting Alfas: a gravel track, a cloud of dust, a green mountainside and, in the distance, the blue of the Mediterranean . . .

The first of the square-rigged Alfas, the little Tipo 103 had a lot in common with the Mini, including its size and its front-drive configuration

This was the Tipo 103 prototype. It used a 66 mm bore, 66.5 mm stroke, almost-square version of the classic twin-cam engine, with a capacity of 896 cc—compared with the Mini's 848 cc. Like the Giulietta engine, both block and head were cast in light alloy, and the valves were set at eighty degrees to one another. The sizes of the valves were reduced to fit the smaller combustion chambers: inlet valves were now down to 26.5 mm diameter, exhausts to 24 mm. With but one single-choke carburetter and 8.5 to 1 compression, the engine produced a useful 52 bhp at 5500 rpm, and was harnessed to a four-speed all-synchromesh gearbox mounted in the same unit as the engine. Like the Mini, the whole engine-transmission assembly was turned sideways and connected to drive the front wheels.

The car was designed to use the compactness of the transverse engine-gearbox arrangement to save as much space as possible. The track was an inch narrower than the Giulietta at the front and two inches narrower at the rear, while the wheelbase was a good six inches shorter. But these measurements were deceptive: like the Mini, the wheels had been set right at the corners of the car, so that it was more

compact than the figures indicated. With a length of 11 ft 11 in (compared with the 10 ft of the basic Mini), a width of 4 ft 11 in (compared with the 5 ft 5 in of the Mini) and a height of 4 ft 3 in (two inches lower than the Mini), the Tipo 103 was well in the running in the super-small stakes.

How did it compare on performance grounds? The power output of 52 bhp was higher than any model in the Mini range with the exception of the later 1275 GT (and Cooper S models), which in any case had an engine almost half as large again. Unfortunately, as with many earlier Alfas, the weight was the problem—at 1600 lb, the car was heavier than its size might have suggested. This meant that its performance was slightly down on that of its British competitor, at a maximum of just over 80 mph. But at the very beginning of its development career, it was clearly no slouch.

What is not so clear is how the smallest Alfa would have compared in the all-important area of handling. The Mini's revolutionary rubber suspension (itself an amazingly effective stopgap for the later Hydrolastic system which was originally intended to be used for the

The Tipo 103 was a victim of shortage of factory space—by the time the move to Arese had made room available, its market would have been taken over by the equally revolutionary Alfasud instead

Far left
The same shape, in a bigger box. The shape of the Giulia TI, though surprisingly effective aerodynamically, was essentially Satta's own idea

Below left
Still the same supple suspension and tenacious roadholding—a TI shows its paces on a slip pan

Left
One of the keys to improving the Giulia's drag coefficient was this lip along the top edge of the boot, which cut turbulence behind the car quite considerably

Mini) made it virtually unbeatable on corners. Whether the Alfa's coil spring and wishbone front suspension and coil springs and trailing arms at the back could have been as effective, we can only guess. For the Tipo 103 turned out to be another of those promising enigmas which crowd the Alfa story. Despite its distinct possibilities, it was another occasion when the development department had bitten off substantially more than it could swallow. With development of the Giulia taking first priority, closely followed by the thorny problems of expanding production and finding more factory space, the Tipo 103 came well down the list.

So, almost inevitably, the project was put on the shelf until the Giulia was in production. Once the new range was safely on sale, and once the factory-space requirements had been dealt with, then the 103 design surfaced again. But by this time—early 1967—new ideas and new possibilities had emerged. Alfa Romeo, as a Government-backed company, had to play its part in revitalizing the impoverished south of the country.

What this meant, in practical terms, was the building of a new plant at Pomigliano d'Arco (on the outskirts of Naples), which had been the site of a wartime Alfa Romeo aero-engine factory. Here the firm would turn out a low-cost, high-volume small car which would extend the range into this new market sector at last, and bring valuable new jobs in an area of horrifyingly high unemployment.

In some ways, the Tipo 103 was tailormade for the role. But ideas had moved on since the design had first been carried out: front-wheel drive was still a popular idea, but it was eventually decided to go ahead with a new engine rather than use the old twin-cam power unit in this, its smallest form. Instead, the Alfasud (or Alfa South) design opted for the form we know today, with a horizontally opposed four-cylinder engine with a single overhead camshaft for each pair of cylinders. With 80 mm bores and a stroke of 59 mm, the 1186 cc engine was well over-square—though its power peak of 63 bhp at 6000 rpm was less for its size than that of the Tipo 103, and though the car was heavier at 1800 lb, its top speed was up to 90-plus.

So the 103 was relegated to a page in the record books: only one

The Giulia's squared-off lines made an estate-car version fairly easy to shape—but this Carrozzeria Colli design, like the earlier Alfa estates, never appeared on the market

prototype car was ever built, and only three engines were ever assembled. But in one unexpected way, it still had a part to play: its body design was to set the style for one of the best-known of all Alfa Romeos. This was odd, for the 103's shape owed little to fashion: it was the simple requirements of packing as much inside room into the smallest practicable set of exterior dimensions which dictated its boxy style. But because of its very simplicity, it stood out from the other designs of its time, and Satta himself felt, as did many engineers, that this was a long overdue triumph for functional design over the demands of the styling department. He became determined that, when the Giulia replacement for the graceful and popular little Giulietta saloon finally made its appearance, it would have the same bluff, no-nonsense square-rigged styling—or absence of styling—to distinguish it from its possible competitors.

Much was made at the time of the role played by wind-tunnel testing in the design of the Giulia's 'three box' body shape. There was a programme of testing to improve the aerodynamics, certainly: but this was to tidy up and reduce the turbulence produced by the square angles of the bodywork which Satta insisted upon, rather than the testing of alternative body shapes to find the one with the best aerodynamic performance. Whatever the shape of the car, a lot could be done—and was done—to reduce the local drag-inducing effect at places like window edges, door openings and the like. But given that the basic body shape was decided, only minor questions remained to be answered. For example, the body proportions were fixed by the styling department, under Satta's instructions—but how long should the tail of the car be? To fit the styling of the rest of the bodywork, a long and carefully curved tail was out of the question; however aerodynamically efficient it may have been, the combination would have looked ridiculous. The alternative was to use a sharply cut-off Kamm tail—but at what point should the cutting off be done?

This is where the wind-tunnel testing came in. The results were surprising: the Kamm tail was reasonably efficient at reducing turbulence, and therefore drag, *behind* the car to an acceptable level. But the unexpected factor was that the shorter the tail, the better the freedom from drag. So in the end alternative longer-tail models were rejected; as often happens in engineering, the solution which looked right *was* right. The Giulia saloon was to make its appearance with a cropped tail entirely in keeping with its sober styling.

Was Satta right? By now he had proved his value to Alfa Romeo a dozen times over on a succession of projects, and clearly his judgement was worth backing. Most cars evolve as a compromise between engineering ideals and styling demands, and if in this case the engineers (or rather one in particular) had more say than usual, then this was all to the good. 'When there is a genius, he can have his way,' says Edo Mazzoni, one of Satta's team at the time—and by the only yardstick which really matters to a commercial company, that of popularity with the customers and the resulting sales figures, the Giulia was all the better for having its creator's personality stamped so firmly all over it. In any case, the florid ideas of the late fifties were

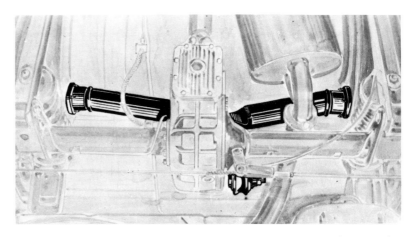

The Giulia TI used the same suspension systems as earlier Alfas, but in this case the reaction triangle of the 1900s was replaced by a thicker, tougher T-shaped member connecting the differential to the chassis and preventing unwanted sideways movement

giving way to neater, cleaner, simpler designs; not only was the Giulia firmly in touch with the fashions of the times, it carried the ideas a stage further and was to survive in its basic shape well into the next decade.

But the new model was a great deal more than just a new body. Clearly the engine size had to be increased from the 1290 cc of the Giulia—but by how much? The next logical step was to shift from the under 1300 cc classes in racing to the under 1600 cc classes, which dictated a displacement in the high 1500s. Simply widening the bores might have caused problems with ensuring efficient combustion at the higher speeds at which the engines were now running. On the other hand, simply lengthening the stroke would be a very retrograde step, effectively reducing the safe engine speeds and cutting the power output rather than increasing it.

The engineers compromised by widening the bores *and* increasing the stroke. They increased the diameter of each of the cylinders from 74 mm to 78 mm, but they lengthened the stroke by a greater margin, from 75 mm to 82 mm, which took the engine back to the bore-to-stroke ratio of the old 1900 series. This ruled out any large increases in engine speed, and it was significant that the Giulia TI engine's power peak was at the same speed—6200 rpm—as that of the later series Giulietta TI.

All the same, there were clear benefits from the increase in engine capacity: the Giulia engine displaced 1570 cc, and the power produced rose to a new maximum, thanks to a step up in compression ratio from 8.5 to 9 to 1, of 92 bhp, which was fractionally better in terms of power output per cubic centimetre than the later Giulietta TI's 74 bhp. There were other detailed improvements: larger valves to admit the larger quantities of fuel and air needed by the bigger engine. Exhaust valves now measured 31 mm in diameter, and inlet valves a full 38 mm across, but the combustion chambers were still the flatter type used on the Giulietta, with eighty degrees between the valve rows. A double-choke vertical carburetter was a standard fitting, and the engine was harnessed to the splendid Alfa five-speed gearbox, though the steering-column change was still normal equipment.

*Suspension on the Giulia TI
used coil springs front and rear*

The new square-rigged body was slightly heavier than the much more graceful-looking Giulietta: the car's kerb weight was a solid 2200 lb, but aided by the five-speed transmission and the extra engine power, the top speed was higher, at just over 103 mph. Part of the weight was used in providing more comfortable interiors than the still fairly austere Giuliettas: gone, or almost gone, was the Spartan tradition of the 1900, though the early series Giulias still featured the front bench seat similar to that of the earliest postwar cars.

The Giulia TI was the first version of the saloon to appear. It was shown to the motoring press on 27 June 1962 at Monza, where its unusual lines and increased performance created a great deal of interest. *Autocar* noticed particularly the sharply descending bonnet line for good visibility (it also helped the car penetrate the airstream easily and smoothly at speed) and the quadruple headlamps—in this case the larger outermost pair of lamps for dipped beam, and a smaller pair inboard of these for the long-range beam. Because of the lower bonnet line, and the engine's longer stroke than its predecessor, the engine was tilted very slightly towards the right (looking from the front)—though the high-mounted carburetters, surmounted by a large disc-shaped air cleaner, overtopped the cam boxes by several inches.

Much of the car's engineering followed the by now traditional lines for postwar Alfa Romeos. The differential was cast in light alloy to reduce the unsprung weight, an idea first introduced on the Disco Volante and used also on the Giulietta range—but the rear suspension was changed in shape if not in its basic system. The differential was still precisely located against sideways movement, but instead of this being done by the triangular member fastened to the differential by two points at its apex, and having its base corners fastened to the bodywork of the car, the Giulia made use of a forged steel three-piece T-bar to do the same job in a slightly different configuration: the cross-bar of the T was fastened to the body sections of the car, while the bottom of the vertical leg of the T was bolted securely to the differential box, ensuring even less unwanted sideways motion for the rigid rear axle, while giving it complete freedom to move up and down over bumps in the road or under cornering loads.

Right
*Giulias (1.6 TIs) galore for
the Italian police—squad-cars
delivered under contract line up
outside the factory*

The original TI stuck to the drum-brake system, again opting for
the three leading-shoe arrangement first pioneered on Alfa's wartime
rear-engine Tipo 512 racing car project, though before long the
Giulia was to be the first Alfa saloon to be fitted with Dunlop disc
brakes, servo-assisted, operating on all four wheels. These, too,
proved to be inadequate, especially at the rear, and were subsequently
changed to ATE. The engine carried no surprises, apart from the
increase in size and power: the twin overhead-camshafts, hemispherical combustion chambers, wet cylinder liners and five-bearing, fully
counterbalanced crankshaft were all parts of the prescription which
customers had come to expect. The car was still high enough off the
ground to possess the tendency to roll on entering corners, as did the
Giulietta—but it held the road, progressing from initial understeer to
almost neutral cornering, just as its predecessor had done.

The TI was tested for the *Autocar* by Count Johnnie Lurani, who
found that one welcome consequence of the new body style was that
drivers who, like him, were more than six feet tall, found themselves

Left
*Some of the grateful new
drivers parading with their
machines on taking delivery
in 1964*

better catered for than in any earlier Alfa models. He also reported the car's handling as 'really outstanding, with excellent adhesion and a comfortable ride over rough surfaces'.

In many ways, the Giulia TI was to represent the full flowering of the postwar Alfa ideal. Here was a saloon with functional styling which owed everything to engineering and nothing to fashion; even the slightly recessed contours in the square-cut tail had been determined by the wind-tunnel test programme (although these contours were removed for the sake of fashion on the final versions of the 1.3 and 1.6 Nuova Supers). The twin-cam engine had reached the peak of its performance for its size, and the rigid rear axle was approaching the limit of its development. It could still cope with the two irreconcilables of providing good handling while dealing comfortably with bumpy road surfaces in a way which was the envy of many independent systems. Everything about the car, apart from the no-compromise approach which had produced the original engine design from a series of sports and racing cars, was closer to practicality than sophistication for its own sake. No wonder that an *Autocar* reader, a few months after the car had been introduced, referred to it as 'the nearest to the perfect motor car for the practical man at present produced'. Many people felt the same: at least enough to send sales figures soaring. New markets were opening up: gone were the days when right-hand-drive versions had to be produced by importers, converted by dealers or produced in small numbers as a very special variant by the factory. From the autumn of 1962, right-hand-drive Giulias were turned out in increasing numbers—and in November it was announced that Alfa Romeo representation in Britain would pass from the hands of Thomson and Taylor of Cobham and Byfleet, who had been doing the job since 1934, to a new subsidiary company. This would be called Alfa Romeo (Great Britain) Limited, whose location changed several times to eventually settle in the Edgware Road in North London.

The TI was not the only Giulia to make its appearance on that day, though: alongside the new saloon were two already familiar shapes. These were the Giulia Sprint, which used the same Bertone bodyshell as the 1300 Giulietta Sprint, and the Giulia Spider, which used the Farina two-seater body used for the Giulietta Spider. Apart from the slightest of detail changes—like the '1600' in chrome numerals on the Spider's bootlid, and improved instrumentation—these merely inherited the Giulia engine along with the existing mechanicals. In this case though, the compression ratio, carburation and power output of the engines were to be the same as that used in the TI; only the lighter bodywork (1991 lb for the Sprint and 1947 lb for the Spider) allowed faster acceleration and top speeds of 107 mph for both versions.

Although the Giulia was intended as a replacement for the Giulietta as the mainstay of the range, it never blotted out the smaller model entirely. Even after the Giulia's introduction, the Giulietta TI remained in production for another three years. In 1963, the year after the Giulia's introduction, more than 12,000 Giuliettas were produced,

Left

The Swiss police too—here in the Italian-speaking canton of Ticino at least—are Giulia users while on duty

Even in faraway Malaysia, the Giulia TI performs its valuable role in helping to keep the peace

the vast majority of them TIs—and even when the model was officially dead and buried in 1965, it reappeared immediately in another guise, as we shall see in the next chapter.

But it was still the Giulia which would set the pace in production figures. In the first half-year of the model's existence, 13,873 Giulias were turned out. In 1963, 36,536 were made—almost three times the total of the dwindling Giulietta production—adding up to a company total for the year of 53,249 cars in no less than twenty different variations, split up among Giulias, Giuliettas and 2600s. And this was the problem: whereas in the 1950s, Alfa's first priority had been to find work for its wartime-inflated labour force, now the difficulty was to find enough factory space to turn out the increasingly mechanized production of ten times as many cars a year. The old Portello factory, built on the edge of Milan in the early

nineteen-hundreds and long since hemmed in by the expanding city, was quite literally bursting at its seams.

The only way to find more space was to move: to move far enough to leave the fast-expanding urban area behind once more, and to lay out modern production lines, test-track facilities, stores and office space in a totally new location. So plans were drawn up to re-site Alfa Romeo at Arese, a village on the flat Lombardy plain to the north of the city, close to the autostrada.

Here there was ample scope for expansion—more than half a square mile of potential factory space which could be built up in stages to allow a peak annual production of 150,000 cars eventually. But setting up a new plant on this scale would take years; years during which the firm would have to strain the resources of Portello to the utmost, to keep up with increasing demand for the Giulia range.

Another necessity, for a company which set such store by the performance and behaviour of their cars on the road and on the track, was a proper test circuit where cars could be driven and studied under almost laboratory conditions. More and more of Alfa's competitors had set up their own tracks, and without them the Italian company was unfairly handicapped. So another site was found among the ricefields lining the autostrada to Turin, at Balocco: here could be built a high-speed circuit, a skid-pan, rough-surface sections, hills and a proper road circuit to match the best.

While these vital new facilities were being designed and built, new advances were needed on the production front. Up to now, the

With production continuing to increase, the company was outgrowing the old Portello plant—so the only solution was to move out into the fast-receding countryside outside Milan, where a new purpose built factory was established at Arese in the early 1960s

company's policy had always been to offer a choice of a few basic models only. But now the ever-increasing production figures allowed them to offer more permutations and combinations on these basic models, to attract still more customers. So successful had been the Giulia's beginning that it was to be a beginning in more ways than one: over the next few years, a series of new versions and variations would make it the most complex and coveted of all Alfa models. Yet, as always, its essential character depended on the engine and suspension which had been developed for the 1900 years before — amply justifying the original decision to go for efficiency and quality in design rather than simplicity and conventionality.

Chapter 6
GIULIAS GALORE

The first of the new additions to the Giulia range was not long in coming. The year after the introduction of the Giulia TI and the reappearance of the Sprint and the Spider in their 1600 guises, a new Giulia coupé was to make its appearance. This was once again a Bertone design, with similar proportions to the original Sprint: but the idea was to broaden the appeal of the car by offering similar lines, similar individuality and similar extra performance, but with more interior space for four genuine seats, rather than the two-plus-two-very-occasional seats offered by the Sprint's restricted dimensions.

Before this, however, there had been two more subtle variations to the range. Bertone himself had revised the beautiful Giulietta Sprint Speciale to take the Giulia engine: with revised instrumentation and detailed inside improvements such as a map-lamp and an ashtray, the car was all set for a new lease of life as the Giulia SS. Oddly enough, the new engine made no difference to the top speed of the car, probably because of its already excellent aerodynamics. Although the power was higher than the Giulia's existing version—with 9.7 to 1 compression, twin double-choke carburetters and revised cam profiles, it turned out 112 bhp at 6500 rpm—the real increase was in the torque delivered in the lower speed ranges. All of these improvements produced a car which, though no faster than its predecessor, did behave more responsively and more flexibly. Not surprisingly, it was a great success: although it was still more expensive at £1468 on the Italian market than the £922 TI, and although the small Bertone workshops were restricted in their production, more Giulia SSs were built and sold than their Giulietta equivalents—1400 as opposed to 1366.

But Alfa Romeo had other things in mind for the more powerful version of the engine used in the SS. The Sprint Speciale appeared in March 1963—and a month later there was a new version of the squared-off Giulia saloon. In a way, the company had shown the way things were developing by introducing the TI as the first of the range rather than a more pedestrian Berlina version, as they had done with the Giulietta. Now they were underlining the message by putting on the market a still faster and more powerful version of the saloon, which used the same engine as the Sprint Speciale.

This was the Giulia TI Super, which was unveiled at Monza on 24 April 1963. Apart from the engine, there were detail changes in the parts of the car which were hangovers from the old family-saloon philosophy which had operated on the basic Berlina models of the 1900 and the Giulietta. Gone at last was the steering-column gear change; gone was the strip speedometer; gone was the bench front seat. Instead the Giulia Super driver sat in a properly shaped bucket seat, facing a trio of round instrument dials, at his side a fairly long but precise gearlever controlling a change which was spring-biased to the third-fourth plane, which was soon to become a byword for fast, accurate shifts. Careful alterations cut the weight of the car by 200 lb, and the speed went up to more than 115 mph. This extra performance was emphasized by the reappearance of the old Alfa Racing four-leaf clover on the side of the bonnet and, unfortunately, by an increase in price to £1409 on the Italian market. For all that, it proved a popular model with the sporting fraternity, though it never sold in numbers approaching those of the ordinary TI.

By September of 1963, work on the new Bertone coupé was complete: the ingenuity of the design was shown by the fact that though the wheelbase was actually an inch shorter than the Sprint, the interior accommodation was vastly improved. The rear roofline was lifted to give adequate headroom in the rear seats, and the old fastback rear end was replaced by a flatter rear screen and a more squared-off

The Giulietta SS was too good to lose—so Bertone built another version around the Giulia, to be known as the 1600 Sprint Speciale

Above
*Still rubber mats on the floor,
but comfortable cloth seats and
a nicely laid-out dash: the
1600 SS from the inside*

Right
*The Giulia SS took over the
competition role of the smaller
car too: here's one against a
backcloth of Sicilian mountains
in the Targa Florio in 1966*

bootlid. In comparison with its predecessor, it was slightly less a
coupé and more a sports saloon, though it still looked a lot sleeker and
faster than the TIs.

This was just as well, for the Sprint GT, as the new model was
called, had a good deal to live up to. Earlier in the year, *Autocar* had
tested the 1600 version of the Sprint and though they assessed it as 'a
mixture of the very good—and the ordinary', they found little
enough to criticize beyond poor headlights, windscreen wiper blades
which tended to lift off the screen at 80-plus, and an almost totally
useless handbrake. On the other hand they hammered it over the
roughest pave at 45 mph and found it 'fully controllable, which is
more than one finds with a great many others'. They took it over
washboard corrugations at 35 mph without distress, and praised the
comfort of the driving seat. They didn't like the small needles and the
confusing reflections which made the instruments difficult to read,
and they found nowhere to rest the left foot, except on the clutch
pedal.

In spite of a lot of insulation material, they found the car noisy, and
complained of strong engine resonances at around 4000 rpm, while
the gearbox came in for criticism—not on the grounds of
performance, though second-gear synchromesh began to fail during
the test—for the spacing of its ratios. They also noticed the body roll

on corners, inherited from the Giulietta, and complained that gusty cross winds demanded a lot of minor adjustments to the steering. They also, like many Alfa drivers, found the steering on the heavy side at low speeds but 'light and extremely accurate with no kickback at fast cornering speeds'. Small movements and little effort at the wheel kept the car on course through sweeping bends though there was some initial roll oversteer on the entrance to a bend, 'but once the car is stabilized, the characteristics are neutral up to the point of breakaway, when the rear wheels slide out quite gently'.

Accommodation was the main problem: the space provided in the boot was taken up almost entirely by spare wheel, battery and toolkit, while the space behind the front seats was a baggage platform which could be fitted with padded cushions at £12 10s the pair, but which still presented a cramped space for fully grown passengers. Performance, on the other hand, was the trump card. Apart from its handling ('unless one made a monstrous error of judgement, and

The 1963 Frankfurt Show—and a new version of the Sprint, this time based on the Giulia chassis and mechanicals, with a genuine rear revised back end, and a new name: the Giulia Sprint GT

entered a corner far too fast, the car would always help one out of trouble') it was fast enough to reach 60 mph in 13.2 seconds, cover the standing quarter-mile in 18.8 seconds, and put up a timed top speed of 112 mph on its best run.

The Sprint GT set out to improve on this: not least by being available in much larger numbers than the body production of Bertone's workshops could cope with. Though the design was still by Bertone, the Sprint GT would be made in the first section of the Arese plant to be completed, using mechanical parts turned out from Portello and sent to Arese for assembly. It had a third version of the Giulia engine, set in between the first two in peak-power terms, with two downdraught carburetters, 9 to 1 compression and a peak power of 106 bhp at 6000 rpm, providing a top speed of 111 mph but using a lazier final drive ratio to make for quieter and less stressful high-speed cruising. Like the later Sprint 1600s, the Sprint GT would use disc brakes on all four wheels, with servo assistance, and though the

A hotter version of the TI, intended for sporting-minded owners—the almost identical (outwardly, at least) Giulia TI Super, seen here on the Monte

gearbox ratios were the same as those which provoked the wrath of
the *Autocar* testers, the revised overall ratios did at least allow a higher
maximum speed in each gear.

But the biggest difference was in the rear-seat accommodation:
instead of the low roof and the padded shelf of the 1600 Sprint, there
were now two cramped but genuine seats in the back of the GT.
Although the car was slightly heavier, at 2090 lb, and slightly more
expensive, at £1386 on the Italian market, this increase in
accommodation brought an immediate widening of its circle of

Front end of the Giulia saloon—this one is actually the 1300 version

potential customers. In four years of production, Alfa would make and sell 21,542 of this model—fully three times the total of Sprint 1600s in three years of production.

In 1964 came still more changes: the 1600 Sprint dropped out of production, though Bertone's long-lived design would reappear immediately with the Giulietta engine back in place, as the 1300 Sprint. Carburation, compression and top speed (102 mph) were all identical with its Giulietta Sprint form; the differences included the instrumentation, the disc brakes on the front wheels and the slightly lower price of £1068 on the Italian market, compared with £1096 for the original Giulietta Sprint.

Two months later, on 11 May, there came an even more interesting hybrid. In the last year in which the long-lived Giulietta TI was still produced in any quantity, its engine was boosted from the 74 bhp of the final series production to 78 bhp, and fitted into a lightened and simplified Giulia TI body to produce the Giulia 1300 Berlina. The weight was down to 2150 lb, so that thanks to the body's excellent aerodynamics, the car could still muster a top speed of just under 100 mph with the smaller engine. Not only did the buyer still have performance and the more modern Giulia bodystyle; he also enjoyed both these benefits for less money than for any other model. At only £840 in Italy, the Giulia 1300 saloon was the cheapest of all the Alfas, and though for that price the customer didn't get a five-speed gearbox, he did get disc brakes on all four wheels.

Alfa Romeo were now cashing in on the successful sales figures and the increasing factory space becoming available out at Arese, and were able to embark on two years of almost uninterrupted innovations without parallel in the company's history. Next in the cavalcade was a hotter version of the two-seater open sports car. Unveiled at Monza on the same day as the 1300 saloon was the 1600 Spider Veloce. This used the 112 bhp version of the Giulia engine, as produced for the Super Sprint, to raise its top speed to 112 mph-plus. The only other changes were amendments to the hood and the addition of the word 'Veloce' to the chrome '1600' on the tail. Other

These anxious-looking gentlemen are pressmen evaluating the Touring convertible GTC version of Bertone's Giulia Sprint GT on the track at Monza in 1965

detail alterations to the Giulia TI saloon, shown at the same time, included separate front seats and a floor gearchange, now provided as standard fittings for the model.

This detailed tinkering with well-established models was to pale into total insignificance, however, compared with what was on the way for the following spring. There were already two versions of the Giulia saloon—the TI, and the competition-oriented hotted-up TI Super. Now the company was to make the situation even more confusing by introducing a worthwhile compromise which had the mystifying designation of the Alfa Romeo Giulia Super! What this meant, in fact, was an upgrading similar to the transformation of the old 1900 into the 1900 Super: chrome body strips along the sides beneath the doors, extra badges, a more sporting steering wheel similar to the triple-alloy-spoked wheel used for the Sprint GT, proper round instruments and, most important of all, a power

Back to square one: the GTC convertible has its top closed again by the fitting of an optional metal hardtop, making an interesting pillarless variation on the basic Sprint GT coupé

increase to 98 bhp at 5500 rpm, two double-choke Webers and 9 to 1 compression. These last did at least ensure that not only did the body look better, both inside and out, it also tended to move faster, with a top speed of 110 mph.

Accompanying the Giulia Super in its first steps into the limelight was yet another new model: and if the Super had at least looked familiar enough from the outside, the Giulia GTC didn't look familiar at all. Yet there were recognizable features for those who looked carefully: the car was unique in the Alfa range, although it represented in its type a return to the open tourers which were the first cars the company had made nearly half a century before. It was a four-seat convertible, based on the Sprint GT, but rather confusingly the work was not done by Bertone, who had designed the original body. Instead the bodywork, which was now produced by Alfa themselves, was sent to Touring, who lopped the top off and did the necessary strengthening and tidying-up operations, and the fitting of the hood and the trim. The engine used was the 106 bhp version belonging to the Sprint GT.

These two models were greeted enthusiastically: the Super's modest power increase and detail embellishments were only the obvious outward signs of a comprehensive improvement programme which virtually transformed the car's driving appeal. The fitting of two Webers instead of a twin-choke Solex and other improvements to aid the breathing had improved the torque, particularly low down the speed range—it was now 110 ft lb at only 2800 rpm, where the TI produced 88 ft lb at 4000 rpm. This improvement was put to good use by changing the final drive ratio from 5.13 to 1, to 4.55 to 1, allowing easier cruising, much more flexibility and longer engine life.

The GTC too was surprisingly successful. All too often designs which are modified as cruelly as this one was—having its roof sliced off above the waistline and aft of the windscreen pillars—end up looking unspeakably ugly. Either Bertone's design was so brilliant that it could cope with this kind of thing without looking hideous, or the process was carried out with great sensitivity, or perhaps Alfa and Touring were simply lucky—probably the truth is a combination of all three—but the car looked attractive and worked well. *Autocar* tested it soon after its introduction, along with the Giulia Super, and pronounced themselves delighted with both. The Super was 'much quicker . . . than the TI', and it was very easy to reach an indicated 100 mph while 'in characteristic Alfa fashion the handling gave every confidence through the turns'.

The GTC's convertible roof folded 'quickly and easily after two clamps are released from the top of the windscreen rail. There are small rear quarter-windows which wind down out of sight, as does the glass in each door. Travelling in the back with the hood down and neatly hidden under a tonneau cover, we found the car surprisingly quiet but rather draughty around the back of the neck. The rear seats are comfortably shaped and there is enough room for legs and feet if those in the front are prepared to compromise a little.'

The only criticisms were, of the Super 'once or twice the outside rear suspension seemed to bottom as the body heeled over accurately towards the limit', and of the GTC: 'The car we drove did not feel entirely rigid, and there was some scuttle shake when travelling over the rougher parts of the track. Like the Super, however, it handled impeccably with all the precision and predictable behaviour which have kept Alfa models so well established in sports car markets throughout the world.'

Sadly, the GTC never quite lived up to its initial promise. In the bleaker climates of northern Europe, convertibles were of limited appeal anyway, and basing the operation at Touring's body workshops meant limiting production to a small figure by comparison with the lines now developing at Arese. Only 1,000 were produced in two years—a figure which the target production at Arese would turn out in little more than the same number of days. So it's hardly surprising that the entirely Alfa-produced Giulia Super sold 36,000 examples in the same time, out of an eventual production total of 124,590 up to 1972—and this despite its having close competitors in the company's own range, which the GTC certainly did not.

By the following year, 1966, the next gap in the Alfa range to be filled by a new variation was that still existing between the Giulia 1300 Berlina and the larger 1600 saloons. By taking the Giulietta engine and fitting it with a double-choke Solex with 9 to 1 compression, a power peak of 82 bhp was produced—only 10 bhp below the Giulia TI 1600! This warmer 1300 was linked to the five-speed gearbox and fitted to the TI body-chassis. The result was a car which looked like its bigger sister, performed like its bigger sister with a top speed of 100 mph, but which undercut the price of the 1600 TI by selling at a keenly competitive £831. In view of this, and the taxation advantages which the smaller engine conferred on the model in its home market, it's hardly surprising the Giulia 1300 TI became a very popular model indeed, selling 144,213 units in just six years.

A month later, and it was time for another pair of new models. The beautiful little Spider had been introduced as part of the Giulietta range back in 1955, and though sports two-seaters never date as quickly as saloons or coupés, the company thought it was time for a more up-to-date body style. Like its predecessor, this was designed and produced by Pininfarina, and owed much to several of his earlier special-bodied projects: in particular to the coupé he had built on the Alfa 6C 3000 CM chassis. The new sports car had a similar front end treatment, with faired-in headlamps and deep scallops running horizontally along the sides between the wheels to a gently tapered tail, though fortunately without the hideous fins and glasshouse hardtop fitted to the original design.

In fact, the body which was to be fitted to the Spider had been produced in prototype form as early as 1961, when it appeared at the Turin Show on Pininfarina's stand in the body-building section. Since then, successful sales of the old Spider, coupled with the long list of more urgent models awaiting introduction, had held it back. Now, five years later, it was given the go-ahead, to be fitted into the seemingly never-ending list of new model introductions now being arranged by the works.

Yet there were many features of the new Spider which hinted at a hasty introduction. The 1600 Spider had become the Veloce only two years before; in spite of a significant performance improvement (107 mph to more than 112) and a price increase which was relatively modest (£1063 to £1110 on the home market) sales had dropped off steeply. After selling 9250 Spiders in three years with the 1600 engine, only 1091 Spider Veloces were sold in the following two years, a drop of eighty-three per cent. So it was high time for a successor to take over and revitalize a flagging model.

Not everyone liked the new model. It was very difficult to improve on a design with the classic beauty and simplicity of the original Spider, and in any case familiarity in car body styles brings acceptance and even appreciation in its train. It was lower and wider than the original car, with a sleek profile and a gently rounded tail. It had all the creature comforts, with an easily removable hood, sun visors, quarter-lights and wind-up windows (still relatively new among non-Alfa sports cars), not to mention a tough but frighteningly expensive optional hardtop. It even had a new engine: less powerful at its peak than the Spider Veloce engine, it was yet another hybrid. It had the twin double-choke Weber carburetters introduced on the Veloce version, but the 9 to 1 compression of the original Spider 1600 engine (or the Giulia TI, come to that), which in this case was a combination which added up to a power peak of 109 bhp at 6000 rpm.

All the same, the top speed of the car, in spite of its being 200 lb heavier than the old Spider, was more than 115 mph—faster even than the Veloce. The reason was once again the engine: different cam profiles and improved breathing, aided by larger 37 mm inlet valves, made the power unit more flexible, so that the final drive ratio could

Quart in a pint pot: the twin-cam Giulia engine fitted (just!) beneath the bonnet of the Giulia Spider 1600

be changed in the same way as was that of the Giulia Super. All the car lacked, in fact, was a name: for the first few months of its life it was called the 1600 Spider, only distinguished from its predecessor by the official dropping of the Giulia name.

Yet to those who knew it well, the Spider was a thoroughly delightful car. My own introduction to it was a demonstration blast round the newly finished Balocco test track a year after its introduction, with one of the company's test drivers at the wheel. This must be the ideal way to make the acquaintance of any car. When I bought one a year later, I'd already seen how the car handled on the very limit of adhesion in skilled hands on a closed track, at cornering speeds I would never have had the skill or courage to approach in ordinary driving. In spite of its nose-heavy weight distribution, its handling varied from slight initial understeer to almost perfectly neutral cornering—the only time the lack of weight over the rear wheels betrayed itself was in a certain lack of traction in muddy or icy conditions.

It certainly belied its sports-thoroughbred image in its practicality and reliability: in nine years it ran for close on 150,000 miles all over Europe with unfailing performance. Engine wear was almost nil: the only failures and replacements in all that time were a water pump and three exhaust valves. The clutch was relined once; apart from brakepads and other consumables, the only other problem was worn universal joints on the propeller shaft. Although a genuine two-seater, there was room enough behind the seats for cases, or for passengers who didn't mind a little discomfort—on one occasion the car coped with three adults, four children and a Labrador in a rescue operation after a friend's car broke down miles from home!

If the car had a fatal flaw, it wasn't in the engineering department: mechanically it was good for another 100,000 miles. But like so many of its fellows, it was prone to the deadly and eventually terminal disease of body rust. In the early sixties, Alfa Romeo, like many other continental car manufacturers expanding into wider markets, found themselves up against entirely new climatic problems. After Alfa had set up their British subsidiary, and introduced their own right-hand-drive versions of their best-selling models, they channelled an increasing proportion of their production to countries like Britain.

Unfortunately many of these cars were not adequately protected against the rigours of northern winters. Body sealing and paint finishes that were adequate in Italian conditions couldn't cope with weeks of wet weather on end, corrosive fogs, slush mixed with salt thrown up from the road which could lodge in moisture traps and chew away panelling from the inside. After *Motor Sport* drew attention to the problem in 1964, there followed a succession of letters from anguished owners complaining that otherwise good cars were beginning to fall to pieces after a frighteningly short life.

To do Alfa credit, they weren't the only makers to suffer from this problem: and once production shifted to Arese, then they were able to install more elaborate coating and paint preparation processes which did at least ease the problem. But so high were their own standards of mechanical reliability that it would be a long time before body life would ever begin to match up to the engineering. By the time the new Spider was introduced, Alfa's own body protection had been greatly improved—but the Pininfarina Spider body still proved vulnerable along the wheel-arches and under the doorsills (though in the case of my own Alfa much of the blame must have gone to an inadequate repair by a dealer who had been involved in an accident with the car while road-testing it after a routine service—hardly a common hazard, one would hope!).

Despite its hurried introduction and lack of a proper christening, the new Spider revitalized sales of the open-top Alfas. In less than two years, 6325 were sold, which represented a higher production than the best of the 1600 Spider (earlier version) years. *Autocar* timed the Spider at better than 115 mph, and though standing starts were hampered on occasion by wheelspin (that light tail again!) they recorded a time of ten seconds to 60 mph. With the hood down 'we could enjoy that characteristic Alfa exhaust note only a few feet behind us', and they reported that 'the Spider handled splendidly, helped no doubt by its shorter wheelbase [its wheelbase was in fact the same as the earlier Spider, though the front track was an inch wider] lighter weight and its low centre of gravity'. They went on to criticize 'the dashboard painted in the body colour', but noticed with pleasure that 'we were able to throw it about with spirit after only a few minutes' driving'.

Introduced alongside the Spider was another model which, though it appeared to be a much simpler modification of an existing model, was to become in the eyes of many Alfa enthusiasts one of the best Alfas of all time. This was a more sporting version of the Sprint GT, called logically the Sprint GT Veloce, soon known as simply GTV.

This car was, like the old Spider Veloce, outwardly almost identical to the non-Veloce version: in this case the only outward changes were a revised set of grille bars on the front end and, once again, the addition of the word 'Veloce' at the back. But the fitting of the same twin-Weber, 9 to 1 compression, 109 bhp version of the Giulia engine as fitted to the Spider, transformed the car out of all proportion to the increases in power and flexibility. Bertone's beautiful four-seat coupé was a familiar enough design by now, but this was surely the engine it had been waiting for. The two halves came together to make a car which totally outclassed its predecessor, and which even now is eagerly sought after on the collectors' market.

When *Autocar* first met the GTV, they considered it slightly less stable than the Spider. Later, in a fully detailed road-test back in Britain, they assessed it as 'a pure-blooded sports car which impresses immediately and goes on endearing itself to the driver the more he sits behind the wheel'.

The five-speed gearbox they described as 'delightful', though in this case they found the engine rather less flexible than on other Alfas: 'Instead of being able to pull away cleanly from as low as 20 mph in fifth, the GTV would only drop to 30 mph in this overdrive ratio before the pick up became "fluffy".'

First step towards the successor to the original Giulietta/Giulia Spider: a Pininfarina prototype at the 1961 Turin Show was to re-emerge, with alterations, as the Duetto five years later

But it was in the handling department that the testers found the greatest cause to revise their opinions: 'In terms of roadholding, this Alfa is without doubt the best we have tried. The characteristic "twitchiness" of all other Alfas barely exists, and it is not necessary to choose one's line through a corner and set the car up so early. It is a much more forgiving car, with first-class stability. Understeer is predominant, and the ultra-sensitive steering tells the driver exactly how much cornering power he is using, and how much more he has in hand. When rushing through a long turn, the car keels over to take up quite a noticeable roll attitude and stays firmly glued to the road, with some front tyre squeal occasionally. Even after the tail of the car has reached the apex there is no oversteer, regardless of how much power is then turned on, so the driver can keep to a steady line at very high speed. It is extremely difficult to kick the tail round under power, and in a straight line the Alfa runs true as an arrow.'

Praise indeed: especially when one recalls that the basic suspension layout of the GTV had been developed for a production saloon a decade and a half before. But over rough surfaces—inevitably the bane of most sporting suspensions—the *Autocar* found the car's performance even more remarkable. 'Suspension movements are soft in an accommodating kind of way, and the car traverses bumps and dips very smoothly with only the minimum of disturbances transmitted to the body. We were able to rush the MIRA concrete waves at 40–50 mph without being bucked in the air, and on pave the Alfa only began to kick its tail about at 45 mph. All the time the structural stiffness was impressive, with no rattles or signs of deflection.'

But perhaps the most remarkable qualities of the GTV showed up in contrast to its competitors on the market. In terms of its sporting pedigree and its accommodation for two people, comfortably, in the front and two more, rather less comfortably, at the back, the GTV's closest opposite numbers were the Porsche 912, the Lancia Flavia coupé and the Jaguar E type 2-plus-2. On all performance figures the Jaguar won hands down—with an engine more than twice as big as the Alfa's it was bound to—but it paid for this pre-eminence by consuming by far the most fuel of the quartet. The Porsche had a better maximum speed than the GTV, but in its acceleration to 60 mph and in its time for the standing quarter-mile, it came second only to the Jaguar, for a fractionally higher petrol thirst than the other two. But the most remarkable comparison was in price: while the Jaguar sold on its home market at £2284 at that time, and the Porsche's imported price was £2428 and the Lancia's £2357, the GTV sold on the British market for a mere £1950, all taxes and duties paid!

The GTV stayed in production in this form for three years, a year longer than the Spider, and during that time more than 13,000 were sold. Yet the Spider was to prove in some ways the more successful, and certainly the more durable of the two: Alfa made up for its hurried introduction, and the lack of a separate identity from its predecessor, by holding a competition to suggest a name for the car, with one of the cars itself as a prize. The lucky winner was Guidobaldi Trionfi of Bari—in a contest which produced ideas as varied as 'Patrizia', 'Edelweiss', 'Lollobrigida', 'Sputnik', 'Hitler' and 'Nuv-

One of Pininfarina's original sketches for the Duetto—it portrays the car as considerably lower and wider, and far less attractive, than it really was

olari', his suggestion was the simple but appropriate 'Duetto'. Yet the name disappeared at the next engine change and body modification, when there was no longer any danger of confusion with the earlier model; most dealers never knew the name anyway, so that ordering spare parts for the car was always a nightmare.

In its ultimate Kamm-tail form, the 2000 Spider, the car and body-style is still with us, though it is no longer imported into Britain as, having been passed for sale in America, the demand is so great that it is no longer worth producing a right-hand-drive version for this country. But it's still the only Alfa from the middle sixties still recognizable in today's range. Over the years it has been popular with opera singers and footballers, film stars and shiekhs; it played a role in the 1967 film *The Graduate* hardly less important than that of Dustin Hoffman, it made its first appearance in America after a luxury trip across the Atlantic in the liner *Raffaello*, and it was in fact the last design of Battista Pininfarina himself, founder of the coachbuilding company which bore his name in 1930.

After the brilliance of the Spider and the GTV, it seems hard to imagine there were still two more cars in the Alfa range due to make their appearances in that same year of 1966. The first of these was no world-shaking new design, but another valuable gap-filler: the GT 1300 Junior, which was a GT Sprint fitted with an even hotter 89 bhp version of the 1290 cc engine. Using two double-choke Webers and 9 to 1 compression, like the GTV, the little engine produced enough power to push the identical body to 106 mph-plus. Once again, the five-speed gearbox and disc brakes on all four wheels were standard fittings in the inclusive price of £995 in Italy—remarkable value for money at the time.

But the other new model wasn't obvious at all: in fact it looked anything but new at first sight. It relied upon the Giulia chassis with an inch-longer wheelbase and a narrower front track to provide a

The real thing: the original Duetto, with its rounded tail and the light and airy hardtop. The style seemed strange after the earlier and more familiar Spider, but soon became very popular

A very familiar view—the 'office' of my Duetto was the right-hand drive mirror-image of this Italian version

basis for a Zagato tubular frame rather like the one used on the Giulietta SZ, but this time reproducing the contours of the immortal 1750 of the early thirties. The engine was the standard 92 bhp TI 1600 unit, which was enough to push the light but virtually unstreamlined open two-seat body to a top speed of 97 mph, and the combination of modern mechanicals and vintage-style bodywork gave many enthusiasts severe attacks of the vapours.

In numerical terms, this was probably one of the least successful Alfas ever—certainly it stood out from all the postwar models in that only ninety-two were ever made. Many people poured scorn on it as a counterfeit imitation of a great original, yet surely this was missing the point: it was a replica, of course, though not an exact replica made with intent to deceive. But it was made by the two companies who had collaborated to produce the original, using (in Zagato's case) similar methods and (in Alfa's case) mechanical parts which still owed much in their approach and ideas to the ones used more than thirty years before.

The idea had come from the prestigious Italian motoring magazine *Quattroruote* ('four wheels') and though there were many differences enforced by time and progress—smaller road wheels, wider track, four cylinders rather than six and the absence of a supercharger—the performance was around the same 100 mph mark. *Autocar* tested one

and criticized the awkward hood and the draughty, badly fitting, fiddly side-screens. But I drove one through one bitter January week with hood down and screen folded flat, and bare as it was, no car in twenty years has ever provided more sheer fun in driving.

Autocar's testers found something of the same quality in the car. 'You sit there like God in his Heaven, with a superb view of everything round you; there are no screen pillars to obscure your view, and the wind whistles past your ears, making certain that in no circumstances whatever do you feel drowsy.' 'The steering, though moderately low-geared with 3.5 turns from lock to lock, is splendidly quick and precise, the car answering almost to tightenings or slackenings of one's grip, like a racing car. One has, therefore, almost to "lean it" through fast bends.' 'It shows not a trace of roll on corners, nor does it seem to over- or under-steer, being as well balanced as any car which I have ever driven.'

In terms of numbers, the 4R Zagato was no commercial success—but it was an extremely interesting car. Almost no one else could have built a car using present-day parts which succeeded in getting as close to the spirit of the early thirties, because few manufacturers had such a design continuity extending through almost four decades. Achilli Motors did, in fact, make a successful attempt in 1975 to reproduce the 4R Zagato with their 'Leontina', but production only ever

A step back into the past, with Zagato's version of the Giulia: using the shape and the techniques of the 1930s to re-create a model with the appeal of the old 1750s and something of the same pedigree . . .

reached very small numbers. Even as a new model in its own right, it deserved better from its public: it was more stylish and more beautiful than many present-day sports cars, yet it competed with the best in terms of handling. With a little more refinement and a cut in price—traditional nineteen-thirties coachbuilding was prohibitively expensive in the nineteen-sixties, and Zagato did well to hold the price down to just over £1500 in Italy—it might have sold in considerably greater numbers.

Yet the car itself, and the year in which it appeared, set the seal on the whole remarkable Giulia range. Not only did the 4R Zagato re-emphasize the links with the past which were part of every one of its more modern-looking contemporaries, but its daring idea also underlined the confidence which the Giulia's success had brought the company. Even the brilliant record of the Giulietta had been totally eclipsed, and the move to Arese had been completely vindicated. Production in 1967 of the Giulia range reached 72,763 cars, almost double the total of the best of the Giulietta years, and it seemed that every square foot of the vast new factory space would be needed to keep up with the ever-swelling demand.

Chapter 7
COMPETITION:
THE PACE QUICKENS

The Giulia range had taken Alfa Romeo to new heights in commercial success, as the Giulietta had done—on a more modest scale—before it. But there was another measure of achievement which in Alfa's past had been equally important, and which still could have a very direct influence on future sales figures: racing success. The importance of a good set of competition results could be seen in Alfa's own advertising during the nineteen-sixties.

The class win to the credit of a racing Giulia TZ in the automobile Tour de France was the subject of a British advertisement in the early sixties: 'First in its Class—ALFA ROMEO—in the 13th Tour de France Automobile, Sept 11–20. First in the Grand Touring Class from 1300–1600 cc was the Giulia TZ driven by Jean Rolland and Gabriel Augias. This team finished in 3rd place on handicap and 7th overall in the Grand Touring category. Four Alfa Romeo Giulia TI Supers were in the first eleven places overall in the Touring category: finishing 2nd, 3rd and 4th in the 1300–1600 cc Touring class and 2nd, 4th and 7th on handicap.'

Underneath the results, the copy went on to emphasize the link between these racing Alfas and the production cars: 'The winning Alfa Romeo Giulia TZ has the same mechanical assemblies as cars in the Giulia 1600 range, available from your Alfa Romeo dealer.'

This sort of publicity was meat and drink to a maker like Alfa—even better, in some ways, than the single win was the succession of results which gave the definite impression that victories were happening all the time. One American advertisement from the same period had the copy line 'Not all auto makers engage in braggadocio about winning races' over a list of results, labelled intriguingly as a *partial* list of Alfa Romeo victories during 1964. It began with a win by a Giulia Super in the 1600 cc Touring class of the Monte Carlo Rally and ended with a win for another Super in the Touring class of a Brazilian endurance race. In between came forty other victories and class wins in events ranging from Le Mans (Giulia TZs, first and second in class) to Sebring (ditto), ranged above the splendid throw-away line 'At Alfa it's simply a tradition.' Underneath, the advertisement said that 'Winning races has been a steady diet at Alfa since 1911. You can see it reflected in the new Giulia TI, a 4-door, 5-passenger sports car with five forward speeds (fully synchronized), all-aluminium engine and double overhead cams. It's easily capable of over 105 mph and 31 miles to the gallon. At 60 mph, you're using

Some of the earlier Alfas were still giving their owners the thrills of racing after a surprisingly long time: this 1900 coupé is racing in the 1963 Targa Florio!

only half the engine's power. Now look at the Giulia TI's equipment: bucket seats, disc brakes, heater-defroster, windshield washers, tachometer, hand accelerator, Robert Bosch electrical system, back-up lights, undercoating and many, many more which others charge for as "extras". There's also a variety of Spiders, Coupés, 2 + 2s. Ask your dealer about Alfa's Owner–Driver Racing Program, including availability of racing options.'

Advertisements like these were what the customers liked to read: and both were the fruits of a resurgence of the works racing efforts to win back some of the ground lost since the brilliant but expensive programmes of the nineteen-fifties. These successes were due partly to a fundamental rethinking of the racing programme, partly to the establishment of a new Alfa-sponsored racing organization, and partly to a series of new racing-car designs and variations on the production range which gave them the material they needed.

It all started with the Zagato-bodied Giulietta Sprint Zagato of 1960. This light, nippy, agile little coupé had powered many an enthusiastic owner to class wins in local races and hillclimbs all over Italy. This was exactly the class of racing in which Alfa had begun their sporting history, and in financial terms it made a lot more sense than the more specialized classes like the Grand Prix programme, which had brought Alfa Romeo three world championship wins in a row since the war.

Obviously Grand Prix racing was not contemplated, on the grounds of sheer complexity and cost. But Alfa had tried to switch their plans to purpose-built sports prototypes instead, and this had proved to offer no savings at all. According to engineer Edo Mazoni, the 3000 CM six-cylinder sports car had cost more to develop than the Tipo 159 Alfetta Grand Prix car, and had produced nothing in the way of victories to match the single-seater's record.

A compromise policy seemed to offer more sense: using production cars and components, which had already effectively paid for themselves, as the basis for new racing contenders would clearly save money. It would also tie any successes won by the new cars more closely to the versions in the showrooms, with an obvious effect on sales. But there was still the problem of providing the effort: earlier ideas had foundered, often at their most promising stage, because the company's technical staff could not be spared from their primary duty of working on new production cars and their development problems.

So the company began to look around for someone who could be put in charge of a racing subsidiary, which could use cars developed by the company, tune them and improve them and use them to implement a full racing programme. In the old days, Alfa had provided likely drivers with parts and other help, but what was needed now was a much more professional set-up. Nicolis's efforts with the SZ, producing more power and greater speed, showed what could be done—but he could not be spared from production priorities.

The car was already on the way. Before deciding who should race it, Satta and his engineers had begun to follow up the Giulia in 1962 with a full-blooded racing version, using a totally different chassis but as many of the production mechanical parts as possible. In view of the success of the Giulietta SZ in the hands of experienced top-class drivers like Sanesi and Rodriguez, Baghetti and Bandini, it made sense to involve Zagato again, but in this case the design was entirely a factory effort.

The secret of the new car was its tubular space-frame, designed by Edo Mazoni. He used various diameters of tubes, ranging from 20 mm to 40 mm across, and he built up a close-mesh birdcage of several kilometres of tubing. The spacing and the thickness of tubing were determined by careful experimentation: the frame was pinned at three points, a load placed on a fourth point and the deflection was measured. If the stiffness was insufficient, a thicker tube was fitted instead, and stage by stage the whole complex shape was built up into

Engineer Carlo Chiti, chief of the Alfa semi-works racing organization, Autodelta, set up originally in Udine in north-east Italy

Above
*Autodelta's efforts would begin
with Zagato's Giulia-based
successor to the Giulietta
SZ—this was the tubular
space-frame Giulia GTZ,
or Tubolare Zagato*

Below
*This Tubolare cutting the
corners to the nearest
millimetre in the 1964 Le
Mans 24 Hour race, shows the
sleekness and purposefulness of
the car to perfection*

Left
The sharply cut-off trefoil tail of the Tubolare was part of a highly aerodynamic shape which weighed very little and which handled to perfection: pitwork in the 1964 Nurburgring 1000 Kilometres

Below
Another Tubolare delighting the crowd in the 1965 Targa Florio

*Bianchi and Rolland drove
this Autodelta Tubolare to
seventh place overall and a
win in their class in the 1965
Targa Florio*

an extremely rigid skeleton which weighed just 88 lb, including the mounting points for the front and rear suspensions.

The bodywork which was fitted on top was built by Zagato, and owed nothing at all to the production Giulias. On the contrary, it was a stretched and more streamlined version of the SZ body with a longer tail which, after similar wind-tunnel tests to those undergone by the Giulia TI saloon, was modified in the same way. It was shortened and recessed to cut turbulence and drag to the minimum — though in this case, because of the body contours, the shape of the tail panel was not rectangular like the TI but a curved trefoil shape, which identified the car instantly to those which it succeeded in overtaking.

There were more modifications under the skin of the Giulia TZ, as the new car became identified. The TZ stood for Tubolare Zagato,

Two Tubolares playing follow-my-leader round the bends at Le Mans in 1965

but it was a major redesign in its own right, owing little to the Giulia beyond the engine and transmission. For the first time in a postwar production-based car, the TZ adopted independent rear suspension instead of the set-up introduced on the 1900. The system used coil springs and single lower wishbones with upper transverse radius arms to provide independent suspension within the fairly limited movements acceptable on an out-and-out competition car.

The radical design took a long time to complete: the project had begun as long ago as 1959, and the first prototype had been built during 1960, so that development testing had begun the following year. The disadvantages of involving production experts were obvious by 1962, when work on the TZ had to be stopped while all hands turned to the pumps to see the Giulia safely launched; but by

Another shot from the same race: the original TZ (right) contrasts with the lower and more angular shape of its TZ2 successor on the left

1963, the first production version, using the 112 bhp Sprint Speciale engine, was ready for the customers. In this form the TZ, weighing just 1450 lb ready for action, was capable of a top speed of 135 mph, scorching acceleration and handling which could match any of its likely opponents on the track.

So the car was ready: but where was the team to develop it, supply it, maintain it and race it? During the years when the TZ project was being developed, a former Alfa Romeo employee named Carlo

The TZ2 on test with Autodelta: Chiti is at the far left, De Adamich and Zeccoli are behind the car, wearing helmets

Chiti, an aeronautical engineering graduate of the University of Pisa, who had worked in the experimental department for five years until 1957, was busy working on the 1.5-litre Grand Prix car which would win the 1961 World Championship for Ferrari.

Despite this triumph, Chiti left Ferrari following a disagreement at the end of the season, and in 1962 he joined four friends to work on the ATS project (the initials stood for Automobili Turismo e Sport) under the sponsorship of one Count Volpi. There Chiti designed a ninety-degree V8 1.5-litre engine for the current GP formula, which was fitted to a six-speed gearbox in a space-frame carrying all independent double-wishbone suspension and a single-seat racing body. The company produced two cars, for Phil Hill (who had won the 1961 Championship for Ferrari and had then left the company following the same dispute as that in which Chiti had been involved) and Giancarlo Baghetti: they entered in three Grand Prix races, retiring in two and finishing in eleventh and fifteenth places in the 1962 Italian Grand Prix.

The financial strain of this single season finally broke ATS. Count Volpi withdrew his support, taking away with him the design for the 2.5-litre GT car which had been the company's other major project, and Chiti was left high and dry. It was at this point, early in 1963, that Alfa Romeo contacted their one-time employee to see if he would be willing to put his experience to work in a totally new area, in running their proposed racing subsidiary. For Chiti, the offer could hardly have come at a better time: after the fall-out with Ferrari and the failure of ATS, the chance of working for a company with the strength and the background of Alfa Romeo on a challenging new programme must have seemed like a gift from Providence.

Chiti accepted the offer and began work quickly. With fellow-engineer Ludovico Chizzola, he founded the organization which was soon to become famous in European racing—Autodelta. Initially it was run from garage premises in Udine, to the north of Venice on the route to Austria, but this geographical separation from the Alfa plant made little sense, and by 1964 the team was relocated in the industrial suburb of Settimo Milanese, ready to embark on a full-blooded and ambitious racing programme.

During the months at Udine, Chiti's first priority had been to assemble, develop, tune and prepare the series of 100 TZs. During these years up to 1964, the work which could be done on cars was limited under the international regulations then operating. Basically the position was that parts could be taken off cars, but not added—and development work was limited to careful rebalancing of the moving parts, polishing of ports and the tuning and adjustment of exhausts; all this and more was now done by Autodelta, rather than by the factory's racing support department.

By this time, five long years of development work had gone into the TZ. Would it be another might-have-been, like the corpses of other racing dreams which littered the company's museum? In this case, something more than the modest but worthwhile results of the Giulietta SZ were needed to justify the whole exercise. The TZ was a

The pits at Le Mans in 1965:
behind a trio of the angular
and aggressive TZ2s is a
GTZ with its bonnet open

A TZ2 chases a Porsche up a
village street in the Targa
Florio: note the Udine number
plate and the Autodelta
symbols on either side

specially developed design which was far more expensive to produce: setting up Autodelta had been expensive in its turn, and even though it was Chiti's team who were doing the racing programme, the factory's own prestige was involved to a greater degree than with the earlier car. For all these reasons, results were vital—but could Chiti and the TZ deliver the goods?

The 1963 season was almost over when the TZ programme began—but it was a promising beginning, with a class win at the FISA cup race at Monza. Whether the car could maintain this promise into a new season was by no means sure, however, since everyone had the benefit of the winter close season to develop and tune their cars to higher peaks of performance. But there was no need to worry: within its strictly limited objectives (class wins rather than outright victories, which could clearly tend to go to bigger, more powerful and infinitely more expensive machines), the TZ was to establish a domination approaching that of its equivalents in the 1930s. In the 1964 season alone, the TZs chalked up class wins at the Sebring 12-hour race, in the Tour de France, in the Targa Florio, in the Nurburgring 1000 Kilometres, and in the Le Mans 24-hour race. Not content with putting up first and second places in the 1600 cc class in many of these events, the TZs went on to win the Coupe des Alpes and the Tour de Corse overall, in the same brilliant season. Alfa's decision to re-enter the world of racing by this carefully controlled development programme had been triumphantly vindicated.

Yet almost as soon as the TZ had appeared, Alfa and Autodelta were moving on to something new. Another twenty-four cars remained to be built under the TZ programme, half of them to be finished in fibre-glass rather than metal as the second-generation TZ2, which would eventually replace the TZ in Autodelta's own racing entries during 1965. By this time, the Giulia engine would be developing 170 bhp at 7500 rpm, turning the car into a more formidable contender still; but this was a by-product of a different kind of racing challenger, with even closer affinities to the production cars.

The reason for the switch in Alfa's efforts was the change in racing rules affecting the all-important touring cars events. The old stipulation that parts could be removed but not replaced had given way to a number of strictly specified modifications, like changes to the rear axle and the front suspension to lower the roll centre, and changes to production engines to produce more power for racing purposes. The effect of these alterations was to make the production GT Sprint much more attractive as the basis for a racing car, provided the power unit and the suspension could be made competitive within the framework of the new rules.

The first step was to cut the weight as far as possible: out went the sound-deadening fitted to the production cars, and the steel body panelling was replaced by light-alloy panels in the same shapes. This reduced the car's total weight from the 2250 lb of the Sprint GTV to a mere 1540 lb; at the same time the engine was boosted to 115 bhp at 6000 rpm, raising the top speed to almost 120 mph, though it was in

The view which many of the TZ2's opponents in the 2-litre class may find the most familiar . . .

the acceleration and the handling that the main improvements were made. This was the GTA version of the Giulia, the A standing for Alleggerita, or lightened, and it was aimed at the competition-minded owner. For the factory's own team, the GTA was modified even further: the limiting factor in raising the engine speed was the time taken for the flame front to travel right through the combustion space on each ignition. But by fitting two plugs, still set on the centreline of the cylinder but offset slightly fore and aft of the centre when looked at from the side of the engine, this time could be cut dramatically, and the speed and power of the engine increased to new heights.

The improvement effected by the twin-plug engine was dramatic indeed. With 10.5 to 1 compression, the racing engine delivered a resounding 170 bhp at 7500 rpm. The suspension was lowered and tightened to keep as much of this power on the track as possible, and the GTA *corsa* combined fierce acceleration with a new top speed of 136 mph.

This was a formidable prescription, and it was not long before the GTA began to make its presence felt on all the tracks of Europe. The first GTAs had been ready for private customers in 1965, while Autodelta had been busy collecting class wins in events like Sebring and the Targa Florio with the last of the original steel-bodied TZs. Now for 1966, the Autodelta team would be carrying the factory flag with the TZ2s in the GT classes and the GTA *corsas* in the touring classes. It added up to a doubly difficult challenge for Chiti's still relatively inexperienced team, at a time when the factory was

developing still more complex material for them to cope with, in the shape of the T33 sports prototype; but they set out to do their best to make the two cars worthy of their places in the record books alongside the 1500s and 1750s, the Monzas and the P3s and Alfettas.

The TZs did well enough on a fairly limited front: De Adamich and Zeccoli came in first in the 2-litre 'Sport' class in the Monza 1000 Kilometres race, and three of the cars took the first three places in the 1600 cc Sport class in the Targa Florio. Bianchi and Schutz and De Adamich and Zeccoli took first and second place in the 1600 Sport class in the Nurburgring 1000 Kilometres. And across the Atlantic the Geki/Andrey car won the 1600 Sport class in the Sebring 12-hour race, setting a class record in doing so.

This was a splendid achievement, but it was to be completely dwarfed by the scale of the GTAs' successes. They took first, third, fourth, fifth and eighth places in the Sebring 4 Hours against much bigger machinery like the 4.5-litre Dodges and Plymouths on their home ground. The winning driver, Jochen Rindt, not only put up fastest lap but set a new class record for lap and race average. De Adamich and Zeccoli went on to win the Nurburgring 6 Hours, beating Lancias and BMWs to do so, and Pinto and Parmigiani won the touring class in the Circuit of Mugello. De Adamich and Zeccoli won the Snetterton 500 Kilometres, and Pinto and Giunti won the Grand Prix of Budapest. These were but the highlights in a season which included class wins in Holland, Sweden, Germany, Italy, Spain, Belgium and France, as well as in the United States, where GTAs won the Transamerican Touring Car Championship with

Teodoro Zeccoli and Geki Russo drove this TZ2 to third place in its class in the 1967 Targa Florio

victories at Marlboro, Danville (Virginia International Raceway) and St Louis, ending up with thirty-three points to Ford's works Lotus Cortinas with fifteen, BMW's three and Volvo's two points. In Europe too, the Alfa GTAs upset the by now almost traditional Lotus-Cortina domination of the Touring Car Championship in this their first season to win the series.

But this was no mere flash in the pan. The GTAs had won more than their share of Alfa's 200-plus victories during 1966, but they were to do even better in 1967. Not only did they win the European Championship again, this time beating the formidable 2-litre Porsche 911s rather than the Lotus-Cortinas to do it, but they went on to win other events all over the world from Warwick Farm in Australia to Oulton Park in England. Works driver Ignazio Giunti came second in the first qualifying round for the European Hillclimb Championship for touring cars—but he won every one of the remaining six rounds, adding yet another Championship to Alfa's score.

In 1968 the story went on, with another win in the European Touring Car Championship records making it the hat-trick for the GTAs. By 1969, 500 of these tough, fast racing machines had been built, and Autodelta were busy adding other strings to the Alfa bow. They fitted the twin-plug competition engine into the Duetto Spider, giving it a top speed of 133 mph—Duettos won their classes in events like the Cesana-Sestriere hillclimb, the Targa Florio and the Circuit of Mugello. Next in line was an obvious step in the progression; if the

Right
Jochen Rindt driving the Autodelta GTA which won the 1966 Sebring Four Hour race

Below right
Rindt carving his way through a field of bigger and more powerful American machinery in the Sebring Four Hours

Below
The new contender for Alfa's racing fortunes—the GTA— seen against the background of Autodelta's racing workshops in 1966

De Adamich and Galli share the driving of this GTA, which won its class and took fourth place overall in the Nurburgring 1000 Km of 1967

Giulia-based 1570 cc GTA had done so well in the up-to-1600 cc racing categories, why couldn't a Giulietta-engined equivalent enjoy a similar monopoly in the 1300 cc class?

In fact, Autodelta went a great deal further. Not only did they take the light aluminium alloy body of the GTA, and not only did they fit all the different parts of their full-race prescription, including extra oil coolers, competition exhaust system, modified starter motor and generator, wider alloy wheels, anti-roll bar and heavy-duty locating member on the rear suspension, heavy-duty clutch, competition suspension parts, twenty-gallon fuel tank, racing seats, roll-over bar and limited-slip differential, they also produced an entirely new engine to complete the treatment.

The capacity of the engine of the GTA 1300 Junior was the same as that of the Giulietta—but instead of the 74 mm bores and 75 mm stroke, the new version had wider 78 mm bores and a shorter 67.5 mm stroke. Fitted with the twin-plug head used for the bigger

Another GTA in the 1969 Monte Carlo Rally

The GTA, based on the Giulia engine and body, gets a smaller but still competitive stablemate: the 1300 cc GTA Junior

GTA, this engine developed 96 bhp at 6000 rpm as supplied to the customers. In Autodelta's own version, using carburetters, the engine finally delivered 160 bhp at 7800 rpm, the extra power and speed being made possible by the revised dimensions of the engine. Later, a fuel-injection version turned out 165 bhp at an even higher 8400 rpm, both versions having phenomenal acceleration and a top speed of more than 130 mph.

The GTA 1300 was to carry on the Alfa domination of touring car racing into the smaller classes, at the same time as the Tipo 33 sports cars were beginning their long struggle which was to end seven years later in another racing World Championship for the company. Yet Autodelta and the Alfa development department really had the bit between their teeth now: from this moment on they would get to work on virtually every new production model, giving it the treatment it needed to turn it into potential race-winner or rally star—for in the coming seasons Alfa Romeo would add not only the world sports car championships to their long list of sporting laurels but they would collect the European Rally Championship too.

Before returning to the production-car story, which provided the raw material for the later stages in the Alfa-Autodelta racing programme, there were three more unexpected offshoots from the competition cars of the sixties. Two were special-bodied prototypes by Pininfarina and Bertone on the frame and mechanical parts of the GTZ. The Pininfarina coupé was a beautifully sleek design, with a

front-end treatment not unlike a lower, leaner version of the Duetto, and a flatter radiator grille, faired-in headlamps and humped wheel-arches curving back to an extravagantly curved windscreen, a closed coupé top and a sleek sloping fastback tail.

But the Bertone coupé, christened the 'Canguro' (or Kangaroo) was in the eyes of many enthusiasts the most beautiful of all his many designs for Alfa Romeo—or indeed for anyone. Styled with gentler, more subtle curves in rich Italian red, rather than the white of the Pininfarina car, the Canguro had that rare property of seeming always ready to leap into action, even when standing still—a quality it shared with the lovely Alfa P3 Grand Prix car of the nineteen-thirties. The front end of the car was beautifully moulded around a stylized Alfa radiator, set in between deeply cowled headlamps. The body had a high waistline, curved slightly upwards where it passed over the wheels, with the coupé top as curved, convex and clear as a fighter aircraft's bubble hood.

The advantage these cars had over the average exotic prototype was the quality of the car on which they were built: the combination of competition car and one-off bodywork was rare indeed. I was lucky enough to drive the Canguro for several laps of the Pirelli test track at Lainate just outside Milan four years after its first appearance. On the outside a real showcar, on the inside its racing background was more obvious, with ventilated semi-reclining seats, functional instruments and the framework tubes in plain view. The noise from

Hezemans' and Van Lennep's GTA Junior in the Jarama Four Hour race, where they won their class and took fourth place overall

213

the tuned Giulia engine was loud and purposeful, the acceleration exhilarating and the roadholding like glue. It was comfortable, fast, agile and lovely to look at; ultimately it was a saddening car, for as one stopped the engine and climbed out, one couldn't help wondering why all cars couldn't be like this?

But the third of the special spin-offs from the competition programme was in its way more unusual and exciting than even the Canguro. The Bertone car, for all its sleek lines, was orthodox enough. No one, however, could call the Osi Scarabeo orthodox, whatever they thought of its lines.

Jochen Rindt watching the pitcrews at the 1966 Nurburgring 500 Km: the cars are GTA Juniors

First of all, it was unusual in that it used the GTA racing engine for
its power unit. Secondly, its design went back to another of the
interesting would-be racers in Alfa's past. This was no more successful
than many of the others that had failed to make a competition
appearance, though it was much more unusual in design: built in the
early fifties, this had been the Grand Prix Tipo 160 which had been
built around a flat-12 4-cam 2483 cc engine developed specially for
the car and producing 285 bhp at 10,000 rpm.

The idea had been to put the engine at the front of the car, and
locate the driver right at the back of the long wedge-shaped body, just

behind the rear axle. Whatever the advantages of this long wedge shape from the streamlining point of view, the peculiar weight distribution promised handling problems in plenty, though the design included the unusual feature of four-wheel drive under the driver's control.

The engines were built, but the car was not; another project to fall foul of production preoccupations. In this case the Giulietta was on the way, which was the official reason for cancelling the project, though no one could have blamed Alfa for having cold feet with such an unusual design on the books in the expensive and unforgiving Grand Prix world.

Now the idea was to revive the wedge-shaped design, suitably re-formed and updated. In this case the driver and engine were to change places, with the driver sitting forward of the rear axle and the engine turned sideways and located right at the back of the car. The engine was fitted with clutch and gearbox in a single unit along with the differential, driven through an angled drive shaft and a set of conical transfer gears. The rear wheels were suspended independently, using coil springs and wishbones and driven through swing-axle half-shafts, and the rear disc brakes were mounted inboard, close to the car's centreline.

The main frame of the car was built around a pair of large-diameter tubes, which were used to carry the fuel. Front suspension was also by wishbones and coil springs, and the whole car weighed a mere 1500 lb. The initial version was shown at the 1966 Paris Show, and a top speed of 125 mph was predicted. Certainly the car's aggressive

Above left
Bertone's beautiful Canguro—based on the same frame and mechanicals as the Tubolare, but with comfortable road-driving rather than racing as the priority

Below left
The interior, with its reclining, ventilated seats and the unusual repeat speedometer for the passenger

Above
Pininfarina's essay on the same mechanical theme, while interesting and stylish, lacked the real beauty of the Bertone Canguro

wedge shape, with its low front end and humped wheel-arches suggested high performance. The careful streamlining—for once there was no Alfa radiator at all, except for a rectangular air intake and a shield-shaped line on the body panelling which carried an Alfa badge in the centre—promised good aerodynamic performance, and the airflow may well have helped to counteract the car's undoubted tail-heavy weight distribution.

Nothing more was heard of the Scarabeo, however, after its first show appearance; only recently was it revealed that a Spider version had been produced with the engine and transmission moved forward of the rear wheels, and the driver's seat located in the middle of the car behind a low wrap-round racing screen. This promised a much more tractable set of characteristics, and plans were apparently made to go into limited production.

But the most interesting of the Scarabeos was the third and final prototype—a closed version of the Spider, with the engine ahead of the rear wheels, the driver seated midway between the wheel axles, and the extravagant wedge shape of the original toned down to a smoothly aerodynamic profile. This at last looked like a real racing car, and with the undoubted performance and reliability of the GTA engine could have been an extremely interesting contender.

Alas, the promising Scarabeo was to disappear from the scene. At the deserted Osi workshops two years later, all that was left was the original wedge-shaped show car, covered in dust and sitting on four flat tyres. The company's financial troubles had killed the project stone dead, and all that remained was an interesting sideline on the blossoming Alfa racing success story.

OSI's interesting, unusual, but ultimately disappointing Scarabeo featured a deep wedge-shaped body and a tranverse engine mounted behind the driver

Chapter 8
THE STORY SO FAR–OLD NAMES FOR NEW DESIGNS

By the late nineteen-sixties, the Giulia range had broken all records for Alfa Romeo production: whereas the peak year for Giulietta output, 1961, had seen 35,711 cars leave the factory, by 1967 the various Giulia versions made up a total of 72,763 cars for the year. But during that time the output of the largest cars in the Alfa range—the four-cylinder 2000s and their six-cylinder 2600 descendants—had decreased dramatically. In 1961, 2000 production had dropped to 1680 cars, and though things had recovered with the introduction of the six-cylinder models, the 1963 peak of 4595 soon declined to 2568 cars in the following year, and went on dropping. By the 1967 peak of the Giulia's career, only fifty-six of the six-cylinder cars were made, with another thirty to come in the final two years of the 2600's career. Designed-in production rundown or lack of success?

At the same time, the competition which the Giulias were meeting, from cars like the BMWs, were progressively uprating their models. When the Giulia had appeared, 1.6-litre cars had made sense in the commercial world as well as on the race track, but now the other cars which appealed to would-be Alfa buyers were beginning to leave the Giulia behind in terms of size and power. Styling, too, was becoming a problem with the saloon versions: Satta's personal vision of a no-nonsense, squared-off body shape was efficient enough and certainly individual at a time when many cars were beginning to look more like their competitors than ever. But the reverse side of the individuality coin was that the design tended to date quickly, and some customers might actually prefer a car which looked more orthodox in its shape.

These two trends, added to the lack of a top-of-the-range model to attract buyers who had the funds on hand to buy extra size and performance, amounted to a clear and urgent requirement for a new model—an uprated Giulia with a bigger engine and higher performance, preferably in a restyled and more acceptable body. Should it be a four- or a six-cylinder car, however? Or should it have an entirely new engine design altogether—was the classic twin-cam configuration approaching the end of its long road at last?

The answer, to anyone familiar with Alfa history, was obvious from the start. Since the end of the war, the old positions of six-

Right
The 1750 wasn't really a 1750 at all, but the capacity was near enough to use the old designation—the saloon was basically Satta's square box shape as used for the Giulia, but the details were carefully tidied up by Bertone to give a neater and fresher appearance

Right
The 1750 GTV was likewise the same as its Giulia predecessor, but minimal changes to body details did manage to prevent the design from looking dated

Far right
Graphics in metalwork—the simple but well-balanced combination of traditional grille and quadruple headlamps on the 1750 GTV

Above

The 1750 dash was rearranged with the subsidiary instruments sharing the centre console with the gearlever—despite the odd-looking arrangement, the change was as easy and precise as ever

Right

The 1750 Spider was likewise the mixture as before—except that the rounded tail of the Duetto was replaced by a more sharply cut off rear end

cylinder and four-cylinder cars had been reversed: long gone were the days when the RL sixes had been the most important model, with the RM fours turned out as a grudging concession to customers who wanted something cheaper and more economical. Ever since the introduction of the 1900, it was the four-cylinder cars that had been dominant in marketing terms, in production, in competition and in everything else save only size and absolute performance.

So the Giulia's bigger sister was to be another four-cylinder car, and another version of the standard engine would be used to deliver the power. But the way in which the new version of the engine was produced would be surprising on two counts: on the modesty of the increase in engine size, and on exactly how that increase was achieved.

At a time when BMW for example was providing instant performance by fitting a full 2-litre engine into its compact 1600 saloon, Alfa went for an intermediate increase in size, to 1779 cc. Once again, this was done by a combination of increasing the width of the bores and the length of the stroke, but these two dimensions were not enlarged in proportion. Instead, the bores were merely stretched by 2 mm in their diameters, to 80 mm across, while the stroke was stretched a full 6.5 mm to 88.5 mm—the result was an engine which, in its ratio of bore to stroke, was more old-fashioned than the original 1900.

This meant that the increase in size produced only a limited increase in power, since the maximum speed of the engine was unchanged—and even keeping the rotational speed the same meant increased stresses. There were clearance problems with the wider bores, and the alloy casting for the cylinder block was modified to make it stiffer and more resistant to local stresses. The other parts of the engine not directly affected by the size changes—the camshafts, the carburetters and the manifolding—were left unchanged, with the exception of the dynamo, which was replaced by an alternator.

The version of the engine fitted to the new car was essentially that used in the Giulia Super—9 to 1 compression, two twin-choke Webers—but the increase in size lifted the power peak from 98 bhp at 5500 rpm to 118 bhp at the same speed, which was a significant increase in power per cubic centimetre, though not as high as the more powerful versions of the Giulia engine fitted to the Duetto and the GT Veloce. The ratios of the five-speed gearbox and the final drive were also identical to the Giulia Super, so that any increase in performance would be proportional to the engine's increased output.

The bodywork, by contrast, represented much more of a change from the Giulia concept. The new car now had a body styled by Bertone, but this was a very clever and subtle reworking of the Giulia 'box' rather than a completely new design. The dimensions were almost identical: front and rear track were exactly the same as those of the Giulia, and only the wheelbase was fractionally larger, by just over two inches. Yet by rounding off the edges of the severe Giulia shape, by softening the contours, by fitting a revised four-headlamp configuration at the front of the car and a less sharply chopped-off tail, Bertone managed to make it look considerably larger, sleeker and

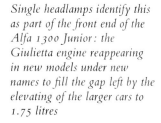

Single headlamps identify this as part of the front end of the Alfa 1300 Junior: the Giulietta engine reappearing in new models under new names to fill the gap left by the elevating of the larger cars to 1.75 litres

more imposing. They achieved the best of both worlds, by giving it a strong family resemblance to the Giulia while making it unmistakably a new design in its own right. Perhaps this was the way the Giulia should have looked from the start? Certainly a lot of devoted Alfa enthusiasts were never entirely happy with Satta's body design, and in many ways the car triumphed in spite of its appearance—the performance was good enough to overcome the styling characteristics. Some say it's a style you grow accustomed to.

The new car had less to overcome in the appearance stakes: but would its performance match up to the Giulia, and to the expectations which the bigger engine would create? Alfa themselves fanned the expectations by the name, or rather the number, they chose for the new model. After the Giulietta, and the Giulia, there was nowhere else to go in that particular progression without losing sight of the fact that the car *was* a new model in its own right. On the other hand, the engine size was close enough to indulge in a little nostalgia—many other manufacturers had already jumped on the back of the good-old-days mood of the late sixties by naming new models after the stars of the past. Alfa's trump card in the early thirties had been the 1750, which Zagato had used for a model in his vintage-replica 4R a few months before—that designation had originally been a misnomer, since the original 1750 had in fact displaced 1752 cc. What was wrong with stretching the point a little further—twenty-seven cubic centimetres to be precise—and calling the new car by the same magic designation?

The first blown Alfa since before the war: the neat underbonnet layout of the supercharged GTA SA racing Alfa, a link back to the classic racing Alfas of the 1920s and 1930s

After the racing treatment: the squat, aggressive frontal features of two of Autodelta's competition mainstays. On the left, the bigger and more powerful 1750 GTAm, on the right the GTA Junior

So the 1750 it became, and it was unveiled as such in January of 1968. But this was not to replace the entire range of Giulia saloons—at least not yet. The TI disappeared from view, but the Super and 1300 saloons went on selling successfully for another four years, and the only other Giulias that vanished altogether were the GT Veloce and the Duetto, and this was for the very best of reasons. If the saloon benefited from a bigger engine, then the two high-performance versions would put the extra power to even better use.

So alongside the 1750 Berlina (the TI designation was dropped with the change of model) there appeared a 1750 GT Veloce, and a 1750 Spider Veloce. Now that there was no need to avoid confusion with the 1600 Spider Veloce, the Duetto name could safely be dropped after its short career. Yet for the first time the 'Veloce' part of the name was really redundant, since both the Spider and the GT coupé now had exactly the same engine as the Berlina, with identical carburation, compression ratio and power peaks. There were subtle changes to the GTV coupé to go with its new designation, and more obvious ones to the Spider, like the sharply chopped-off tail instead of the rounded tail of the Duetto. Some felt the new design looked better, others that it looked worse.

Performance from the new engine was improved on that available with the Giulia unit: the Berlina was slightly faster, with a top speed of better than 112 mph, but much of the extra performance went into hauling around the 150 extra pounds of bodywork and appointments. Even the two faster versions were 50 lb heavier, so that top

speed was only edged up to 118 mph, though acceleration was better up to that figure.

Perhaps the biggest changes between the Giulias and the 1750s were those which accounted for much of the extra weight penalties suffered by the new models. Gone were the last vestiges of austerity which had been all too obvious on the 1900 insides, slightly less so on the Giulietta and still present in some measure in the Giulias. Wood-finish dashboards, plusher carpets, carefully angled instruments set in deep dashboard cowls or an angled centre console, softer seats and a gear lever which disappeared into the aforementioned console instead of into the floor of the car, all added up to an impression of greater luxury and more careful finish which some welcomed and others did not, fearing it as a symptom of age and respectability, out of place in a car where performance should come first.

Each model came in three basic versions, an indication of how much more complex marketing cars in different countries was becoming, with contradictory and confusing requirements on safety and pollution. Added to the basic left-hand-drive and right-hand-drive versions (for Europe and the UK respectively) was a new variant to meet the laws of the United States, Alfa's other big export market: apart from modified lighting (the Spider, for example, lost the transparent headlamp cowls which followed the contours of the bodywork) the American versions of the cars had the Weber carburetters replaced by Spica indirect fuel injection.

Autocar tested the Berlina and enjoyed the experience very much.

As always, the engine was the heart of the car, and came in for the highest praise: 'There is never any fuss or bother from this highly tuned sports engine, and it pulls smoothly and evenly from idling right up past the start of the red line at 6000 rpm. . . . There *is* a noise, a mellow blend of cams, chains, induction and exhaust which never rises above the pleasing, muted roar even at maximum revs . . . the 1750 is one of the most relaxed high-speed cruisers we have come across.'

Handling, the testers found, was characterized by much stronger understeer than on the Giulia, but was otherwise worthy of high praise: 'The steering is just as lively as ever, working back through the driver's hands on every bump and twist, giving a superb responsiveness and a perfect "feel" of the car's attitude when cornering. . . . The 1750's handling is impeccable. There is slight, predictable under-steer, with the car always feeling completely balanced and well under control. When "chucked", in rally drivers' style, into a corner, the Alfa will lift an inside front wheel yet remain perfectly stable, with just a slight chopping from the front. . . . Damping is firm, yet the ride never becomes harsh, and even the radial-ply roughness, so often noticed, is absent from the 1750.'

But there were faults, though they were faults of detail rather than fundamental shortcomings. 'The brakes seem almost too savage,' said the test report, though 'once one has become used to the small

Left
How Zagato build their bodies: the light but complex sub-frame built up to carry the carefully shaped body panels. In this case the car is the GT 1300 Junior Zagato

Below
And this is the result: the sleek Junior Z out on the road. This limited-production variation on the standard range had little family resemblance to any of its stablemates

Inside, though, the Zagato version was typically Alfa in the neat layout of its easily-read instruments, and its functional finish

range [of pressures] needed, the brakes are easy to use progressively. Fade was negligible.' The dashboard layout was also less than perfect, with the smaller dials set on the centre console: 'One has to peer round the clutter of steering wheel, lamp and direction indicator stalks and gear lever to see them.' But the sharpest criticism was reserved for the pedals which, though bottom-hinged, were set at such an awkward angle that they were uncomfortable to operate. For all that, though, *Autocar* summed up the 1750 Berlina as 'still an Alfa through and through, and the best Alfa yet'.

It was just as well. Apart from the problems with reliability and finish which had plagued the company (and, to be fair, its customers) since the huge expansion of production during the nineteen-sixties, there were ominous signs that the basic 1900 design was soon to reach the limit of its progressive updating process. Increasing power output has brought out shortcomings on the clutch of the Giulia—this had been cured by modifications on the 1750, but changing the design of the rear suspension to cope with more powerful engines would be much less easy. Weight distribution too might be a problem, as the greater the bias towards the front wheels, the greater the tendency to understeer rather than the ideal of perfectly neutral handling.

The 2000 saloon was the 1750 shape with a larger engine—but enthusiasts could tell the difference from details like the broader radiator shield on the 2000

For the time being, though, the 1750 was a shot in the arm for the company's sales record. Though 1968, the year of the new range's introduction, saw the Giulia production dip from 72,763 cars in 1967 to 55,168, this drop was more than outweighed by a total of 42,114 of the 1750s, pushing the company's total production closer to the magic 100,000 mark for the year. The new model's competition debut was promising too: four 1750 Berlinas were entered for the Spa-Francorchamps 24 Hour Race in July 1968 after enough had been made for homologation purposes, and four finished in first, second, third and fourth places in the Group One production touring-car class. The 1750 did well in the Coupe des Alpes too, with the car driven by Bianchi and Jacquemin taking first place in the series-production touring car category.

This was a return to the old tradition of first-time-out Alfa victories from the heady pre-war days, yet in a way it was not surprising at all: so powerful had the company's grip on production-car racing become by 1968, that the 1750s' results were simply fitting into their proper context. The twin-plug racing GTAs were still winning races all over the world: in the 1968 season, they came first in class at the Daytona 24 Hour Race on 4 February, first in class at

*The 2000 saloon (apart from details like the radiator the 1750 was exactly the same)
outside the showroom of Thomson & Taylor, who had acted as Alfa importers until
the formation of Alfa Romeo (Great Britain) Ltd in the early sixties*

Kyalami in South Africa on 7 April and first overall in the Pimentel Grand Prix in Brazil on the same day, first overall at the Pietermaritzburg Easter race on 15 April, first in its class in the Belgrade Grand Prix on 21 April, first overall in the Shell Trophy race at Monza on 2 June, first overall in the fifth round of the South African Touring Car Championship at Kyalami on the 3rd, first and second in class at the Francorchamps 24 Hour Race which saw the 1750's racing debut, first and second in class at the Circuit of Mugello and first and second in class (not to mention second overall, finishing behind a specialized sports prototype) in the Coupe des Alpes, plus wins in more than fifty other national and international events in the same season.

This, as a record, was splendid enough. But already the GTA was having to face increasing competition from other cars produced in its own stables. The reign of the specialized racing cars like the TZ was approaching its end, though the fibre-glass-bodied TZ2s, fitted with the hottest of the GTA engines, and dry-sump lubrication, were now so supremely reliable that they were still able to clean up class wins in long-distance events. Yet at the Circuit of Mugello, the class-winning TZ's time of 4 hours 29 minutes 56 seconds was fully 9 minutes 12 seconds slower than a smaller and less specialized Alfa that was already beginning to make its presence felt on the racing circuits: the GTA 1300 Junior, with its wide-bore short-stroke version of the old Giulietta engine, capable of delivering—with the GTA twin-plug head and fuel injection—a power peak of 165 bhp at 8400 rpm in full Autodelta race tune. Small wonder that the modified production car was capable of beating the purpose-built race machine of a few years before—such was the furious pace of development.

Another formidable Alfa contender, and another version of the stupendously successful GTA, began to chalk up a run of competition successes at about this time. This reverted to what had been at one time standard procedure with all racing Alfas—the use of a supercharger—though postwar racing rules had all but eliminated the idea of a separate blower. The GTA was fitted with two centrifugal blowers rather than the lobed Roots blowers used before the war, and instead of direct gearing the blowers were in this case driven by a turbine which was itself powered by a hydraulic pump, chain driven from the engine. The compressors themselves were turning at speeds up to 100,000 rpm, and the engine was given the most boost at the highest revs.

The upshot of all this attention was that the Giulia engine which had been the basis of the original GTA was given the same reshaping as the Giulietta engine had been in the case of the GTA 1300 Junior. The bores were widened from 78 mm to 86 mm and the stroke shortened from 82 mm to 67.5 mm—the result of all this was that the capacity stayed exactly the same, at 1570 cc, but the engine could now turn over much faster for the same stresses. Combustion was no problem, thanks to the use of the twin-plug head, and the use of water injection into the inlet manifold kept the combustion chambers cool enough to allow the use of normal fuel, as required by the regulations.

This ingenious redesign of the engine gave the car a peak power output of 220 bhp at 7500 rpm, which was enough to push its top speed up to 150 mph. The car was shown to the public in February 1967 and later at the Geneva Show, while its first race appearance was in a 100-mile event at Hockenheim in Germany, where the German driver Dau took the car to its first overall victory—again firmly in the old Alfa tradition. It went on to win the Coupe de Vitesse USA at Montlhèry in France the following April, followed by a class win in the Bad Neuenhar hillclimb in Germany, a class win in the Coupe de Spa, first overall in the Belgian Grand Prix des Frontières and first in class in the Chamrousse hillclimb.

Successes like these, won by the more specialized cars, were the highlights of the sports programme, backed up by a steady if less spectacular succession of wins by other production models from the GTV's triumphs at the Surfers' Paradise Four Hour race in Australia to the Duetto's wins at the Cesana-Sestrière hillclimb in Italy and the National Championship in Austin, Texas, won by B. Griffith in a welcome outright victory for an often underrated competition car. At a time when the major factory and Autodelta efforts were going into the ambitious and demanding programme of development for the big T33 prototypes, this was a spectacular record of success for a single manufacturer. And if *that* wasn't enough, the splendid twin-cam engines were being used in another sporting area entirely, one pioneered by the highly specialized Alfetta Grand Prix engines several years before: high-speed motor-boat racing. In that same year of 1968, Alfa-engined craft won world and European championships in four different classes.

Left
The 2000 dash had its critics however—instead of the clear and functional dials used on the Giulias, many people found the white-on-black-on-white figures difficult to read at times

Below left
Even more unusual was this automatic transmission version of the 2000: along with its 1750 equivalent, several hundreds were sold to buyers who were unconvinced of the delights of the manual Alfa gearchange

Below
The Giulia lives on: except it now has the Giulietta engine in the old body box and a 2000 radiator. The name—Nuova Super 1300—is different, but the lively performance is still the same

Right
The GTAm 2000 at the Monza Four Hours in 1970— driven by Hezemans, the car took first place overall

Below
The 1750 GTAm going round a bend with one wheel delicately raised at Brno in Czechoslovakia in May 1970. None the less, its handling was still good enough for Hezemans to win the race outright

But there were problems still to be faced on the commercial front. In 1969, the company's production broke the 100,000 barrier for the first time—but that increase was accounted for entirely by increased sales of the established Giulia models: production of the 1750 range actually fell by more than five thousand cars. What was the reason? Price was hardly a factor, since the 1750 models were only slightly more expensive than their Giulia counterparts. More important in the buyers' eyes was the taxation question: the larger engines lifted the cars into a different tax bracket, which involved greater running costs for extra performance of debatable value.

In a sense, then, the 1750 compromise wasn't working: it hadn't gone far enough. The opposition was tending more and more to opt for the full two litres, and only the special conditions of the Italian market had held Alfa back from this step for so long. For a car like the Fiat 500, Italy was the cheapest country in Europe from a taxation point of view: the complex horsepower formula, which rated cars on a notional power output rated as 0.08782 times the number of

Going one better—with all wheels off the ground—is this GTV 2000 of Karna and Siitonen in the Arctic Rally in Finland. They still went on to win the Group One category outright!

237

cylinders, multiplied by the cubic capacity of the engine raised to the power 0.6541, ensured that Italy was the most expensive country in Europe to tax a car with an engine larger than 1500 cc. The results of this policy had a drastic effect on car ownership in Italy: where the average car engine size in Britain during 1967 was 1385 cc and in Germany 1445 cc, the combination of low wages and capacity-based taxation meant that the average car in Italy was only 890 cc in engine size.

On the other hand, for those owners to whom performance mattered more than cost, then it might well make sense to increase the engine capacity still further, and make a more worthwhile job of it. The way had already been shown by another competition variant on the GTA theme, but this time using the 1750 as a basis, and this

Alfas down under—Chris Cole's 2000 GTV going strong in the 1973 Surfers' Paradise International, where he won his class and took fourth place overall

proved spectacularly successful. The idea was to contest the European Championship for Group 2 touring cars for the 1970 season with a car based on the 1750: the 1600 and 1300 versions of the GTA had won their classes in the European Touring Car Challenge series—the third successive Alfa victory—and the GTAs had also managed to collect the Austrian Hillclimb Championship, the SCCA Sedan Class C Championship in the USA, the Championship of Makes in Brazil and individual events like the National Championship races at Riverside and at Phoenix in the United States, the Jarama 3-hour race in Spain and the Coupe des Alpes, where the GTAs scored valuable class wins, all during the 1969 season. Even the 1750s were beginning to follow suit: Kevin Bartlett won the Bathurst 500-mile race (class E) in Australia with a 1750 GTV, and two of the cars took first and second places in the 2-litre class in the Kyalami six-hour race in South Africa, all of which boded well for future seasons.

For 1970 the focus of interest promised to be the 2-litre class, and though the GTV was well below the capacity limit, the Autodelta team set out to provide the GTA treatment for the larger engine, within the limits allowed by the regulations. The twin-ignition cylinder head was substituted for the original: the carburetters were replaced by indirect fuel injection, fed by twin electric pumps. The valve openings were widened, and 40.5 mm inlet valves and 36.5 mm exhaust valves, all sodium-cored, were fitted in place of the 38 mm and 31 mm valves used on the production GTV. The compression ratio was raised from 9 to 1 to 11 to 1 and—the most significant change of all—the cylinder bores were widened from 80 mm to 84.5 mm, to take the capacity from 1779 cc to an altogether more competitive 1985 cc. In its 1970 form, the engine produced 220 bhp, compared with the 118 bhp of the GTV—and with a body more than 250 lb lighter, the sports version could not only accelerate much faster, but could reach a useful 137 mph top speed.

The new version was called officially the 1750 GTAm. The '1750' was to identify the car with its production basis, the 'm' stood for maggiorata, referring to the increase in cylinder capacity, and the combination soon began to become familiar on the racing circuits. Once again, as so often before during the long story of Alfa's involvement with motor racing, the car proved itself a force to be reckoned with from its first appearance onwards. In the first event in the 1970 European Touring Car Challenge, the Monza 4-hours, Toine Hezemans took first place overall with the GTAm, while first place in the 1000–1600 cc class went to the Truci-Ghigo GTA 1300 against cars with considerably larger engines. Hezemans took the GTAm to the Easter meeting at Zandvoort a fortnight later, and he and the car won again. It was the same at the Budapest Grand Prix in May, while Larrousse won the Paris GP at Montlhèry and the Dijon Grand Prix. De Adamich and Picchi won the six-hour race at the Nurburgring, Roselli won the Cesana-Sestrière hillclimb, and the GTAms came second, third and fourth overall at the Francorchamps 24 Hour Race to win the team prize for Alfa Romeo. Victories at Budapest, Brno and at the Jarama 4-hours, reinforced by second

Rudolf Hruscka—the ex-Porsche engineer who designed the front-drive Alfasud and went on to succeed Satta in the Design and Experimental Departments of Alfa Romeo Nord, where he worked on the Alfettas and the new Giulietta

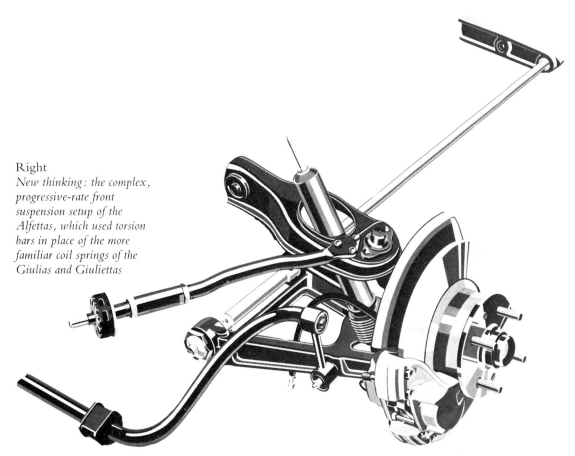

Right
New thinking: the complex, progressive-rate front suspension setup of the Alfettas, which used torsion bars in place of the more familiar coil springs of the Giulias and Giuliettas

places at the Tourist Trophy and in the race for the Trophy of Austria, clinched the European Touring Car Championship for Hezemans and the GTAm in its first competition season—a brilliant achievement, and eloquent proof that the design of the original twin-cam was so efficient that it could still be competitive, even on the unforgiving ground of the racing circuits.

In the meantime, more and more people in markets all over the world were beginning to notice the Alfa name for the first time. Many of the advertisements were beginning to concentrate on the cars' other virtues, leaving the lengthening record of competition achievements to speak for itself among the real enthusiasts. First-time Alfa buyers, or possible buyers, were being wooed by advertisements like this, for the Giulia Super in South Africa:

'There is a certain type of man who stops conversation when he enters a room. When he talks, it's worth listening to. When he listens, he uses his eyes. His clothes and grooming reflect his sensitivity. He knows many women, and treats each one like a queen. He is imaginative and outspoken, yet compassionate and gentle. He reads widely and without prejudice. His only hate is bigotry. He is honest enough to admit that he can never be satisfied with mediocrity, yet confident enough to concede that he will never have to. For such a man there is a car. A car that is the lengthening shadow of his own personality. A car with the same power in reserve. He drives it

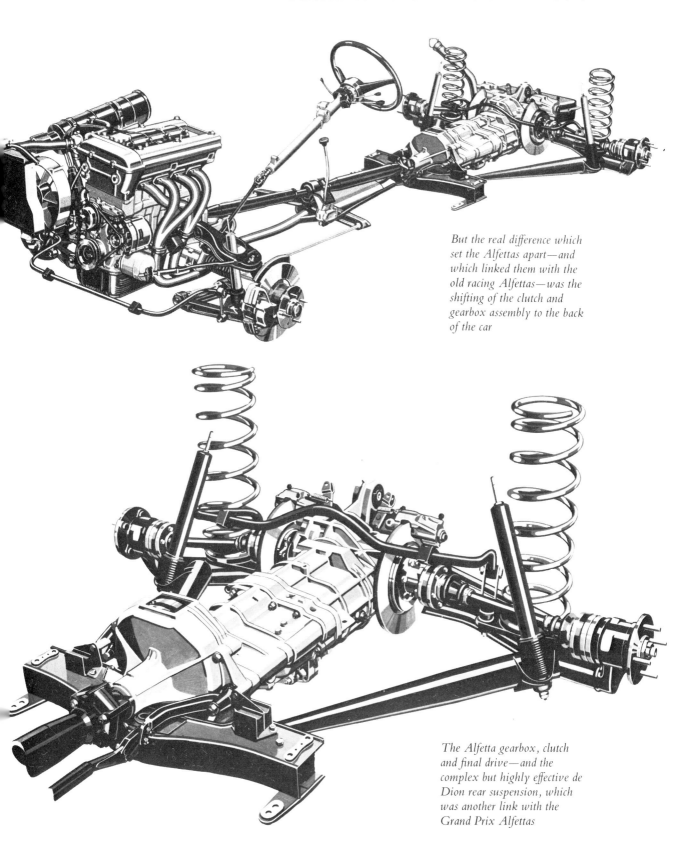

But the real difference which set the Alfettas apart—and which linked them with the old racing Alfettas—was the shifting of the clutch and gearbox assembly to the back of the car

The Alfetta gearbox, clutch and final drive—and the complex but highly effective de Dion rear suspension, which was another link with the Grand Prix Alfettas

241

slowly, in the knowledge that the only person he has to impress in the world is himself. The car is Alfa Romeo. Are you the man?'

This splendid piece of Copywriters' Baroque would give most Alfa enthusiasts severe coronary problems, but it had a difficult job to do— the traditional sales lines of racing success and exhilarating road performance could hardly be used to make the car appeal to non-racing buyers in a country where a universal 50 mph speed limit would soon become an ever-present fact of life. For America, on the other hand, where attitudes were very different, the 1750s were heralded with advertisements on much more traditional lines:

'*1969 begins today. The New Alfa Romeo 1750s are in. They'll make your blood race. You haven't really driven yet. Until you drive a new Alfa. Whichever you drive, you're going to experience a sensation no other car ever gave you. Your blood's going to race. Because each new Alfa has a larger, more powerful twin-overhead-cam engine that turns out 132 hp. Each one has a new race-proven fuel injection system. It improves performance. It saves gas. And it's standard. You also get five forward speeds, fully synchronised. New, wide-tread, high-performance radial-ply tyres. New pressure-equalized disc brakes on all four wheels for safe, sure, straight-line stopping. And just look at the beautiful Italian coachwork by master designers Bertone and Pininfarina, with elegant interiors that cradle you in comfort at speeds up to nearly 120 mph. So let us repeat. If you want driving excitement, drive one of Alfa's new 1750s. And feel your pulse pound.'*

In England, on the other hand, safety was becoming respectable as

Left
There have been several different versions of the Alfetta saloon: the smallest 1.6 version, which uses the old Giulia-size 1570 cc engine, has single headlamps

Below left
The original Alfetta had a 1.8 engine inherited from the 1750s—now the 1.8 has the quadruple headlamp installation

Below
Top-of-the-line Alfetta: 2000s can be distinguished by the broader radiator grille (like the old 2000 saloon) and the pair of bigger, rectangular headlamps (except in North America)

The Alfetta 2000 in full cry: although the rear mounting of the gearbox has caused problems, the handling of the car when properly set up is above reproach

a selling argument for motor cars—and in a country where the traditional two-seat sports car had always been looked on as bachelor transport, the capacity of the Berlina was worth stressing:

'The Italians are crazy about women and fast cars. That's why they marry them.

'No one cried at Sig. Mastroni's wedding. Except for the Conte de Nuovarini, and that was from laughing too much. After the wedding, Sig. Mastroni sold his sports car, and bought a family car. His idea of a family car is a fast car for 5 people. A beautiful car that the whole family can enjoy together.

Now he's bought another family car. A new Alfa Romeo 1750. Sig. Mastroni is an excellent driver. On the Autostrada between Turin and Milan he sat the Alfa on 100 mph. And smiled happily. It was all so effortless. And Sig. Mastroni points out that his "family car" is capable of yet another 12 mph. And can zip from 0–50 in 7.1 seconds flat.

Still going strong after more than three decades: the neat and efficient double overhead camshaft, now nestling in the much roomier confines of the Alfetta 2000 bonnet

Alfa insides have been growing ever more luxurious since the Spartan days of the 1900, and this is probably the best yet: but the instruments are more difficult to read than they need to be . . .

He says, and we agree, that a safe family car should be very fast. And that, after all, it's just as important to get out of danger quickly as it is to stop quickly. (Disc brakes all round make sure of that.)

An Alfa 1750 saloon like this costs £1849 13s 1d in the UK (including Purchase Tax). But there are two other equally remarkable Alfa saloons to choose from. And all Alfas have 5-speed gearboxes, disc brakes all round, twin overhead cams and race-proven 5-bearing aluminium engines.

Our slowest "family car" is the Giulia 1300 TI. It does 100 mph. It's the most powerful 1300 cc 4-door saloon made today, in Italy or anywhere else. And it costs only £1199 9s 9d in the UK (including Purchase Tax).

Then there's our Giulia Super. Really super in comfort and performance. And it's probably the fastest 1600 cc production saloon in the world. It does 0–50 in 8.2 secs. And costs £1499 15s 4d in the UK (inc. Purchase Tax).

So now, if you're thinking of buying a new saloon, buy the safe one that's fast. An Alfa Romeo.'

*The one model the Alfetta
range still needs: a Spider.
This one, complete with
Targa top and a rollover bar
is, unfortunately, a one-off
show prototype, unveiled by
Pininfarina in 1974*

Advertisements like these concentrated on the virtues of the
established models—but there were new variants available, on the
home market at least, to those who wanted more individuality. The
model line-up of the late sixties had no equivalent to the Sprint
Speciale and Sprint Zagato versions of the Giulia and Giulietta which
had satisfied this small but important sector of the market. Bertone
was still represented by two out of the three best-selling 1750
models—but there was nothing at the smaller end of the range to fill
the bill, and certainly nothing by Zagato since the last of the
Tubolares had been built two years before.

But these omissions were to be remedied by a totally new Alfa
Romeo model which made its first appearance at the Turin Motor
Show in November 1969: the GT 1300 Junior Z, or Zagato. This was

an interesting combination of the Zagato skill in combining lightness and strength with clever aerodynamics, and the well-proven Alfa marriage of the Giulietta engine and the five-speed gearbox as already used to considerable effect in the Bertone-bodied GT Junior coupé.

The Junior Z was effectively a newer, smaller, more comfortable and less specialist version of the Tubolare. In profile it had a drooping nose sweeping upwards and backwards to an elegantly curving window line, a sloping fastback with a rear hatch, and another sharply cut-off Kamm tail. It was a sleek and attractive little car, weighing just over 2000 lb complete, and with the 89 bhp engine as fitted to the standard GT Junior, it was good for a top speed of 110 mph. There were several interesting ideas in the body design: the front end treatment, with headlamps hidden behind a transparent panel extending the entire width of the car, broken only by a shield-shaped air intake aperture in the centre, for example. Because the car was built by Zagato rather than by Alfa, production was bound to be small: but in three years, 1108 of these elegant little two-seat hatchback coupés were turned out, mainly for the Italian market.

Another addition to the lower end of the company's range made its appearance a year later: a much more familiar, and perhaps more obvious addition, but no less worth while for that. The Giulia 1300 Super—rather confusingly dropping the 'Junior' theme, and calling itself a 'Giulia' in spite of the use of the smaller engine—was essentially an uprated 1300 TI in the same way as the original Giulia Super was an uprated *Giulia* TI. By using the 89 bhp version of the engine as already used in the GT Junior, with its double twin-choke carburetter arrangement in place of the single carburetter on the TI, and by keeping the body weight the same, the top speed crept up to 103 mph. To confuse things even further, the introduction of the Giulia 1300 Super coincided with the dropping, after only a year, of a more obscure variant, which had been called the Giulia 1600S—this had been a single-carburetter 95 bhp version of the Giulia saloon intended as a relatively low-cost long-distance cruiser, and selling at little more than the 1300 Berlina.

But these new modifications, rearrangements and specialist additions and deletions in the existing range were to be over-shadowed by a new series of models in the following year, 1971. By now the writing on the wall stood out all too boldly: the 1750 GTAm had shown that an increase in capacity to the full two litres need not harm the traditional reliability in any way, but it *could* do an awful lot for performance. So the next step was to carry out the same cylinder-widening on the production cars: though in order to avoid shaving clearances too close, the bores were half a millimetre narrower than the GTAm cars at a round 84 mm, giving the production cars a total capacity of 1962 cc rather than the 1985 cc of the racing cars.

Otherwise, everything stayed exactly the same: stroke, carburation, valve sizes, cam profiles, compression ratios, gear ratios and final drive gearing. The simple increase in size pushed the power peak up from 118 bhp at 5500 rpm to 132 bhp at the same speed, and once again the same engine in the same state of tune was used in the Berlina, the GT Veloce and the Spider Veloce, though now the top speed was up to 118 mph for the saloon and 'better than 121 mph' for the more sporting versions.

The 2000s were just what the public wanted. The 1750 GTAm now became the 2000 GTAm (though the 'm' was now only justified by the extra 23 cc of the competition engine, now turning out a scorching 240 bhp at 7500 rpm and giving a top speed of 143 mph, a combination which would give the car and Hezemans their second successive European Touring Car Championship) and the extra performance of the production cars delighted the enthusiasts. *Autocar* tested the 2000 saloon in March 1973 (after pointing out that 'labour troubles in its native Italy kept the Alfa Romeo 2000 saloon from its British admirers for too long'). After some gentle niggles like 'the

clutch is a little on the heavy side by contemporary standards' and 'a sensitive person is reminded not to hurry the first gearchanges from cold by the mildly protesting crunch of sleepy synchromesh', they went on to say that 'once warm, which doesn't take long, the classic power unit is a delight'. They did however point out that the long-stroke 2000 engine had a slightly lower speed limit at 5700 rpm than had the 1750 saloon, with its identical crankshaft throws and 6000 rpm limit. 'Decent pulling power' commenced from 1500 rpm upwards, with a real power surge beginning from 2500 rpm.

When compared with their test of the 1750 Berlina, the *Autocar* test team found the 2000 saloon reached 30 mph from a standing start in 2.8 seconds rather than 3.2, 50 mph in 6.8 seconds rather than 7.8, 60 mph in 9.9 seconds rather than 10.8 and 80 mph in 18.6 seconds rather than 20.2. In fact, the improvement was greater than these figures suggested, as the test was run in very strong winds, with a car which had only a small mileage on the clock. When retested, they found the car reached 80 mph in 17.8 seconds, 2.5 seconds faster than the 1750, while the engine was noticeably more flexible.

But there were other, more difficult problems. The steering was as good as ever: 'No other maker produces steering that feels quite like this. The chief hallmark is . . . the very low friction, the lack of stickiness of action, the mechanical sweetness of it. This delightful quality brings with it at least two great benefits. One is very good self-

Like all its predecessors, the Alfetta has had a vital role to play in competition: here is Jon Dooley's Alfetta 1.8 at Thruxton in 1975 in a production saloon-car race

Above
Underneath all the rallymen's extras is an Alfetta saloon: this one was driven by Guy Frequelin in the Tour de Corse in 1974, and all those extra lamps, oil coolers and bodywork extensions were part of the prescription for success in modern international rallying

Right
The back view of Frequelin's Tour de Corse car is slightly more recognizable: though the dents and scratches show how tough the going has been

centring; even at very low cornering speeds in town, the handsome varnished wood of the steering wheel will spin back through one's hands to straighten the car without effort. The other is superb feel of what the front tyres are doing on slippery surfaces. There is just the right amount of kickback without fight over bumps, and just the right amount of weight.' Likewise the gearbox: 'As before, the quality and ease of the change is a model to all other makers of five-speed gearboxes. Being spring-loaded to just the right degree into the middle of the gate, one can always feel where one is. The extraordinary point about the Alfa change, and something which has been for so long that it is easy to take it for granted, is the sweetness of action of the long gear lever, the lack of friction in its movement. There is, of course, the load of spring and synchromesh to overcome, but no stickiness. It is rather like the movement of controls on a nicely worn high-quality machine tool—a delight to the perceptive driver.'

But the handling seemed to have lost its ahead-of-the-field quality. 'The car is pretty swerveable, rolls only a little and ordinarily understeers to an acceptable degree. . . . On ordinary roads, the only time the tail is likely to come out is by careless use of the right foot round corners in the wet, when the grip of the Cinturatos on the test car left much to be desired. . . . Ride is surprisingly good for a car of

Frequelin's car wasn't unusual in the treatment it received. This is team-mate Beguin's car in the same event, with exactly the same cosmetic additions

251

this weight with a live rear axle and such good "stiff" handling. . . .' In simple terms, the 2000 handled reasonably well, but it was no longer the best in the business. Alfas had grown much faster, heavier, more powerful in the twenty years since the 1900—and while their handling and roadholding was still as good as ever, the opposition had undoubtedly caught up. The engine was still the standard by which others could be judged, but more of the cars which were competing with the Alfas for a share of the enthusiast market now boasted independent rear suspension and handling of at least comparable quality.

It was time, in short, for the 1900 design to bow out at last—in some respects anyway—and for a more up-to-date replacement to take over. But what could the Alfa engineers do to replace the tried and trusty solid-axle layout? The arguments which had held good at its introduction—that a well-located solid axle system was preferable to an inferior independent system—were still as valid as ever. So if it was to be replaced, it must be by an independent suspension system which could really offer something better.

There were other factors which were also contributing to Alfa's biggest model shake-up for decades. For a long time, the Italian Government had been determined to encourage industry to extend itself into the agricultural and impoverished South, and Alfa Romeo, as a Government-backed company, would have to play a key part in the programme. There was already an old wartime Alfa aero-engine plant at Pomigliano d'Arco on the outskirts of Naples, and it was decided to build an entirely new plant nearby to build an entirely new Alfa, about as different from its predecessors as it was possible to produce. Instead of a vertical in-line engine driving the rear wheels it would have a flat-four driving the front wheels—it would be small, compact, simple so that it could be built by workers in an area with no pool of skilled industrial craftsmen existing around which a work force could be built. Big sales were essential, so the plant was designed to produce a relatively cheap Alfa with a high degree of automation.

This was the rationale behind the Alfasud project, and to put it into practice Alfa once again called in one of their ex-employees—in this case a man who had also worked for Porsche and Simca in his thirty-three-year career. Engineer Rudolf Hruska, born in Vienna in 1915 and a mechanical engineering graduate of the University of Vienna, worked on the design of the pre-war Volkswagen project on the Porsche team at Stuttgart. When Professor Porsche had been imprisoned without trial by the French after the war, and Ferdinand Porsche had accepted a commission from Italian industrialist Piero Dusio to design the Cisitalia Grand Prix car, in order to raise the ransom demanded for the release of his father by the French authorities, it was Hruska who was sent to Turin to run the Italian end of the project.

The Cisitalia project folded up in 1950, but Hruska stayed in Italy, joining Alfa Romeo to help in organizing the production of the 1900. He became Technical Manager of the Design and Production

Left
At last, a coupé version of the Alfetta—the sleek and exciting Giugiaro-designed Alfetta GT, which is arguably the prettiest Alfa coupé yet

Below left
Again, a curious dashboard, with the early Alfetta GT's rev-counter set on its own in front of the driver—excellent for a racing car, less practical for speed-limited roads

The Alfetta GT was ideal material for the sporting fraternity: here are the cars of Andruet/Biche and Ballestrieri/Mannini on the dockside at Genoa waiting to board the Canguro *for the voyage to Barcelona for the 1975 Costa Brava Rally*

Departments in 1954, working on the 'Romeo' light lorry and van and on the Giulietta Sprint production development. In 1959, he left Alfa to work for Simca and for Fiat, but returned to Milan eight years later to be put in charge of the Alfasud (or Alfa South) programme.

The eventual target for Alfasud production was 1000 cars a day, and the foundation stone of the purpose-built factory was laid in April 1969. By the Turin Show of November 1971, the first Alfasud was ready to be shown to the public, and the first production cars were on sale in Italy in June of 1972. It was a success from the beginning: although its design was so radically different from the 1900 and its successors, the Sud had much of the same character—indeed the remarks which the *Autocar* had made about the feel of the steering and gearbox of the 2000 Berlina could be applied equally truthfully to the Alfasud.

With the introduction of the Alfasud, all the 1300 models—the GT Junior, the Giulia 1300 Super and the GTA—had been phased out, while the Zagato-bodied Junior Z had been fitted with the Giulia engine in the form fitted to the Duetto and the GTV to become the 1600 Junior Z. This pushed the top speed up to 118 mph, and the new

*Two views of the power
lurking under the bonnet: the
Group Two version of the
Alfetta GT engine as modified
for rallying, but still
recognizably the same classic
twin-cam unit as used since the
1940s*

model stayed in production for another three years. During that time, however, only 402 cars were turned out at the Zagato plant. The other 1300, the 1300 TI, had been dropped the year before, so that for the time being the company's future depended on the 2000s, or their successors, and the Alfasuds.

Unfortunately, the smaller cars were giving problems: but not with their engineering and design, which was good enough to build up long lists of orders. The difficulties were in production—though care had been taken to make the car as simple to build as possible, there were still defects which could be traced back to the inexperienced work force. And there were not enough of them. To begin with, 500 cars a day was set as an interim target, and that took a long time to achieve. Continuing labour troubles—among them the fact that workers all too accustomed to living on low incomes often

Apparently completely unstoppable, the road-hugging stance of the formidable Alfetta GT of Zanetti and Pittoni in the Rally of the Four Regions of May 1975

preferred to take a day or two off rather than carry on to the bitter end for a full pay-packet—meant that production was only up to 800 cars a day after three *years*. At a time when the 1300 cc market sector was booming, the lack of Alfasuds was bad news—and the reintroduction of the 1300 twin-cam range in 1974, with a Giulia Nuova Super in 1300 and 1600 forms, which took place in 1974, was an attempt to fill the gap. It could also be said that the Arese factory had production capacity to fill before the then planned 'New Giulietta' was to be ready.

This new 1300 range was a considerable improvement: the saloon was a neater, sleeker, tidier version of the Giulia box with an engine delivering 103 bhp at 6000 rpm (more than the 1600 Giulia Super!) and a top speed of 104 mph. There was also a restyled four-headlamp version of the old Bertone GT 1300 Junior coupé and an updated

Ballestrieri in action in the San Remo Rally of 1975— the event was won (in group 2) by Fagnola and Novarese in another Alfetta GT

257

Andruet on his way through a typically Corsican village street on his way to third place in the 1975 Tour de Corse

Spider, and both of these versions were offered with either the hotter 1300 Giulietta engine, or the Giulia version delivering 116 bhp at 6000 rpm.

The success of the Alfasuds and the reintroduction of the smaller twin-cam models did not alter the need for a new design at the upper end of the range, however. The 1300 and 1600 cars were unchanged as far as their basic engineering was concerned—and the Alfasud had different priorities. With the engine driving the front wheels, the use of MacPherson strut front suspension gave the flexibility and performance necessary to provide steering, handling and traction up to the standard of its best competitors. The question of the rear suspension was less important, and to keep the rear wheels upright and the track constant it was decided to stick to the live rear axle theme, in this case suspended on coil springs and located by a Watt linkage.

But this did not solve the problem of how to improve the handling of the larger twin-cam cars. So the Alfa engineers approached the problem from the same logical standpoint, using a similar step-by-step argument to the reasoning which had produced the twin-cam engine layout. What factors *could* improve the roadholding? The answers centred on two improvements: evening up the weight distribution between front and rear, and reducing still further the unsprung weight on the rear wheels.

The last requirement was the easier to fulfil. In the late 1930s, the vastly greater power delivered by successive Grand Prix racing Alfas had produced the same problem in delivering as much as possible of that power on to the track. At the same time, the need for more sophisticated independent suspension systems had given rise to a series of experiments with transverse springs, swing-axles and the like, none of which had proved completely satisfactory. In the end, with the return of the Alfa team to Grand Prix racing after the war, the old transverse-leaf-spring-and-swing axle suspension was replaced by the entirely different De Dion axle set-up.

This had two very real advantages, in a passenger car as much as in the Grand Prix Alfettas where it had been so successful—not to mention its use in various Maserati and Ferrari racing cars too. It provided independent suspension so that the wheels can stay in contact with the road even over rough surfaces and under cornering loads, but without the camber changes inseparable from swing-axles, which can cause loss of adhesion at awkward moments. Because of the geometry of the De Dion system, the wheels are kept upright with respect to the ground surface all the time. The second great advantage is that the unsprung weight of the set-up is reduced to the weight of the tube linking the wheels—this allows the wheels to respond more quickly to uneven surfaces so that grip is never lost by hop or axle-tramp.

A system like this made sense for the 2000's replacement—but to make the location as precise as possible was still high on the engineers' priority list. So they fastened the central pivot of a Watt parallelogram linkage to the middle of the De Dion tube, and the outer ends of the two bars to the suspension pivots—this effectively prevented any transverse movements of the suspension under load.

The next priority, again inherited from the old suspension system, was to keep the unsprung weight as low as possible. This, on the other hand, was linked to the need to even up the front-to-rear weight distribution as far as possible. Many manufacturers of exotic and expensive sports cars had opted to fit the engine, as the largest single mass in the car, as close to the centre of the car as possible. This paid dividends in improved handling, but it reduced boot space to the minimum, eliminated rear seats entirely and inflicted on the driver the sensation (and often the noise and vibration) of a large and powerful engine churning away within inches of the back of his neck.

Moving the engine, in the case of cars which had to cope with carrying four or five passengers, in at least some of the versions, was out. The other alternative was to leave the engine where it was, but to shift some of the other weights on to the rear wheels to even things up in a different way. What could be moved? Again Alfa tradition came to the rescue: the pre-war 8C 2900 and the postwar (and pre-war) Alfettas had solved the same problem by moving the clutch and the gearbox back to join the differential. Could the same idea not be adopted for the new production Alfas?

On the face of it, this was an ideal solution. Put the clutch and gearbox and differential together at the back of the car in a compact light-alloy package, together with the inboard disc brakes, and fit the whole assembly to the body of the car so that it evens up the weight distribution without adding to the *unsprung* weight. With less weight left on the front wheels, the steering becomes lighter and the geometry can be carefully revised: the double wishbone configuration was arranged so that the long torsion bar suspension could adjust itself to compensate for the effects of body roll under hard cornering. Though this may have made little difference to the ultimate roadholding of the car, it played an important part in keeping the driver even better informed of the car's behaviour on a corner, and in providing a measure of compensation for cornering loads.

In theory, this was the ideal solution. In practice, it bristled with development problems. The idea, like so many others in automotive history, was not original—it had been tried before but, as Engineer

Frantic action in the service station at night, with mechanics tinkering with the car of Ballestrieri in the 1975 Elba Rally

Mazoni pointed out, all who had tried it had been beaten by problems of reliability. On the Lancia Flaminia it had been a disaster, Buick had tried a similar configuration and, after six months in production, had cancelled it and gone back to putting the clutch and gearbox in the front of the car. Porsche were trying a similar idea with the 924 and 928, but they were using it in a vastly more expensive car—even so they had been plagued by transmission problems, and had compromised by locating the clutch in the front of the car with the gearbox at the back.

Alfa too had their share of problems. The drawback of the system was that the engine crankshaft was now linked to the propeller shaft, which was now turning at engine speed all the time. The different rotating masses caused terrible resonance problems, which it seemed that nothing could stop. The original prototypes could not manage more than 6000 miles without the likelihood of the overloaded crankshaft being shaken to pieces by the vibration. Slowly, patiently, the development proceeded: the rear prop shaft was split into two

It was all worth while— Ballestrieri's Alfetta in full song, on its way to victory in the same event

Andruet's car in that same 1975 Elba Rally, leaving a cloud of dust from the loose gravel surface as it crosses a narrow bridge over a mountain gorge

separate sections, linked by three rubber couplings to transmit the power but damp out the vibrations.

The other problem was a more familiar one to any manufacturer who had changed from the old orthodox engine-drive-train layout: ensuring a precise and efficient gearchange mechanism. The problem here was that the gearbox was a vital part of the Alfa character, and it seemed that in no way could a remotely operated box ever approach the feel and the ease of the traditional direct gearchange. The engineers did their best, using rods and linkages rather than the simpler cables: but they were faced with the need for months of testing and hundreds of small modifications to make the new system work properly. Even then, they realized that they would have to face criticism—not, ironically, because their new gearchange was that much worse than similarly remote competitors, but because the old box was so very nearly perfect in its performance.

There was another problem with the new car: this new and unorthodox design might win over many customers who could appreciate the care which had gone into it and the ideas behind it. But equally it might alienate as many others, who were more than happy for Alfas to stay exactly as they had been for twenty years and more. So to begin with, it was introduced not as a complete range to replace the 2000 series, but as a single model to sell alongside them. It was clothed in a neat four-door saloon body which lost all traces of the Giulia's boxiness—this time Satta let the stylists have a free rein!—and whose only specifically Alfa characteristics were the radiator shield and badge.

But if the exterior lines of the car were unremarkable, the name was not. The new car weighed exactly the same as the 2000 saloon, but in order not to steal its thunder, it reverted to the 1750's 1779 cc version of the twin-cam engine. The 1750 name was out though, as this would have seemed too much of a step back, not to the glorious past, but to the models of only four years before. Instead, it was to be linked to another, even more splendid, period in Alfa Romeo's past, when the Grand Prix cars had humbled all other challengers in the dust of their passing. This was no mere coincidence of engine size to establish a rather tenuous link with an old and honoured favourite— the basic design of the car, the rearrangement which set it apart from all the other production Alfas, was the characteristic it had in common with the last of the Grand Prix Alfas: the immortal Alfetta.

So it was that the new Alfetta 1.8 saloon made its first public appearance in May 1972. But like its 2000 predecessor, its impact was to be postponed by increasing industrial unrest in Milan. *Autocar*, when it finally managed to test one almost two years later, commented: '[The Alfetta] . . . ran into heart-breaking difficulties. Massive labour troubles at the factory . . . meant that production could only stutter into life, and it was not until the middle of last year [1973] that anything approaching full production could be achieved.'

Was it worth the waiting? The body design, they found, was a great improvement on the 2000. Though the wheelbase was two inches shorter, the Alfetta's body was two inches wider and provided

Andruet and Dini's Alfetta GT on the track, at Spa in 1977, instead of on the rally circuit, this time with a flat tyre

the same amount of legroom for the rear-seat occupants. The use of the smaller engine meant that the gearbox had to be used much more enthusiastically to get the best out of the car than was the case with the 2000, though the better aerodynamic shape with its curved sides, clean surface treatment and high, squared-off tail ensured a high top speed of 113 mph on test.

Fortunately, in this case at least, the testers found that 'the gearchange feels typically Alfa with a nice slick action and a positive, sturdy feel to all its movements. The length of the linkage back to the rear axle imposes a weight factor on movement, and the inertia of the additional linkage must be overcome for each gear change. As a result, changes cannot be made with the same lightning speed as with other Alfas . . . but in all other respects the change is a delight to use, with just the right loading towards 3rd and 4th gears.' Subsequent testers were not so impressed, however.

Commenting on the handling, the testers explained that the wider track allowed a slightly softer ride which nevertheless 'remains typically Alfa, with a pleasant taut feel at all speeds'. Less pleasant was a 'continual high-frequency drumming through the structure, which is excited by the engine mountings and transmits a vibration even through the accelerator pedal'. But on cornering, the changes produced very good handling 'of a high standard indeed, with safe initial understeer changing progressively to a well-balanced neutral condition as cornering speeds increase. Hard acceleration at low

The Alfetta name didn't have the same glorious associations in the USA—so the car was renamed the Sport Sedan instead. These American versions feature fuel injection instead of carburetters

speeds will cause the tail of the car to kick out of line, especially on wet roads, but the delightfully quick steering allows the driver to remain master of the situation, and indeed this characteristic can be used to advantage to tighten one's line at will.'

There was another, unexpected bonus resulting from the new design—the clutch and gearbox were now much more accessible for maintenance or repairs, a total of an hour and a half having been cut from the time necessary to change a clutch, for example. The only real problem with the model, in marketing terms, was that Alfa soon found out that a name with such glorious associations in Europe meant almost nothing in America—it dated back to a time when Grand Prix racing had a much narrower appeal on the other side of the Atlantic, and in any case in the words of the American enthusiast monthly *Motor Trend* 'there is nothing deader than a retired racing car, and when that retirement has been on for a quarter of a century, dead is very dead indeed. To the average American with a smattering

Left
The eternal Spider—in this case the Spider Veloce for the American market, which is now enthusiastically snapping up almost all the open cars built for export

Below
Completing the trio of American Alfa models, the Sprint Veloce—like the other two cars, this was photographed outside the gates of one of MGM's country estates

The return of the Giulietta, but with a different more over-square version of the engine *and a very modern wedge-shaped body*

ALFA ROMEO   Giulietta 1.3

Giulietta 1.3

The rear view shows the very high boot and the spoiler at the top of the rear panel to improve adhesion at the rear end of the car

of spoken Italian, Alfetta simply means "little Alfa". And as a number of car manufacturers have discovered, the word "little" is not a selling buzzword in and of itself.'

So the Alfetta was eventually changed, for the American market only, into the Alfa Romeo Sports Sedan. By this time however it had grown up in size: Alfa had begun exploiting the car's appeal and its potential by fitting other versions of the perennial twin-cam engine into the same transmission-suspension-body package. At the beginning of 1975 they fitted a warmer 9.5 to 1 compression Giulia engine developing 118 bhp at 5600 rpm into the car to produce the Alfetta 1.6. Both engines had two horizontal twin-choke carburetters, and the top speeds of the two versions were almost identical, around the 110 mph mark. Outwardly, apart from the figures in chrome on the bootlid, the only major difference between the two versions was that the 1.8 had four round headlamps, the 1.6 just two.

In that same year another obvious version of the car was introduced, with fuel injection, for the American market only. This used the 2000 version of the engine to push the top speed up to 115 mph and provide the extra torque lacking in the original Alfetta, but since partially remedied by the slightly lazier engines fitted to the later 1.6 and 1.8 versions. Again the headlamps were the clue: rather than the round lamps fitted to the smaller-engined models, the Alfetta 2000, when it appeared on the European market in 1977, was instantly distinguishable by the use of a single pair of rectangular

The side view of the Giulietta—originally offered in 1.3- and 1.6-litre versions—shows to perfection the wedge shape of the body

headlamps. (The American 2000 still having four round headlamps, of course.)

But the Alfetta, for all its virtues, is still a saloon—and coupés have been too important in Alfa history to be dropped at this stage in the game of car production. So, in 1974, there appeared a very different Alfetta indeed: different from the saloon, but equally different from the coupé versions of the Giulietta, the Giulia, the 1750 and the 2000, which had all borne a very strong family resemblance.

This was the Alfetta GT, a sleek and very handsome fastback coupé styled by Giugiaro to look very fast indeed and yet to offer space for driver and three passengers in a high degree of comfort. But the Alfa engineers have never forgotten the other requirements which have been borne in mind ever since the 1900. A beautiful shape is not enough: it must be aerodynamically efficient, and this the Alfetta GT certainly is, with a drag coefficient of a mere 0.39. The wheelbase is four inches shorter, but the mechanical parts are arranged in the same way as in the Alfetta saloon. The engine too is the same, to begin with at least: the 1974 version of the GT with the 1779 cc, 122 bhp engine, was good for a top speed of 112 mph upwards. In 1976, this version was dropped and replaced by two new versions: the Alfetta GT, with the old Giulia engine in its 109 bhp form, giving a top speed of 112 mph, and the Alfetta Gran Turismo Veloce (or GTV) 2000, with the 122 bhp 2-litre engine, which has a top speed of more than 120 mph.

Even more complications in the range: April 1979 saw the introduction of an outwardly similar additional version of the Giulietta using the 1750 engine, to produce the Giulietta 1.8

Obviously, the new cars had performance potential in plenty, and they soon provided results which followed in the great tradition set by the GTAs and their fellows. In 1973, the year after the new range was introduced, it was still the 2000 GTAms and the GTVs that provided the lion's share of the 650 wins—outright victories and class wins—during that year, which included the Austrian Touring Car Championship and the Canadian Sedan Championship, won by the GT Junior and the 2000 GTV respectively. But in October of that year, Alfetta saloons won their class in two events, one in Spain and one in Finland. In 1974 there were more wins, though once again the lion's share of the 400-plus victories—including once again the Austrian Touring Car Championship and now the Belgian equivalent, not to mention overall victory in the Central American Turismo Championship and class wins in national championships in France, West Germany, Holland, Poland, Portugal and Venezuela—went to the older and already well-proven models. Yet the Alfettas turned in ten victories, ranging from the Lucky Strike Grand Prix, the Swaziland Trial and the Natal Rally Championship in South Africa to class wins in the Winter Trophy at Vallelunga and in the Foggia-Monte S. Angelo hillclimb in its native country.

The year 1975 was a morale-boosting one for Alfa, when they won the World Championship with their 33 sports prototypes. But as always the twin-cam cars were there in the background, bringing home another 600 wins, including 27 national championships, from

Another highly stylized dashboard, with similar confusing movements of the instrument needles, but otherwise highly functional: the Giulietta control panel

the Czechoslovakian Hillclimb Championship to the French Touring Car Championship for Group One cars. Significantly, two of these titles were won by Alfettas: the Greek Rally Championship by the Alfetta saloon and the CSAI Cup for Special Touring Cars by the Alfetta GT coupé. It was the same in 1976, another brilliant year for Alfa racing—though most of the 600-plus wins still went to the GTAs and Juniors, the Alfetta GT was really beginning to show its class in the second division of the European Touring Car Championship, with class wins at Monza, Mugello, Francorchamps, Silverstone and Jarama, and an outright win in the event at Vallelunga!

Since then, the emphasis has shifted more and more to the Alfetta series, as development problems in racing terms have been ironed out and the cars' real virtues can be used to the full in competition. Even now, in the last years of the seventies, it is probable, if previous form is any guide, that the greatest days of these cars still lie in the future. But in a very real sense, Alfa Romeo is approaching a crossroads in its history, and it's difficult to see exactly what will happen next.

First of all, there are signs that the old twin-cam engine will lose its position at the top of the tree. Soon we shall see the introduction of a new Vee-engined model to take its place at the top of the range, and the production of the sleek and nippy Sprint 1.5 version of the Alfasud version has cut into the Alfetta GT 1.6 sales so much that the Alfetta coupé is only to be offered in GTV form, in England and some other markets, from 1979 onwards. Back in 1976, Alfa themselves admitted that they were losing around £500 on each car they produced, due to a variety of industrial problems.

On the other hand, Alfa's position as a Government-backed organization is not the same as that of many of the companies against which they compete. Possibly the Alfasud venture, in terms of where the factory was built rather than in the design of the car, would never have been begun on strictly commercial rather than social grounds. So if the company is to add the relief of unemployment and economic malaise in the Mezzogiorno to its other priorities as a car *maker*, then perhaps some measure of loss is inevitable.

Unfortunately, engineering of the style and complexity that has become an Alfa tradition can be extremely expensive, and there is a danger that engineers of the old school, who were brought up in this tradition, may eventually be succeeded by more conventional and cost-conscious men who will find it more expedient to adopt consensus ideas used by the rest of the industry rather than the pioneering ideas which have served the company, and its customers, so well for so long.

Of course, there are problems, from the owners' viewpoint as well as from that of the factory. In the old days of the fifties, the sixties and even the early seventies, the perennial enemy of any Alfa owner was rust. The 2000 GTV is greatly in demand among collectors, but road salt and moisture can attack points like the brake master cylinders and the pedal pivots—two weaknesses on my Duetto. *Autocar* quoted a specialist earlier this year in a story on Alfa collectors: '. . . the steel-bodied Bertone coupés were regrettably not built with longevity in

The Alfetta 2300 is a model which you can't buy in Europe—it's produced in Brazil using the Alfetta body but a larger engine and with a different front end treatment with four equal-size headlamps and more chrome embellishments

mind, at least not in cold, wet climates.' One body expert talks of jacking points collapsing in two years. Another gives some idea of the care which many feel should be lavished on these cars: 'After I've been out on snow or ice, I hose the car down underneath to get rid of the salt.'

The Alfettas' greater complexity has introduced another requirement, over and above the pampering which these thoroughbred cars seem to need to keep them in good condition. The sophisticated suspension has to be adjusted to extremely fine limits—the current workshop manual devotes more space to suspension adjustments than to those of the engine—and a tiny discrepancy can make all the difference to the cars' handling. This means, if necessary, plaguing suppliers to get the car *right*: as *CAR* magazine found when they came to test-drive the latest model in the company's range to use the twin-cam engine and a glorious name from the past, though in this case the more recent past.

This was the Alfa Romeo Giulietta, though in this case the car is basically a shorter, lower and wider Alfetta with the same mechanicals fitted into a sharply styled wedge-shaped saloon body with a high boot line and a sharply curving bonnet contour. There are two versions of the car: the Giulietta 1.6, which uses the Giulia engine

Above
Yet another Giulia—with an important difference. This one doesn't have the twin-cam engine, but a totally different diesel unit instead

Left
Back view of the Giulia Diesel—only the chrome writing on the bootlid gives the game away. Note the flat boot lid this time

in its 78 by 82 mm, 1570 cc, 109 bhp form to give a 109 mph top speed, and the Giulietta 1.3 for capacity-tax-conscious Europe. This, oddly enough, doesn't use the old Giulietta unit, but a revised wide-bore, short-stroke version of the trusty engine, measuring 80 mm by 67.5 mm and displacing 1357 cc to produce 95 bhp at a higher speed of 6000 rpm; this version, thanks to the excellent aerodynamics, can still manage 103 mph flat out.

CAR found the Giulietta gave them extremely mixed feelings. One version had an appallingly stiff gearchange and the handling was soft and imprecise, although the unchangeable absolutes of the design, like the driving position, the comfort, the size of the boot, the spacing of the gear ratios and the encouraging care taken to protect

Alfa's entry in an international competition to design a completely new taxi for New York City—the dashboard seen from the padded luggage compartment

the car against rust came in for praise. Another, on the other hand, behaved beautifully, just as the car should—impeccable handling, especially over the most terrible surfaces, and ever-crisp steering. Eventually, the first car was retested some time later, when it performed faultlessly—a case of careful adjustment in the meantime perhaps? Certainly my own experience with road-test Alfas bears this out—handling was better on the Giulietta and the GTV than it was on the Alfetta 2000. Likewise the Alfetta 2000's gearbox proved stiff to use—that of the Giulietta was far better and that of the test Alfetta GTV (the newest car of the three) was hardly distinguishable from the direct gearchange on the Giulia series.

It all boils down, once again, to care. Dealers have to become accustomed to the painstaking checking and adjustment which these new-generation Alfas need. Customers have to educate themselves to make sure the dealers do their job properly—now that the problem of rust has been at least reduced if not completely solved, time spent on getting these small but important adjustments to steering, suspension and gearboxes will be very well spent.

For in the end, an Alfa is still a very hard car to beat, at its size and price. Engineer Mazoni, with the impending retirement of Garcea, is now the only one of Satta's immediate group still left with the company—Satta himself died in 1973, and the Giulietta was the first model to be produced without his guidance—and he speaks eloquently of the satisfactions his work has brought him. 'You spend months and months on a stupid problem. Finally you solve it, it goes into production and eventually you see it everywhere. To help in building a car which is loved and appreciated everywhere because it's better than the others—you can't put a price on that kind of feeling.'

He considers the best tribute to Alfa engineers has been the imitators: from the Triumph Dolomite of the 1930s to the postwar Volvos and BMWs. He talks of the time when the Giulietta's alloy differential casing—the first in the world—was sent to a firm in New York State for machining and drilling, it was returned with a note saying 'You've made a mistake—it's in aluminum.' Now development is proceeding in entirely new directions: a Giulia diesel has already been sold to the public using a Perkins engine. Eventually, production VM diesel engines from Finnmeccanica, another IRI company, will be used in cars like the Fiat 131 and 132, and in a diesel version of the Alfetta saloon.

For the time being though, the future of the classic twin-cam engine is secure, in the middle of the range at least. With the Alfasud at the lower end of the market, and the Vee-engined cars coming in at the top, there is still nothing to beat the Merosi-Jano-Satta design on its own ground. In trying to assemble a list of competitors against which the current models could be assessed, it proved surprisingly difficult: though they were all good cars in their different ways, the cars which came closest to the Alfas in style, in character and in engineering originality were all far more expensive. Cars which were its equivalent in price inevitably suffered in comparison in one way or another.

Exterior view of the Alfa New York taxi design: based on the 1290 cc Giulietta version of the twin-cam engine, the taxi provided a top speed of 75 mph, room for five passengers, a sliding door and a retractable access ramp for wheelchairs

Of course, if the loss of the old traditions which Mazoni and Garcea value so highly were to happen, this happy state of affairs (happy for Alfa fans that is) may soon come to an end. If it did, the automotive world would be a great deal poorer for its loss. Already the car which for me symbolizes the sheer fun of Alfa driving—the Spider, which in 2000 form has carried on since the introduction of the Alfettas, with no re-engineered equivalent—has disappeared from the British market. Originally, it was dropped from its most successful overseas market, the United States, because of problems in meeting the stringent emission-control laws. From early 1977, these were solved and the Spider was able to reappear in California and in a slightly different version in all the other forty-nine states of the Union.

This meant that the American market, where convertibles are now increasingly rare (European sports convertibles that is) could comfortably absorb most of the Spider production not needed for the home market. For the small numbers now left over, it was no longer worth producing a separate right-hand-drive version for the British market, so British buyers lost one of the best-loved Alfas of all. When *Autocar* last tested the car, back in 1976 when the rumours were already beginning to fly, they had this to say about it:

Engineer Gian Paolo Garcea (far right) at a meeting of the Convention on the Child and the use of the Car. Garcea is one of the last of Satta's team of engineers still working with the company

'There is, most happily, no such thing as a dull Alfa. And, to the driver who appreciates unencumbered open two-seater motoring there are now, regrettably, few true sports cars. Widespread misunderstandings of the lunatic excesses of American safety thinking have, for the moment, discouraged convertible production. The strong suggestion that the Alfa 2000 range is to be replaced are backed by some details on this week's Road Test car which could easily be modernized. The Alfa Romeo 2000 Spider Veloce is not perfect, but if it is to disappear soon—we would rather it didn't—then that makes it an even better car for the discerning enthusiast to buy, for it is a contemporary classic. The only snag of buying a Spider as a collector's piece is that you just couldn't store it; for truly, like so many Alfas, it begs to be driven.'

Coming from a sober, technically qualified group of experts who test every kind of sophisticated sports car in the course of their work, that is praise indeed. Nor are *Autocar* the only testers to fall under the car's spell—read what *Road & Track* wrote about the American version of the same model:

'Even the most devoted Porsche-meister on our staff returned from his first drive and said "You know, it'd be fun to have one of these for sunny Sunday afternoon drives down the coast". With the easy-to-operate convertible top in the down position and the wind ruffling your hair, it's easy to look upon drivers in other cars with smug disdain and recall the words from Dante's Inferno, "These unfortunates, who never were alive." '

What the experts—impartial experts—have written about the Spider could be applied with equal justice to any of the twin-cam cars, from the 1900 in its time to the Giulietta and Alfettas of today. If the twin-cam Alfas, a brilliant series of cars which, apart from delighting countless owners, have won on average more than one race for every day of their lives over the last ten years, ever need an epitaph, then quotes like these will do as well as any. But may that need not emerge for a long, long time yet. . . .

And finally . . . John Lyon's Alfetta GT demonstrating in 1977 that body roll is still an enduring part of the Alfa pedigree

Epilogue
A PERSONAL VIEW

One of the problems with writing a book like this is proving one's objectivity. That's why I've tried to rely, wherever possible, on other people's recollections and estimates in comparing Alfas with their competitors—or on the comforting certainty of cold figures and engineering details rather than feelings and impressions of my own experience with Alfas over the years.

Yet I must declare an interest. Henry Ford always said that, whenever he saw an Alfa Romeo pass by, he raised his hat—and I know what he meant. If I hadn't come to respect these extraordinary cars from personal acquaintance, to take an interest in why they are designed and built the way they are, then this book would never have been written in the first place. At least, not by me.

The big problem is that one cannot compare Alfas fairly with any other cars: if you compare them with their competitors on the grounds of price, then their rivals hardly ever boast the kind of engineering sophistication and individuality which the Alfas possess. If you find other cars which share their engineering ideas, and their performance and their driver appeal, then very often you find you are pitting these cars against others which are bigger, more powerful and a great deal more expensive. Just look at the road test section to see the problem clearly.

But what do these cars mean to someone who knows them well? I can claim no vast collection of rare and historic Alfas, no backlog of experience behind the wheel of the great vintage Alfas of the past. I haven't even driven a 1900, or a Giulietta. But in a decade and a half of testing and writing about cars for everything from books to magazines, television to newspapers, a life which involves trying to compare and assess cars from the mundane to the exotic, with as much cynical and professional detachment as possible, I've come to respect these cars as few others. Of course they're not the only cars to be fun to drive, to have exciting performance or to create fond memories: the Jaguar E type, the Porsche 911, the 450 SL Mercedes-Benz, the AC Cobra, the Jensen FF are all highspots in my driving career. But the car which I owned the longest, which provided the least trouble and the most pleasure for the lowest price—that car was, for me, an Alfa.

I can't remember the first Alfa I ever saw: the first one I *noticed* was a vintage 1750 which used to be parked outside the Red Lion in Withington, a suburb of Manchester, in the early 1960s. Compared with the classic beauty of that lean, graceful two-seater, the boxy Giulias seemed to represent the inevitable decline into modern boring tinware which so many other great vintage names had suffered by that time. Then, a few years later, I had my first turn behind the wheel of a modern Alfa: in a way it was a cheat, since this was the Zagato 1750 replica, which might have been expected to have something of the quality of the original in its make-up.

Indeed it did: but the biggest surprise was that the more mundane modern Alfas shared the same quick, lively steering, the same magnificent engine, the same beautifully precise handling, the same solidity and comfort and above all excitement. The Giulia Sprint GTV was next on my list—but that was still a special-bodied sports coupé. Then came the boxy Giulia Super—and in some ways that was the most surprising of all. A car which looked so completely functional and unassuming could still be so much a keen driver's car—that was an achievement which was unusual and increasingly valuable at a time when cost-benefit-analysis and price competition were dictating that various makers' cars were growing more and more like their principal competitors in identity, image, performance and engineering.

But my favourite Alfa was the Alfa I owned for almost ten years: a Duetto open two-seater, coloured the only hue for an Alfa of that shape and pedigree, sanguine Italian racing red. At the time, I nearly didn't buy an Alfa at all: I had set my heart on an E type, but delivery delays at a time when my previous car was showing its age in no uncertain terms, meant I had to look further afield. Having handed back the GTV with more reluctance than was the case with most test cars at the end of their loan time, and having sampled a Spider on a press

'I don't want any excuses . . . it's in a restricted area and I want it moved NOW.' What happens when even an Alfa is pushed too far and the car's agility can't prevent it from contacting the scenery. The policeman is probably Austrian, and the car, from its crumpled radiator grille and Zagato badge on the side, is probably a Gulietta SZ . . .

trip to the then recently-opened Alfa test track at Balocco, I opted for the Duetto instead. I had my doubts—there were those who hinted darkly at complexity and temperament and high running costs as the other side of the coin of a thoroughbred engine design. My insurance broker winced at my change in cars, and when I saw the new premium I wondered if perhaps I *had* made a mistake.

Yet nine years and 130,000 miles later, the car was still going strong. The only mechanical failure had been a water pump at 80,000 miles or so—though the cost of £25 (at that time) for a replacement unit, when my neighbour paid £2.50 for an identical component for his Minor 1000, seemed exorbitant, it was part of a total bill which for that time and that distance, was in fact a great deal less than I might have paid for far less ambitious transport. The car needed new clutch linings, new brake pads at regular enough intervals, new plugs and a new battery, plus a quartet of new exhaust valves over the years. But in terms of the Automobile Association's average list of renewal and replacements for a car over a three-year span, this was remarkable enough—for almost a decade of hard driving, it was virtually unbelievable.

By the end of our time together, the Duetto *was* showing its age. A rumble in the prop-shaft universals was defying all remedies, and replacement was planned: the easy-to-drop hood had chafed on the edge of the bodywork so that it was beginning to leak. Worst of all, a mishap while the car was being road-tested by the local agents (still a round trip of seventy miles for every service) started body decay in a big way: another driver in a Vauxhall Viva skidded on an icy road and bent the Duetto's starboard front wing. Although the garage tidied everything up so that it looked as good as new at the time—the legacy was a persistent steering vibration at certain speeds, an increase in tyre wear and a localized tendency to rust around the site of the damage.

Yet by then the car had driven a distance equivalent to half-way to the moon. In one trip to Vienna and back, across Alpine passes and along crowded autobahns, it had never missed a beat despite advancing age and increasing mileage. It had taken people, children and dogs on sailing expeditions and holiday trips. It had even had a moment of notoriety: in all innocence, we set out to drive to the cinema to see Dustin Hoffman in *The Graduate*, all unaware that his co-star in that film was a red Duetto. For the only time ever, the only parking place we could find was right outside the cinema entrance . . . at the end of the film, we climbed in and drove off, the centre of a crowd absolutely convinced the whole thing was a carefully set-up publicity stunt.

In the depths of winter, a brilliantly effective heater (and this on an Italian car!) made it cosy enough, in spite of increasing draughts through an increasingly threadbare soft top. But it was on summer days when the hood could be safely folded that the car really came into its own: with the breeze in one's face, the crisp boom of that incomparable twin-cam engine in one's ears and the splendid steering telling one's hands all about every tiny facet in the relationship between tyres and road, this was a different kind of driving indeed.

It was too good to last: a growing family was straining the accommodation of that miniature baggage platform behind the comfortable two seats to the utmost. The rust in the wing was beginning to spread, and other ageing problems were probably waiting to make themselves felt—yet at the last overhaul, the mechanic had expressed amazement at the small amount of bore wear showing at such a high mileage. Then, one Friday evening, it happened. After bringing home the weekend shopping, the car was driven into the garage and switched off. There was a second's pause and then the engine began turning over on the starter, faster and faster. . . .

There was just time to get everyone clear and to push the car out into the drive—by the time a screwdriver had been found to lever off the battery connections, the dashboard wiring and the trim were well alight. By the time the brigade arrived, the car was beyond saving, and two days later the charred remains were carried away to the wails of weeping children and a surreptitious tear or two from their parents. One short circuit in the ignition/starter switch had brought nine years of fond ownership to an abrupt and harrowing end.

Since then driving has been a lot less exciting. The occasional road-test cars, like those covered in this book, have been welcome diversions—and day-to-day routine has been catered for by an unexciting but splendidly reliable Volkswagen Beetle, while we looked for a replacement. In two years of careful consideration, the paradox I mentioned above proved impossible to answer: any car which seemed a worthwhile replacement for our Duetto was far too expensive for our finances.

So, to cut a long story shorter, we've finally given up. If enjoying driving without breaking the bank means running the risk of being classified Alfa-fanatics, then so be it. After two years of routine, sober, undramatic there-and-back journeys, we're about to fill the gap left so suddenly and finally by the death of our Alfa. And what are we filling it with? What else but another Alfa—in this case the Alfetta 2000 GTV, latest, fastest and most powerful of that immortal postwar twin-cam four-cylinder family of thoroughbreds?

David Owen
May 1979

Appendix 1
THE TWIN-CAM
FOUR CYLINDER ENGINES

Engines are arranged in ascending order of size, and of power in each size and model bracket. Columns refer to, in order, bore, stroke, capacity, compression ratio, mean piston speed (m/sec), bmep (kg/sq cm), cylinder head material, block material, valve angle, inlet valve diameter, exhaust valve diameter, (both mm), carburation, peak power and rpm, and models on which each particular version of the engine was used

66/66.5/896/8.5:1/12/9.5/light alloy/l.all/80 deg./26.5/24/	1 s-choke carb/52/5500	Tipo 103 fwd
74/75/1290/7.5:1/13.75/6.72/light alloy/l.all/80 deg./31/28/	1 s-choke carb/53/5500	Giulietta Berlina (1955–1960)
74/75/1290/7.5:1/15.00/7.2/light alloy/l.all/80 deg./31/28/	1 s-choke carb/62/6000	(1961–62)
74/75/1290/8.5:1/15.25/7.43/light alloy/l.all/80 deg./31/28/	1 d-choke carb/65/6100	Giulietta TI 1957–60
74/75/1290/8.5:1/15.5/8.33/light alloy/l.all/80 deg./31/28/	1 d-choke carb/74/6200	Giulietta TI 1961–63
74/75/1290/8.5:1/15.75/8.85/light alloy/l.all/80 deg./31/28/	1 d-choke carb/80/6300	Giulietta Sprint and Spider
74/75/1290/9.1:1/16.27/9.66/light alloy/l.all/80 deg./31/28/	2 d-choke carbs/90/6500	Giulietta Sprint and Spider Veloce
74/75/1290/9.7:1/16.26/10.74/light alloy/l.all/80 deg./31/28/	2 d-choke carbs/100/6500	Giulietta SS and SZ
74/75/1290/8.5:1/15/9.07/light alloy/l.all/80 deg./31/28/	1 d-choke carb/78/6000	Giulia 1300 Berlina
74/75/1290/9:1/15/9.53/light alloy/l.all/80 deg./31/28/	1 d-choke carb/82/6000	Giulia 1300 TI
74/75/1290/9:1/15/10.36/light alloy/l.all/80 deg./31/28/	2 d-choke carbs/89/6000	GT 1300 Junior GT 1300 Junior Z, Spider 1300 Junior, Giulia 1300 Super
78/67.5/1290/9.1:1/13.5/11.17/light alloy/l.all/80 deg./40.5/36.5/	2 d-choke carbs/96/6000	GTA 1300 Junior
80/67.5/1357/9:1/13.5/11.4/light alloy/l.all/80 deg./37/31/	2 d-choke carbs/95/6000	Giulietta 1.3 (1977)
76/82/1488/10:1/21.85/10.96/light alloy/l.all/90 deg./35/31/	2 d-choke carbs/145/8000	750 Competizione
78/82/1570/9:1/16.98/8.51/light alloy/l.all/80 deg./35/31/	1 d-choke carb/92/6200	Giulia TI
78/82/1570/9:1/15.05/10.22/light alloy/l.all/80 deg./35/31/	2 d-choke carbs/98/5500	Giulia Super
78/82/1570/9:1/15.05/9.82/light alloy/l.all/80 deg./35/31/	1 d-choke carb/95/5500	Giulia 1600S
78/82/1570/9:1/15.05/10.64/light alloy/l.all/80 deg./35/31	2 d-choke carbs/102/5500	Giulia Super 1971–72
78/82/1570/9:1/16.4/10.013/light alloy/l.all/80 deg./35/31/	2 d-choke carbs/106/6000	Giulia Sprint GT Giulia GTC
78/82/1570/9.5:1/15.3/12.8/light alloy/l.all/80 deg./35/31/	2 d-choke carbs/108/5600	Alfetta 1.6

78/82/1570/9:1/16.68/10.42/light alloy/l.all/80 deg./37/31/	2 d-choke carbs/109/6000	Giulia Sprint GTV, Duetto
78/82/1570/9:1/15.31/11.15/light alloy/l.all/80 deg./41/37/	2 d-choke carbs (or f/inj. for USA)/109/5600	Alfetta GT 1.6
78/82/1570/9:1/15.3/11.6/light alloy/l.all/80 deg./37/31/	2d-choke carbs (or f/inj. for USA)/109/5600	Giulietta 1.6
78/82/1570/9.7:1/17.78/9.9/light alloy/l.all/80 deg./35/31/	2 d-choke carbs/112/6500	Giulia SS, TI Super Spider Veloce, TZI
78/82/1570/9.7:1/16.4/11/light alloy/l.all/80 deg./40.5/36.5/	2 d-choke carbs/115/6000	GTA
78/82/1570/10.5:1/20.5/13/light alloy/l.all/80 deg./36/30/	2 d-choke carbs/170/7500	GTA Corsa, TZ2
86/67.5/1570/10.5:1/20.5/16.84/light alloy/l.all/80 deg./40.5/36.5/	2 d-choke carbs/220/7500 (+ 2 s'chargers)	GTA SA
80/88.5/1779/9:1/16.25/10.87/light alloy/l.all/80 deg./38/31/	2 d-choke carbs/118/5500 (or f/inj. for USA)	1750 Berlina, GT Veloce, Spider Veloce
80/88.5/1779/9.5:1/16.23/11.25/light alloy/l.all/80 deg./38/31/	2d-choke carbs (or f/inj. for USA)/122/5500	Alfetta Berlina, Alfetta GT 1.8
80/88.5/1779/9.5:1/15.65/12.9/light alloy/l.all/80 deg./38/31/	2 d-choke carbs (or f/inj. for USA)/118/5300	Alfetta 1.8
82.55/88/1884/7:1/12.92/7.06/light alloy/cast iron/90 deg./38/34/	1 s-choke carb/65/4400	1900 M (jeep)
82.55/88/1884/7.5:1/15.27/8.27/light alloy/cast iron/90 deg./38/34/	1 s-choke carb/90/5200	1900 Berlina
82.55/88/1884/7.75:1/16.15/8.68/light alloy/l.all/cast iron/90 deg./41/36.5/	1 d-choke carb/100/5500	1900 TI, Sprint
84/88.5/1962/9:1/16.23/11/light alloy/l.all/80 deg./38/31/	2 d-choke carbs/132/5500 (f/inj. for USA)	2000 Berlina, GT Veloce, Spider
84/88.5/1962/9:1/15.65/10.56/light alloy/l.all/80 deg./44/40/	2 d-choke carbs (or (f/inj. for USA)/122/5300	Alfetta 2000, Alfetta GTV
84.5/88/1975/7.5:1/15.27/7.68/light alloy/cast iron/90 deg./38/34/	1 s-choke carb/90/5200	1900 Berlina Super
84.5/88/1975/8:1/16.15/9.54/light alloy/cast iron/90 deg./41/36.5/	2 d-choke carbs/115/5500	1900 TI Super, Super Sprint
84.5/88/1975/8.25:1/15.57/9.02/light alloy/cast iron/90 deg./38/34/	1 d-choke carb/105/5300	2000 Berlina (1958–61)
84.5/88/1975/8.5:1/16.73/9.2/light alloy/cast iron/90 deg./38/34/	2 d-choke carbs/115/5700	2000 Spider (1958–61)
84.5/88.5/1985/11:1/20.15/12.28/light alloy/l.all/80 deg./40.5/36.5/	f/inj./195–220/7200	1750 GTAm
84.5/88.5/1985/11:1/21.1/12.71/light alloy/l.all/80 deg./40.5/36.5/	f/inj./210–240/7500	2000 GTAm
85/88/1997.4/9.1/19.1/10.07/light alloy/cast iron/90 deg./40/34.5/	2 d-choke carbs/138/6500	2000 Sportiva
85/88/1997.4/8.73:1/19.1/10.97/light alloy/l.all/90 deg./40/34.5/	2 d-choke carbs/158/6500	1900C52, Disco Volante 2000

Model	Type	No. of doors	Engine	Transmission	Length (in)	Width (in)	Height (in)	Wheel-base (in)	Front track (in)	Rear track (in)	Front head-room (in)	Front leg-room (in)
1900	Saloon	4	1884 cc, 90 bhp	4 sp. manual gearbox, column change	174.0	63.0	59.0	104	52	52	38	35
Giulietta TI	Saloon	4	1290 cc, 65 bhp	4 sp. manual gearbox, floor change	158.0	62.0	56.0	94	50	50.5	35.5	37.5
Giulietta Spider	Open sports	2	1290 cc, 80 bhp	4 sp. manual gearbox, floor change	153.5	62.2	52.6	88.6	50.8	50	33.5	43.5
Giulietta Spider Veloce	Open sports	2	1290 cc, 90 bhp	4 sp. manual gearbox, floor change	153.5	62.2	52.6	88.6	50.8	50	33.5	43.5
Giulietta SS	Coupé	2	1290 cc, 100 bhp	5 sp. manual gearbox, floor change	167.0	65.3	49.0	88.6	50.8	50	35	40
Giulia TI	Saloon	4	1570 cc, 92 bhp	5 sp. manual gearbox, floor change	163.0	61.4	56.3	98.8	51.6	50	39.5	35–40.5
Giulia Super	Saloon	4	1570 cc, 98 bhp	5 sp. manual gearbox, floor change	163.0	61.4	56.3	98.8	51.6	50	39.5	35–40.5
Giulia Sprint Speciale	Coupé	2	1570 cc, 112 bhp	5 sp. manual gearbox, floor change	162.2	61.2	50.0	88.6	50.9	50	33.2	40
Giulia Spider 1600 'Duetto'	Open sports	2	1570 cc, 109 bhp	5 sp. manual gearbox, floor change	167.3	64.2	50.8	88.6	51.6	50	38.5	40
Giulia 1600 Sprint	Coupé	2	1570 cc, 92 bhp	5 sp. manual gearbox, floor change	158.0	60.5	51.9	93.5	50.75	50	36	37.5–43
Giulia 1300 TI	Saloon	4	1290 cc, 82 bhp	5 sp. manual gearbox, floor change	163.0	62.0	58.0	98.5	52	50	36	35–40.5
Giulia Sprint GTV	Coupé	2	1570 cc, 109 bhp	5 sp. manual gearbox, floor change	161.0	62.2	51.8	92.5	50	51.6	35	32.5–39.5
1750 Berlina	Saloon	4	1779 cc, 122 bhp	5 sp. manual gearbox, floor change	173.0	61.7	56.3	101	52.1	50.1	37	31.5–37.5
1750 GTV	Coupé	2	1779 cc, 122 bhp	5 sp. manual gearbox floor change	161.0	62.2	51.8	92.5	50	51.6	35	32.5–39.5
1750 Spider Veloce	Open sports	2	1779 cc, 122 bhp	5 sp. manual gearbox floor change	162.2	64.2	50.8	88.6	52.1	50.1	34	33.5–43
2000 Berlina	Saloon	4	1962 cc, 133 bhp	5 sp. manual gearbox, floor change	173.0	61.7	56.3	101	52.1	50.1	37	31.5–37.5
2000 Spider Veloce	Open sports	2	1962 cc, 133 bhp	5 sp. manual gearbox, floor change	162.2	64.2	50.8	88.6	52.1	50.1	34	33.5–43
Alfetta 1.8	Saloon	4	1779 cc, 122 bhp	5 sp. manual gearbox, floor change	171.0	66.0	56.0	100	53	53	35	33–41
Alfetta 2000	Saloon	4	1962 cc, 122 bhp	5 sp. manual gearbox, floor change	172.6	66.0	56.0	100	53.5	53.4	37	35–41
Alfetta GTV	Coupé	2	1962 cc, 122 bhp	5 sp. manual gearbox, floor change	171.0	66.0	53.0	94.5	53.5	53.5	36	32–40
Giulietta 1.6	Saloon	4	1570 cc, 109 bhp	5 sp. manual gearbox, floor change	165.8	65.0	55.1	98.8	53.5	53.5	36	34.5–40

We have followed the progress of the twin-cam four cylinder Alfa Romeos since the second war through to the new Giulietta. But how did these different models compare in size, in comfort and in performance over the years? This table gives a direct comparison between twenty-one representative models (rather than a possibly meaningless simple data bank), taken from road tests and measurements carried out in Great Britain, Europe and North America (before US emission controls)

by a number of reputable magazines such as *Autocar, Motor, Road & Track, CAR, Quattroroute, Auto, Motor und Sport* and *l'Automobile*. In some cases the figures given are a healthy average.

Rear head-room (in)	Luggage capacity (cu. ft.)	Fuel tank (Imp gal)	SPEEDS IN GEARS (mph)				Top speed (mph)	ACCELERATION TIMES (seconds)				STANDING ¼ MILE			FUEL CONSUMPTION (miles per gallon) Driven		
			1st	2nd	3rd	4th		0–30 mph	0–40 mph	0–50 mph	0–60 mph	0–70 mph	Time (sec)	Speed (mph)	Average	Hard	Touring
35	9.5	11.5	30	44	65	—	93	5.5	8.9	12.9	18.6	27.4	22.5	62	23.5	21	26
3.5	8.2	8.8	30	48	70	—	97	5.1	8.4	12.2	17.7	24.7	20.8	67	28.8	24	32
—	5.5	11.5	28	47	74	—	100	3.8	6.1	10.1	14.8	21.9	20.1	69	25.7	22	28
—	5.5	11.5	35	59	86	—	107	3.9	6.9	9.7	14.2	18.5	17.7	69	28.6	27	33
—	3.5	14	33	51	80	108	120	4.0	6.0	8.2	12.4	16.8	18.5	73	29.2	26	32
36	12	10.1	26	44	64	88	102	4.7	6.9	9.8	13.3	17.7	19.0	72	27.1	25	30
36	12	10.1	27	45	64	88	108	4.0	6.0	8.3	11.4	16.1	18.3	77	25.1	22	27
—	3.5	14	32	54	79	106	112	4.0	6.2	8.5	12.1	15.3	18.4	76	24.4	21	26
—	7.5	10.1	30	48	69	93	114	3.4	5.6	8.1	11.1	15.3	18.2	78	27.5	24	32
—	14	11.7	26	42	62	86	112	4.3	6.4	9.8	13.2	18.6	18.9	71	26.8	24	30
34	12	10.1	27	42	62	83	101	5.1	7.5	11.2	15.3	20.8	19.7	68	24.7	22	28
32	9.5	10.1	30	52	75	102	112	3.3	5.5	7.2	10.6	14.4	17.8	75	27.7	24	30
34	12.5	10.1	30	49	73	99	117	3.3	5.4	7.7	10.8	14.4	17.9	75	23.6	20	27
32	9.5	10.1	31	52	77	104	118	3.6	5.8	8.0	11.2	14.7	18.1	78	24.5	22	27
—	12.2	11.2	26	46	68	93	115	3.4	4.9	7.2	10.0	13.6	17.7	80	25.5	21	29
34	12.1	11.6	29	48	72	96	118	2.9	4.6	6.6	9.7	13.1	17.3	78	23.8	20	27
—	12.2	11.2	30	50	74	100	120	3.2	4.8	7.3	9.6	12.9	16.9	81	24.9	21	28
34	18	10.7	31	52	75	100	110	3.2	5.3	7.6	10.7	14.6	17.6	77	24.5	22	26
5.5	21	10.7	30	50	70	90	113	3.2	5.0	6.8	9.4	13.0	17.1	80	23.0	20	26
—	10.2	11	32	52	76	101	114	3.2	5.0	6.8	9.4	13.0	17.2	80	25.0	21	28
4.5	9.5	11	30	51	75	98	106	4.0	6.2	8.9	12.2	16.4	18.1	73	24.0	20	28

Appendix 3
ALFA ROMEO
IN NORTH AMERICA

The Alfa Romeo story in America started rather late. Before the war there had been isolated if brilliant incidents like Tazio Nuvolari winning the Vanderbilt Cup race in 1936, run on a cinder track on the very field which had seen Lindbergh take off in the *Spirit of St Louis* on his solo Transatlantic flight seven years before. But as far as *cars* were concerned, there were only the few rare examples brought over by collectors, like the end-of-series 1935 twin-cam 1750 which was tested by the American enthusiast magazine *Road & Track* in the middle fifties. They found the experience overwhelming: 'Second only to its performance is the perfect road manners of the Gran Sport. The ride is very firm, almost as if there are no springs at all, but cornering is absolutely a joy. The wheel takes only $1\frac{1}{2}$ turns, lock to lock, and when sliding a corner there is neither front end "plough" nor rear end "breakaway". If you want a little more drift angle go into a tighter turn—if the drift is too severe, turn out a little. Correction is easy and instantaneous.'

It was the same with another of the Jano twin-cam pre-war cars, the straight-eight 2.3-litre two-seater they drove a year later: 'The clutch, steering and gear control all feel inordinately heavy around town. Yet to give the car full credit, its engine is remarkably reliable, and gives no show of temperament under such treatment aside from a tendency to overheat if traffic delays last too long. A car such as this is not in its proper environment until one hits the open road. Above 50 mph everything about the car changes. The rough ride smooths out, the controls feel light and positive. A curve posted at 45 mph can be taken in 3rd at 60 mph in ease and confidence. Only on sharp, right-angled corners does the heavy tail become noticeable, but even then a mere flick of the wheel will straighten things out and allow full throttle once more. Over-exuberance in cornering and too much throttle can produce violent oversteer, and eager neophytes have been known to make 360 degree loops until they learn to restrain themselves'.

But as far as the ordinary customer was concerned, delights like these were far out of his reach.

The name of Alfa, apart from mentions in occasional stories like these, was only heard as a distant echo from the other side of the Atlantic. Even by 1955, with the Giulietta range firmly established and the company moving slowly but definitely into the mass-production big-time, North America was still an almost totally untouched market. In April 1956, *Road & Track* wrote: 'Proof that the Italian automotive industry is at last serious about entering the American market is offered by the long-awaited "$3000" Alfa Romeo. Many of us have heard, read about, and occasionally seen one of the sleek, expensive Italian imports, but of the 1 per cent of our population who could readily afford such a car only a few hundred have been willing to give up the luxurious floating ride and six passenger spaciousness of their $5000 "prestige" automobile.'

The car they were writing about was the Giulietta Spider, already almost a year old on the Italian market. Was it worth the wait? In an America where the virtues of the European thoroughbred sports car—crisp performance, agile handling, compact dimensions and sophisticated engineering—were enjoyed by a fortunate few, the first relatively low-priced Alfas hit the market with all the impact of a keg of iced lager in the middle of the Sahara Desert. 'Without a doubt the 1300 Spider is the most fascinating small sports car we have ever driven,' said the testers. 'With an engine of only 78.7 cubic inches displacement it provides a performance which approaches the modern American behemoth so closely that one wonders if claims of 300 bhp are not closer to an honest 150. An acceleration time of under 15 seconds for 0 to 60 mph, and an honest top speed of 100 mph were impossible less than four years ago, from our lowest priced "big 3" makes . . . the adhesion to the road is absolutely uncanny. In cornering there is moderate understeer, very light castor-pull on the steering-wheel rim, no noticeable body roll and no squeal from the Pirelli tyres until the absolute limit of adhesion has been exceeded. . . . Second only to the impeccable handling and roadability of the Giulietta must come the brakes, which are close to if not absolutely the best we have ever encountered . . . the engine is both a delight to the eye and a joy to drive.'

Nor was this naive and uncritical adulation from an unsophisticated market. American sports-car enthusiasts knew a drawback when they saw one, and when they felt criticism was needed, they were quick to point it out. 'The interior appears to have been designed only for drivers between the heights of 5' 4" and 6' approximately. Anyone shorter than the lower limit will find himself (or herself) peering under the steering wheel rim, and our 6' 4" staff member found that when the top was in place it fitted rather like a hat. . . . The less said about the column-mounted shift lever, the better. It was next to the worst we have ever encountered, especially on the shift from 2nd to 3rd. The travel on this shift was too short, and there was insuffient leverage to make the change quickly and positively. We estimate that all the acceleration figures from 0 to 50 and up could be reduced by one full second with the new floor-mounted shift lever. . . .' But the mixture was so much to their liking that only one problem remained to worry the test team: 'When is the factory going to come through with enough Spiders to fill orders?'

By the time the Spider Veloce appeared on the US market, there were enough keen Alfa owners in America to constitute a real pressure group. *Road & Track* tested a car which had just earned three class wins in a row, but all the magazine earned from their test was a howl of rage from loyal Spider-drivers, who complained that the figures obtained constituted an insult to both marque and model. Ever thorough, the magazine tested another Veloce: in this case the personal property of the Technical Editor and tuned according to the experts at the Service School of US Alfa importers, Hoffman Motors. . . . They showed a 0 to 60 mph time of 11 seconds and a top speed of 112 mph. 'perhaps the speeds shown may not seem very high to those who own Corvettes, but for a 1300 cc machine with rather heavy touring bodywork, they are utterly fantastic.' The gearchange too was very much better: 'The new gearbox virtually eliminates the second-gear crash that plagued earlier Giuliettas. The ratios are unchanged, which pleases us because the gear spacing was perfect already. Shifting is still a bit short of being foolproof: a sharp, hacking shift from first to second gear will produce a crunch, but just the barest hesitation in neutral will overcome this.'

The amazing quality of the Giulietta, in American eyes, was the performance it achieved with an engine whose total capacity was not that much bigger than the volume of a single cylinder of some of the larger American sedans. In a sense the larger Alfa models, like the 2000 Spider, had a more difficult job to do, in that they were closer to the home-grown product in terms of sheer size. But though the larger car behaved slightly differently from its smaller sister, its heart was clearly still in the right place: 'Steering is neutral, and in spite of its length, the car is noticeably more willing to go round corners than earlier Giulietta models . . . the road-holding qualities very much depend on adjustment of the dampers, and they do their job faultlessly.' (This last point is one being made in Britain about the need for careful suspension adjustment on the current Alfetta models.)

Less popular over the years than the open two-seater—in terms of cars sold on the American market—has been the closed coupé. But the original Bertone-bodied Giulietta Sprint came in for similar high praise as 'the first of the present crop of Gran Turismo cars, and even now, after nearly six years, the car fits the meaning of the term as well as anything since introduced. To be sure, there are faster cars and certainly more flamboyant ones, but there are precious few that can match the Giulietta for clean and classic styling, or for the refinement of its mechanical elements.' On handling too, the coupé was assessed as the complete equal of the open cars: 'When pressed really hard, the Giulietta begins to lose the pronounced understeer that it shows when negotiating very slow, tight corners and becomes quite neutral in its steering response. Due to the very soft suspension, there is a considerable amount of tilting and leaning, but this does not upset the handling in the least. After the car is started into a corner and the initial roll-angle is taken, it seems to brace itself and never gives the driver any feeling of being tippy. Some complaints have been heard regarding the amount of roll—but this has come from people who haven't driven a Giulietta. The rolling doesn't affect the stability and one certainly can't have a soft ride without some roll.'

One of the best descriptions I've ever read of the handling of the Giuliettas—but there was another aspect of the car which came in for much less praise: '. . . the effectiveness and reliability of its electrical system . . . just isn't up to the job. This is a great pity, for the rest of the car just never lets you down . . . in view of the excellence of the rest of the machine . . . it is silly to have such a marginal-quality electrical system.' What was the problem? 'It centers around a generator, battery and starter that just aren't quite "heavy-duty" enough for North America.' Certainly this was no fault confined to the test car alone—it was to crop up in several other Alfa tests, so that years later, when driving a Giulia Spider, the writers could still say

'One of the big Alfa bothers, and the one that brings more correspondence from owners than any other single item, has always been the electrical system. With the Giulias, a change has been made to Bosch electrics and, presumably, the trouble has been corrected.'

By this time, constant praise of the characteristics of the earlier Alfa models had come in for reader criticism, at a time when more and more competitors were catching up on the excellence of the basic Giulietta/Giulia package. Perhaps because of this, their praise of models like the Giulia Sprint GT was a great deal less extravagant and a great deal more heavily peppered with criticism: 'After a few minutes in the car, we noticed three minor but irritating faults. The first was an undue amount of distortion in the glass of both the windshield and the rear window. The second was an annoying engine vibration at about 2600 rpm which made itself felt through the accelerator pedal, and the third was the gross speedometer error which seems to be a feature of all Italian cars.'

But two features of the car—the gearbox and the handling—still came in for praise, if rather diluted by the standards of the earlier quotes. 'For those who are enamoured of gear shifting, the *pièce de résistance* of the whole car is undoubtedly the five-speed transmission. All forward speeds are synchronized and there is considerable spring loading in the 3rd/4th position to prevent accidental shifts from 2nd directly to 5th. In the past, there has been some criticism of the sturdiness of the Alfa synchronizing mechanism, however, and only time will tell if there will be deterioration in the 5-speed model.'

'For those people who are convinced that independent rear suspension is essential for fast driving, the handling of the Alfa will come as a surprise, because the car is an excellent example of what can be done with a live axle if it is correctly located. Under certain conditions, there is a suspicion of the rear wheel steering which one normally associates with swing axle suspensions, but it never becomes exaggerated and is normally indiscernible. It is presumably caused by movement of the complete rear suspension in the big rubber bushes in which it is mounted.'

So Alfas were still clearly highly popular with their American fans—though now as older and trusted friends rather than amazing newcomers. The *Road & Track* test team described the styling of the original (pre-Duetto) Giulia Spider as 'somewhat dated, but . . . still better after seven years of steady production than some newer efforts. And in this day of disc brakes and 4-wheel independent suspension the Alfa drum brakes and live rear axle may seem archaic, but try the car before you

condemn it'.

One of the 'newer efforts' was of course the Duetto, and here the testers' reaction was unanimous. 'No one liked it as well as the Giulietta or the Giulia. One condemned it as a contrived design with meaningless styling gimmicks. Another said: "I think Pininfarina missed the ball this time." Somebody else commented: "They did this shape five years ago on a show car and it isn't any better now." Several people compared it, unfavorably, with the Lotus Elan.'

Other aspects of the car made them much happier: 'The transmission is the fine Alfa 5-speed that we like so much. In fact, we've come to like it so well that we find ourselves using it as the standard with which to compare other 5-speed gearboxes we encounter. It is a delight to operate, the handle is in the right place, the knob is the right size, the throws are the right length and the movement is crisp and precise.' Likewise the handling: 'Pushed very hard, the Duetto plunges into strong understeer, requiring lots of minor arm action to hold a precise line. At this point, it becomes a matter of "twitching" the front end to and fro across the limit of adhesion, all the while applying power to keep the rear end poised. Thus, it lacks the ultimate cornering power of some of its competitors, but it does warn the driver before he does anything clumsy.'

Styling of other Alfas had been criticised, albeit gently. When Alfa announced that limited quantities of the Giulia TI would be imported into America from the middle of 1965 onwards, this was for many Americans the first acquaintance they had with one of the Alfa saloons, rather than with the more obviously sporting models. 'An earlier TI, based on the 1300 Giulietta, was also rare in this country,' explained *Road & Track* to its readers at the time, 'but was a familiar sight in Italy where, unless you were going very fast indeed, you would probably be passed by one.'

Although they admitted the TI 'won't win any beauty prizes', they also said that 'underneath the unprepossessing exterior . . . there is as fine a set of 1600 internals as you'll find anywhere'. At the end of the test, they summed the car up by claiming 'if there's another car that offers more for $3000 than the TI, we can't think what it is. Matter of fact, we can't even think of one that comes close.'

Yet just three years later, they found one—'This is the Alfa Romeo Giulia Super and it, friends, is a car. It's nothing much in the way of pretty, what with slab sides and boxy lines, but it sure is everything else a car of this type ought to be. If you're under the hood, attached to the gearshift lever, holding the steering wheel or motoring down the road, it says Alfa, Alfa, Alfa—and that's a pretty nice thing to say to any enthusiastic motorist.' But when the car was tested, it was about to disappear from the American market: 'We expect it to be replaced by a larger sedan with a 1767 cc engine and a larger price tag about the middle of the year. So if you want one, you'd better get it soon.'

Sure enough, the promised replacement did turn up on schedule, with a 1779 cc engine instead of a 1767 one. But by that time, there were signs that the increase in engine size was not only long overdue, but was not in fact far-reaching enough. In a comparison test with the BMW 2002 Tii and the Mazda RX2, there was ample evidence of how much catching up had been done by the opposition: 'The Alfa needs a lot of revs and gearbox work to move with brisk traffic and, as the Noise table indicates, makes a lot of fuss at it. Surely the new 2-litre engine will help here.' Even the 5-speed gearbox only rated a 'satisfactory', though the steering was classed the best of the three, but 'in handling the BMW wins hands down'.

There was worse to come: the 1750s had been the first Alfas to feature fuel-injection for the American market, in order to meet increasingly tough emission-control regulations, without losing performance. Even when the 2-litre Alfetta made its appearance, much of the engine's extra promise was lost to the complexities of the new legislation. When assessed against seven other mildly sporting sedans in 1977, the Alfetta was clobbered because of its driving position, its gearbox and, for the first time ever, its *engine*. Handling, thanks to the rear mounting of clutch and gearbox, was excellent: 'simply heap praise upon praise. It's absolutely superb at speed with no surprises and near perfect balance. It's totally predictable and controllable at all times. . . . It's hard to get into trouble with the Alfetta, but easy to recover if you do.' Straight-line performance, on the other hand, was 'anemic. The Alfa took 14.4 seconds to reach 60 mph and required nearly 20 sec to cover the quarter-mile. Sporty? Hardly!' They went on to describe the gearlever as 'like a broomstick in a bathtub. The throws are so long and mushy that a driver never knows if he's going to get it into gear or not.' On the other hand, though the BMW 320i came out top overall, the Alfetta still came out in the first three, together with the Saab 99EMS, ahead of such worthies as the Audi 80, the Fiat Mirafiori, the Lancia Beta, the Mazda RX4 and the Volvo 244DL.

There was better to come, however. Later in the year detail changes which included a revision of the exhaust system to include a double-outlet manifold as fitted to the European-market cars, together with a larger catalytic canister of 2-litre rather than $1\frac{1}{2}$-litre capacity, revised valve timing and improved adjustments to the distributor produced a dramatic improvement—the 0 to 60 time was cut from 14.4 seconds to 10.8 for example, while the top speed went up by 4 mph to 101 mph. The 'balky' gearbox seemed to respond 'to a firm and aggressive hand with crisper shifts'—overall the improvement was amazing.

'How well does all of this work? Damn well! So well in fact, that you have to drive to believe it . . . the California version Sports Sedan is the feisty, sporty Alfa we all knew it could and should be. The performance has zip, the exhaust note is sporty and the handling is excellently balanced. . . . Welcome back, Alfa Romeo, to the land of the living and breathing.'

But the real success story of Alfa on the American market, in recent years at least, has been the Spider. In Europe, the sales of open two-seaters have been dropping, compared with their increasingly sportier closed coupé equivalents, for many years. In America—partly because of increasingly strict speed limits, a warmer climate, a strong convertible tradition combined with a shrinking number of models still available and above all the affluence which allowed an increasing number of families to buy a good-weather car to back up more practical family transport—the reverse has been happening. This was one reason (there were others!) why British Leyland came so severely unstuck with their Triumph TR7, aimed first and foremost at the American market. Instead, the Americans went on buying open cars like the ageing MGB.

The result is that for the last years in which detailed sales figures for the European and American markets are available—1967–72—the Spider has almost monopolized Alfa's market in the States. In 1968, 141 of the new 1750 Berlinas with fuel injection were sold in America, with 147 of the GTVs—but 259 Spiders were sold in America in the same period. In five years, Spiders represented 8922 cars sold on the European market out of nearly half a million of all models—a proportion of around 1.7 per cent. But in America, out of a total of 11,540 Alfas sold in the same five years, no less than 5073— or 44 per cent—were Spiders!

This leaves Alfa in a strong position in an important overseas market—but as much at a crossroads in the company's fortunes as in Europe itself. The company's best-selling model in America is also its oldest—the only one of the twin-cam range not to have the rear-mounted transmission and De Dion axle of the Alfettas. At the same time, the competition has become steadily fiercer—only time will tell whether the company can maintain its position on the other side of the Atlantic when the Alfettas too need replacements.

Appendix 4
ALFAS AND THEIR
CURRENT OPPOSITION

This has been a book about Alfa Romeos. But in real life cars never have the world to themselves—they exist in furious competition with all kinds of other designs and models, and the measure of their success is how they manage to sell against others of similar appeal. So to provide a more objective assessment of Alfas from this point of view than one could normally provide in a model series history like this, I submitted each of the current models to a week-long test, and then set out to do the same to as many potential competitors as possible. In order to arrive at a comprehensive list, I included cars which compared with Alfas on the grounds of engine size, design philosophy, performance or price. These are the results of that marathon test session which lasted for the best part of a year: a brief design background and driving assessment of each car, and then a detailed breakdown of the figures for all the models covered, arranged in a table for easier comparison.

Audi 100LS

Behind its unassuming exterior, the Audi 100 is technically an advanced car—introduced originally under different sheet metal as the Audi 90, the 100 came in 1968. The Audi 100 predecessor not only revived one of the long-dead company names which had helped to form the Auto Union combine before the war, but it also introduced the front-wheel-drive concept to the fairly large and luxurious sporting saloon market. In the ten years since the 100's first appearance, the model has gone through a major restyling and revision which has produced the lower, wider and sleeker body style of the current version, together with a succession of worthwhile detail improvements, from the revision of the steering geometry to a negative roll radius system which automatically tends to keep the car straight in the event of a blow-out on one of the front tyres, or if one of the front wheels should hit anything from ice to loose gravel and cause a sudden sharp imbalance, to the fitting of a vacuum gauge on the dashboard which allows the driver to use the engine as economically as possible in these days of rising petrol prices.

Other improvements have been less obvious: over the years the Audi engineers have been progressively eliminating the sources of noise and vibration to make the car as smooth and quiet as possible. This brought them up against their next problem: the 4-cylinder single overhead cam 2-litre engine fitted to the LS I tested was an efficient unit, with its wedge-shaped combustion chambers and over-square dimensions, but the company wanted extra smoothness to match the refinement they were trying to build into the body structure. They felt they could not achieve this with 4 cylinders, however hard they tried—but switching to a six would mean too much weight over the front wheels, which would affect steering and balance.

They compromised by going for 5 cylinders instead—and the current Audi 100s have a single overhead cam five cylinder unit with narrowed bores and a longer stroke than the 2-litre engine we tested, though power output of the basic models is exactly the same. The suspension is a combination of McPherson struts and wishbones at the front with a torsion beam axle with a Panhard rod at the back, and long-travel coil springs all round, set up so as to try to reduce pitching and rolling to a minimum.

Have they been successful? Up to a point, yes. Even the 4-cylinder engine was notably smooth, quiet and responsive—so much better than many of its competitors that one could not help wondering whether all the trouble and expense of developing the 5-cylinder design was really justified. The long, wide body provides plenty of room for five people in comfort, and it squats firmly down on the road even under hard acceleration, braking or cornering—almost too firmly, since compared with say a Citroën, or a Mercedes, or an Alfa for that matter, the ride is definitely on the hard side.

A firm ride is often part of the appeal of a sporting car—but despite its advanced specification, the Audi is scarcely that. The contortions the drive train has to go through imposes a similar problem to the rear-mounted gearbox on the current Alfas, that of a complex linkage in the gearchange mechanism. In the case of the Audi, the change is precise enough, with a nice narrow gate, but the long fore-and-aft throws of the lever prevent really snappy shifts from one speed to another. It's a reasonably light car, so the acceleration is good, and the handling is reliable: like many front-drive cars it tends to understeer fairly noticeably, but its ultimate cornering power is very high.

Yet it isn't a car which *invites* press-on driving. The careful engineering improvements have produced a car which is very smooth and refined, and almost for that very reason, the car tends to lack a definite character. The seats are very soft and comfortable, especially for a German car, the heating and ventilation highly efficient, the controls and instruments are nicely laid out. It's fairly expensive for what it offers, but that's the value of the Deutschmark rather than the fault of the manufacturer—for a long motorway journey, it's a well-balanced, comfortable and civilized car. It will corner quickly if you force the pace, it will accelerate sharply, stop efficiently and do all the things which more sporting-minded machinery will do—it's just that you cannot help feeling all these things are out of character, and against the designers' intentions.

BMW 320/6

Ask anyone at Alfa Romeo who their major competitors are, and sooner or later (usually sooner) the initials 'BMW' enter the conversation. For this reason I've included two BMWs in the test list: the compact little two-door 2-litre 320/6 and the more spacious and powerful 525. In spite of the closeness of the competition, neither model is directly comparable to a particular Alfa, but the design, the philosophy and the character of the two marques are so similar that it's hardly surprising the competition should be so keen.

In its styling, the 320 is definitely a sporting saloon rather than a coupé, and its similarities with the Giulietta are closer than to the other Alfas. Yet in its use of two doors, and the concentration of comforts on the driver and front seat passenger, with the back seats regarded as occasional accommodation, the 320 is closest in its philosophy to the Alfetta GTV. But in terms of its engineering, the BMW could hardly be further away from its Milanese opposite numbers.

Though Alfa have stayed with four cylinders right up to the 2-litre limit of the current range, BMW have now opted for six: in this case a firmly under-square single overhead camshaft unit which, though 28 cc nearer the exact 2 litres than the Alfa unit, produces an identical power output at a rather higher engine speed. Compared with the Alfas, the BMW's drive train is orthodox, though in the case of the test car the ease of the gearchange didn't enter into the comparison: it was fitted with the optional ZF automatic transmission, which must be one of the smoothest, most flexible and most efficient systems on the market. Instead of the Alfas' de Dion axle at the rear, the BMW has a fully independent system based on semi-trailing arms.

All this adds up to a package which is every bit as attractive to the sporting driver as an Alfa—hardly surprisingly, for the two firms are long-time rivals on the racing circuits as well as in the market place. The BMW goes quickly, though there are inevitable losses in relying on a three-speed automatic rather than five closely-spaced ratios in a manual box. It handles extremely well—in spite of the weight of the six-cylinder engine over the front wheels, its handling is neutral except when pushed really hard into a bend, when it will begin to oversteer. Though all the wheels are suspended independently, the movements are kept to a smaller range than on current Alfas, so that the ride is perceptibly harder, a difference which is reinforced by the beautifully shaped but distinctly firm seats.

Another problem caused by the use of a six-cylinder engine is the extra weight over the steering front wheels: the manual steering is distinctly heavy at parking speeds, though like many sporting machines of the past, it wakes up at speed to a nicely balanced feel of the road. You can avoid the effort by specifying power steering, though this is a fairly expensive option: in fact the BMW's competitiveness on price (in Britain, at least) rapidly evaporates once you start tacking on extras. But it's a very attractive car, and Alfa's engineers are right to worry about it: from its beautifully laid out dashboard, complex as an aeroplane's, with every dial angled toward the driver, to the generous boot, it offers a combination of the practical and the exciting. The only real difference is that the BMW is fast and comfortable in the German manner—quiet, smooth efficiency rather than the more flamboyant style of Italian sports cars. The only real drawback of the 320 is the restricted room in the rear seats, in a car which lacks the extra individuality of real coupé styling.

BMW 525

If the BMW 320 compares more closely with the GTV than the Alfa saloons on the grounds of accommodation, then perhaps a fairer competitor is the bigger and more powerful 525 with its four doors and five seats, and its larger alternative six-cylinder single overhead camshaft engine. Once again, the test car was fitted with the excellent ZF automatic transmission, and in this case the extra 28 bhp delivered by the engine is very welcome in a car weighing nearly 550 pounds more than its smaller stablemate. Like the 320, the 525 is commendably quick off the mark for an automatic: what was more unexpected was the engine noise output, which was much more sporting and less subdued than the 320, and was far more like the Italian cars in this respect.

The 525 has the same suspension setup as the 320. The ride is still on the firm side, though in this case the comfort of the passengers would only really be upset by bad potholes or bumps taken at speed. Even though the car is larger, its handling is similar to that of the 320: well-balanced, neutral cornering, ending in progressive and controllable oversteer if pushed beyond reasonable limits by a really determined driver. The power steering has a first-class combination of lightness and sensitivity, essential to make the best use of the car's cornering ability.

The 525 looks a big car: its styling is more dignified and less sporting than the Giulietta and the Alfettas or, for that matter, the BMW 320. But seen from behind the wheel, it doesn't feel nearly as large, and all its responses are every bit as quick and as sensitive as more obviously sporting machinery. Its only drawback from this point of view is its price—in Britain, at least, this tends to place the cars among the limousines rather than the roadsters.

Fiat 131 Supermirafiori

At first sight, the Mirafiori doesn't seem to be a competitor to any of the Alfas. Described in the pages of one magazine as Italy's Leyland Marina (a comparison not meant to be a flattering one), it was aimed at the conventional, economical, bread-and-butter market at a time when the October War in the Middle East had pushed up oil prices and cut supplies, and put Economy firmly at the top of everyone's list of priorities. But since then, with old requirements reasserting themselves, Fiat have been making changes to the car which have edged it further into the sporting sectors of the market.

Its background and pedigree ensure that the Mirafiori is a basically conventional car: front engine, rear drive, McPherson strut front suspension, trailing arms at the rear, styling which is neat and inoffensive rather than sporty. But in the Supermirafiori version, the car enjoys one component change which brings it much closer to its compatriots from Milan: a 1.6-litre engine with

twin overhead cams which is linked to a five-speed gearbox!

In fact the Mirafiori's more sporting sister makes a very enjoyable prospect for the driver who enjoys press-on driving. The twin-cam engine has more modern proportions than the 1.6 version of the Alfa unit, though it seems rather less flexible as a consequence, when asked to pull away from low down its speed range. On the other hand, use the available revs to the full, and the car hums along to the manner born—aided by a gearchange which, though it was always difficult to use for first or reverse, seems happier in the upper ratios.

Cornering too is a revelation, bearing in mind the exceedingly conventional suspension design. As Alfa themselves proved years ago, a simple suspension setup, when properly located, can provide excellent handling at the expense of a harder ride—and this is what happens all over again with the Supermirafiori. If left alone, as far as the throttle opening is concerned, the car will understeer its way gently round the corner. But apply enough power, and the resulting oversteer will balance this tendency into a neutral and highly efficient response. The quick, precise steering helps here—though given the engine's narrow power band, choosing the right gear for the speed of the bend before you start the corner is absolutely crucial.

One consequence of its unexciting beginnings is that the Supermirafiori is well provided with all the practical necessities: reasonable interior room, a useful boot, good visibility, and all the other essentials of bread-and-butter cars which sporting drivers still need. Other, more unexpected benefits, like comfortable seats which provide good location, are also part of the package—the only real drawbacks, apart from odd features like the sliding doors to the glovebox which jam at the slightest excuse, are a general heaviness to the controls and some minor but irritating resonances inside the car when travelling at speed. Against these, however, the car is very keenly priced for a combination of good performance and a nice engine-gearbox package in an otherwise conventional but efficient design.

Fiat 132 2000

If the Mirafiori was Fiat's Marina, then the 132 is their Alfetta 2000. This model was introduced to fill the gap left at the top of the Fiat range by the demise of the earlier 130, and the 2-litre version of the 132 is itself evidence of a further step up-market. It uses a twin overhead camshaft engine like the Super-mirafiori but with the stroke lengthened to raise the capacity to 1995 cc and the power to a useful

112 bhp. Once again the five-speed gearbox gives a good spread of ratios, though the movements tend to be rather long and awkward for a conventionally placed box.

The car is a little heavier than the Supermirafiori, but the engine's extra power more than makes up the difference, so that the 132 is quite fast off the mark. The seats are very comfortable, and those in the front grip quite well: the steering column is adjustable, so that the driver can make himself thoroughly at home. There are some nice details, like the Perspex tinted sun visors, and others which are less successful, like the instrument needles which swing through a mere right angle rather than the greater part of a circle on the usual speedometer configuration.

But the 132 is more limousine than a sporting proposition: at high speeds in a straight line on the motorway it's stable and quiet and comfortable. But try to throw it about and the car is not so reassuring: although it behaves reliably enough, the brakes feel over-sensitive and the handling lacks the taut precision of its smaller and cheaper stablemate. Its final cornering power is still high, but by that time the message about how the wheels are behaving against the road surface is a matter of educated guesswork rather than precise information.

Even though the 132 is appreciably more expensive than the Supermirafiori, it's still a good bit lower than the most directly comparable Alfa models, however. Its only problem as a genuine would-be competitor, is that it's also lower on real sporting qualities—though in other respects it's a likeable and worthwhile car.

Ford Capri 2.0

Ford's Capri was the first in the field as far as the true mass-market combination of family car and sporting coupé was concerned, and even now the variations and permutations on the Capri theme must outnumber anything their competitors can offer on a single model. In terms of competition for Alfas, probably only the two top-grade versions—the sporty S and the more refined and luxurious Ghia—really qualify.

There's no doubt about Ford's racing and rallying experience. Both versions feel taut and responsive, though the suspension settings on the Ghia version offer a softer ride at the expense of some of the S version's flat stance even on sharp bends. The clutch is sometimes fierce, and the steering quick—the only drawback is that the hard suspension can be thrown into confusion by bumpy

surfaces, and a car which is a delight to handle in the dry on a smooth road can become transformed into a positive handful in the wet. The overhead camshaft 2-litre unit pulls well, but the car is heavy enough to need all the power the engine can deliver to put up even reasonable performance, and this sends the noise level up, even in the carefully insulated Ghia version.

But both Capri versions are highly practical cars: the genuine hatchback, aided by rear seats which fold individually, give a wide series of options of passenger/luggage space to suit most requirements. When passengers do occupy the rear seats, they find plenty of legroom, but the sleek coupé styling means that headroom is still rather short. The instrumentation is well laid out, and the pile carpets and brightly patterned upholstery give an air of quality, but the steering and the brakes—though efficient enough—are rather on the heavy side.

In a sense the Capri is a great deal more practical than the original design first introduced a decade ago. But it feels a little as if the fire of youth has been damped by middle-aged respectability, compared with an out-and-out sporting machine like the Escort RS2000, for example. Part of the problem is that the Capri has been a victim of its own spectacular success: a car which was intended to look rare and exclusive has been snapped up by so many eager buyers that it no longer succeeds in turning heads as once it did.

Ford Escort RS2000

Some sporting drivers delight in keeping a low profile: rather a modified touring car than an obvious sporting machine, but one with the performance and the roadholding to see off most specialized machinery. In a sense the RS2000 is one of these wolves in sheep's clothing. Except that there's nothing subtle about its looks—though it's based on the sober and respectable family Escort, the changes and modifications are obvious enough to make it look more like a wolf in wolf's clothing With alloy sports wheels, a new, shovel, matt black nose and a spoiler across the bootlid, not to mention tinted glass, new seats and a black paint finish, it's obvious from a hundred yards away that this is something special.

The RS2000 is a real sporting machine, not a cosmetically prepared car to give the buyer a mere illusion that he's paying for something special. The 2-litre overhead cam engine delivers 110 bhp and it feeds through a four-speed gearbox to the rear axle. The front wheels are suspended on McPherson struts and coil springs, but the rear wheels go back to an arrangement which would have been familiar enough to Alfa drivers of forty years ago: a rigid rear axle hung on semi-elliptic springs, though in the case of the RS2000 these are located by radius arms.

This unpromising material has been revised and tuned to give cornering power of a very high order indeed. But as with the works rally cars, this has been possible only by limiting suspension travel very strictly, so that the ride tends to be choppy and bumpy roads and wet conditions add to the difficulties of the driver. The actual handling under good conditions is nicely balanced, and the steering—though definitely heavy at low speeds—is light enough and positive enough to inspire confidence.

The RS2000 isn't a comfortable car. Rear-seat passengers have their room eroded by the intrusion of the wheelarches, and by the fitting of the excellent German-made Recaro seats at the front. The body drums with vibration from the suspension and from the raucous engine, and it's a question of balancing the exhilaration of handling a genuinely specialized high-performance machine against the harshness and roughness which the extra power and response bring in their train.

Mercedes-Benz 230

Mercedes have an enviable reputation for high quality, and the 230 is no exception. Yet to the driver unfamiliar with Mercedes, it seems rather austere in its interior appointments. Instrumentation is sparse compared with many cars in its high price bracket: a single stalk switch on the steering column controls most of the functions of lights and indicators. The seats are well shaped but firm, and the car is big enough to provide plenty of room for five occupants.

But Mercedes have their priorities right: the 230 is no softly sprung motorway cruiser, driveable with confidence only at processional speeds in as straight a line as possible. The price buys you engineering excellence, and painstaking attention to all manner of small but ultimately important details, like stainless steel inner walls to the exhaust system, a vertically-opening bonnet to provide greater servicing accessibility and specially shaped rear lamp lenses which can still shine through built-up layers of road dirt and grime.

What this means for the driver is a life which, though rarely exciting, is never worrying or uncomfortable either. A sports car the Mercedes is most assuredly not: the overhead camshaft 2.3-litre engine has a large, heavy, solidly engineered body

to move around, and on sheer performance grounds there are many cars which will go much faster and accelerate more quickly. But its most enduring and reassuring characteristic is the confidence it gives the driver: securely cushioned behind the steering wheel, able to rely on the supremely smooth and efficient automatic transmission rather than a manual shift, he tends to feel the scene outside is as remote as the picture on a television screen. Going on a long motorway journey in the Mercedes is rather like watching a film of the trip in your own armchair at home—steering suspension and the solidity of the car cushion you from involvement in your surroundings.

In many cars, this dissociation from reality would be dangerous: but the Mercedes stability and sureness of foot, even when pushed at speed through unexpectedly tight corners, is always there to protect its occupants. For many sports-car drivers, it's *too* undramatic in its style and quality. But it personifies the sober unemotional, efficient German ideals of engineering excellence as does no other car.

Peugeot 504 TI

Peugeot have long been renowned for building tough, solid, conventional cars. More recently, especially in their smaller models, they have turned to new ideas like transverse engines and front-wheel drive, but in the case of the 504 the configuration is more orthodox, with an overhead-valve four-cylinder engine mounted north–south and driving the rear wheels in the usual way. The bodystyle was new and individual in 1969 when the car first appeared, but now seems slightly old-fashioned: the interior room is only really adequate for four people, and the decor is rather dated. Apart from the steep steering-column angle, which is half-way to the bus-driver's position of the original Mini, the dashboard is given a satin-finished chrome panel which, added to boldly marked circular dials which still tend to harbour reflections, can be distracting.

But the car performs well: the four-cylinder unit is smooth and quiet, except when pushed hard, and the gearchange is quick, though the movements are rather too long for really outstanding ease of operation. There are extras fitted as standard on the TI version like fuel injection, electric windows in the front doors and a sliding steel sunroof panel, all of which are welcome: but on the test car the sunroof was rather awkward to operate (by hand) and there were some starting problems.

On the road, the fitting of power steering makes the car pleasantly light to handle. Its typically

French combination of soft seating and soft suspension make it more like an Alfa than a Mercedes or a BMW in its cornering behaviour: though its good roadholding is wasted to a certain extent as the high degree of body roll, reinforced by seats which though comfortable do not provide firm enough location, produces uncertainty and discomfort long before breakaway.

This stops the Peugeot 504TI being a really competitive sporting car. But its trump card is its undoubted toughness: Peugeots seem to go on and on for ever, and their enduring success in much harsher motoring environments like those existing in parts of Africa, can only encourage would-be drivers in our much easier conditions. Definitely a car for long-term investment rather than short-term sporting pleasure.

Porsche 924

In many ways the Porsche is the closest to the Alfa range in its basic design configuration, even though its pedigree, its evolution and its price set it apart from the Italian cars. Developed originally as an extra model which would extend the Porsche range a little further down-market, the 924 broke virtually every rule in the company's own book: instead of the old flat-fours and sixes inherited from the company's Volkswagen-based beginnings, the 924 had an in-line overhead camshaft four, tilted over to allow a low bonnet line and mounted at the front rather than the rear for the first time!

Porsche, like Alfa, wanted to ensure the ideal weight distribution of a mid-engined car without the problems of space. So they opted for a similar solution, by mounting the engine at the front of the car but shifting the gearbox to the back—in the case of the Porsche the clutch was kept at the front, next to the engine, and this was linked to the rear-mounted gearbox through a torsional drive shaft carried inside a transmission tube and located by no less than four sets of bearings.

Cheap the 924 may be—by Porsche standards at least—but it's a very sophisticated motor car. As with the Alfettas, the trouble of relocating the gearbox away from the engine has been amply recompensed in the car's handling. Porsches were always agile cars, but there was little doubt that the rear-engine models required a great deal of careful handling as they approached the limit, in order to have enough warning of the basic dynamics of the car taking over and promoting terminal oversteer. The 924 by contrast is always well balanced, right up to the limit and even beyond.

Its defects are mainly those of refinement, especially when set against its older and more traditional (and admittedly more expensive) sisters. The four-speed manual gearbox fitted as standard has more precision than many of the Alfetta boxes, but the movements are still wide and rather stiff compared with a good direct change. The steering is undeniably heavy, though at speed it does tell you exactly what the front wheels are doing—or are about to do. The fuel-injection four-cylinder engine, inherited from the Audi 100 before the fives took over, is powerful and responsive, but it tends to be noisy in the same harsh way as the Escort RS2000. In fact noise is a problem: not wind noise, but engine noise and road noise, transmitted up through the hard though all-independent suspension system, which becomes very tiring on long trips.

This isn't to say the 924 doesn't have a great deal going for it. It may be strictly a two-plus-two, with restricted room in the rear seats, though it does have the benefit of a hatchback—but the buyers aren't going to worry too much about that anyway. They will buy this car, if they can afford it, because by any real definition of the term, it's an out-and-out sports car. It goes quickly, handles beautifully, its lines rate a second glance in any company, and above all it has the magic of the Porsche name at a much more practical price.

Renault 20 TS

There are two basic versions of the Renault 20—the TL, which has the 1.6-litre engine, and the TS, which uses the new 2-litre four developed for Renault, Peugeot and Volvo. Like the Alfa engines, this is an all-alloy unit using steel cylinder liners and incorporating hemispherical combustion chambers, though in this case the valves are actuated by but a single overhead camshaft. The test car featured the optional automatic transmission, itself a joint Renault-Peugeot system which uses electronic control for easy and flexible changes and precise operation.

Although the 20 bears a strong family resemblance to the familiar and well-loved 16, in many ways it's a totally different car. The seats are still as soft and comfortable as on any French car, though the soft suspension and body roll which are usually part of the package don't seem nearly as obtrusive as usual. The result is a car which feels much faster and more sporting—it corners well, responding to the throttle even through the automatic transmission, and the power steering is noisy but extremely efficient, providing the ease and the sensitivity of the very best of manual systems.

There are only two drawbacks to the car as it stands: the engine noise becomes obtrusive at high speeds, which can be tiring when using its excellent high-speed cruising stability to the full on long motorway trips. And—ironically in view of the Renault 16's versatility in this respect—the seat-shifting arrangements, to boost the luggage space when rear-seat passengers aren't being carried, are fiddly and awkward to carry out.

As a sports car, the main problem is that it doesn't look like one. But in terms of comfort, response and roadholding, it can give many much more sporting-looking competitors a good run for their money. As a basis for a coupé version, it would be a highly interesting proposition.

Rover 2300

In a way, including the Rover 2300 in this test-car line-up may not seem fair, as the car is a cheaper and simpler derivative of a much more expensive model, the Rover 3500. But in the market-place it must find its own level alongside the other models in my sample, however it may compare with its own maker's model range. It shares the same body shape as the 3500, but most of the rest is modified: the engine is an in-line six with a single overhead camshaft, linked to a modified gearbox with the top ratio of five removed to leave a closely spaced set of four speeds. The suspension is simpler too, with constant-rate springs set to give a stiffer and less supple ride—other missing items range from extra instruments to electric windows, centralized door locks to sound insulation in certain areas.

All this makes the car lighter and cheaper—it certainly needs the weight saving, as the smaller engine has to push a body which is still on the large and roomy side. Yet the car is no slouch—and although the engineering paring-down sounds like a recipe for disaster, it's a viable model on its own account. The engine pulls well, and moves the car along briskly, aided by the precise and well-matched gearbox. Handling is good too, even on twisty roads—in fact the only penalties suffered by the buyer going for this cheaper version, apart from the fact that the BL's ideas on what constitutes a full set of instruments and extras is noticeably less than those offered by their competitors in this price range, centres on the harsher ride and the higher noise level, coming mainly from the engine, suspension and rear axle. These things, though often acceptable on a genuinely sporting car, seem less appropriate on an otherwise comfortable and

dignified saloon like this one though.

SAAB 99GL Combi coupé

The Saab is certainly something completely different. In spite of the marque's brilliant record in the toughest of international rallies, it's arguably the least sporting-looking of all the cars in our test series. The clue is in the initials—SAAB stands for Svenska Aeroplan AB, or Swedish Aircraft Company, and does in fact make fighters like the Draken and the Viggen for the Swedish defence forces. Aircraft engineers tend to have to concentrate on fundamentals of performance and behaviour and therefore have little time for the niceties of styling—hence the Saab's almost contemptuous disregard for automotive fashions.

Yet the design has very real virtues of its own. In terms of the average Italian design, it has almost no sporting soul at all. It feels narrow and high and old-fashioned from the inside, with a high window line and narrow door openings. Yet the front seats are firm but comfortable, the instrumentation is functional as an aircraft's, the driver's seat adjusts for height as well as for rake and position, and the rear seats fold flat below the opening hatchback. The finish is first-class and the car feels solid and tough without being too heavy.

Its entire character seems to change once it starts moving. The gearbox is a delight to use, with a quick and easy change—it needs to be, as the weight of the car's body means that the engine has to be kept pulling over a fairly narrow speed range to produce real performance. All the same, the ungainly body shape conceals a good aerodynamic profile and top-speed performance is good, though reaching it may take some time as acceleration tails off at the upper end of the performance graph.

The car handles well, as befits its maker's competition background. With the engine driving the front wheels, the car's balance does depend on the throttle setting as you enter the bend, but controlling it is easy and its responses are reassuringly predictable. The only problem is a certain sensitivity to side winds at speed—this is unusual for front-drive cars, and may possibly have its cause in the car's aerodynamics rather than in its nose-heavy weight distribution. Fortunately, the car's quick steering makes adjustment and compensation easy—it's just that you have to concentrate extra hard in very gusty conditions.

Volkswagen Scirocco GLS

For those drivers to whom 'Volkswagen' means the trusty but undramatic Beetle, the Scirocco must be one of the biggest automotive surprises around. Based on the floorpan and running gear of the Golf, but blessed with a really elegant little coupé body styled by Giugiaro (who was responsible for the Alfetta GT), and fitted with a 1588 cc in-line four in its 85 bhp version as used in the Passat GLS, this is one of the most brilliant little sports cars on the market.

It's also a very practical little car: blessed with a hatchback and a folding rear seat which adds a lot to its load capacity but takes nothing away from its looks, the Scirocco is easier to live with than many specialist sporting designs. The seats used to be very hard, even by German standards, and headroom was limited. Now both areas have been improved, though taller passengers are advised not to try sitting at the back: the front seats are very much more comfortable, they locate driver and passenger precisely, and both have height adjustments in addition to the usual rake-and-reach variations.

Volkswagen finish is legendary, and the Scirocco's no exception, from the engineering viewpoint at least. Metallic paintwork, tinted glass, alloy wheels and tailgate wiper and washer are all standard fittings on the GLS version, and the build quality is excellent—only some loose bits of trim material and the cheap-looking gaiter round the gearlever let down the otherwise very high standard inside and out. This was a pity, because the cost of rectifying points like these must be negligible compared with the extras.

But all these are forgotten once you drive the car. Its character is extraordinary: it's like a dog begging to be taken for a walk, though in this case a very fast run would be nearer the mark. With a powerful engine in a light, compact and simple body, its response to the throttle is electrifying—it cries out to be driven hard in the same way as the early Minis. In just the same way, it corners as if on rails, with such completely unruffled balance that talk of understeer or oversteer becomes irrelevant. This resemblance to the Mini may be more than just coincidence of course—both cars share the prescription of a transverse front engine driving the front wheels, which seems in this case to produce almost identical handling characteristics.

The Scirocco is at its best along winding roads: the boom of the responsive engine, the snappy gearchange as precise as a Swiss watch, the beautifully sensitive steering, all conspire to make driving a pleasure. On a motorway it's less of a pleasure: the engine noise rises to a roar, the ventilation isn't really up to the job, and resonances start to creep in through the bodywork. If only the splendid gearbox could be given a fifth ratio, if only

the rear windows could be made to open, then many of these problems would disappear—but as things stand, it's a better car off the motorway than on it.

About the only other fault from which the Scirocco suffers is its name: the Volkswagen tag stands for quality and reliability rather than competition records, and many possible buyers may never come to realize exactly what the car has to offer. Now, if they'd been able to market it under the Porsche umbrella...! But the increasing number of Sciroccos one sees on the road is proof that the car's very real (and unfortunately increasingly rare) sporting qualities are making themselves known to an ever-widening band of fortunate owners.

Alfa Romeo Alfetta 2000

This is the largest and most powerful version of the Alfetta saloons, though the intention was to use the opportunity to widen its appeal among business buyers rather than turn it into a sporting tearaway. Consequently it has slightly larger, though outwardly unchanged, bodywork with more boot and passenger space, softer suspension settings and a slightly more flexible engine. On the other hand, the basics which gave the range its sporting character are still there: the classic twin-cam engine, the five-speed gearbox and the sophisticated suspension.

The Alfetta, like most Alfas, is essentially a driver's car, though perhaps in this particular model comfort for the passengers has been taken further than usual. It's also a car which prefers the open road to urban streets: the gearchange on the test car was awful on first, second and reverse, remarkably good on third, fourth and fifth. The difference was so great that the car might have been fitted with two separate gearboxes rather than a single unit. The steering is light enough in town driving, but only really comes alive in the old Alfa manner once you leave the traffic jams behind—as the speed rises, the feel and character of the car is transformed.

In one sense, the 2000 model represents a step away from the old ideals. The old combination of steep body roll and high cornering ability is still there, but the car now holds so much space for passengers and luggage that if it is really loaded to the gunwales, then it feels too ponderous to throw into a bend in normal Alfa style. The boot space is really astonishing: returning from a European trip in the test car, we had to transfer our luggage into a Fiat 132 (itself a roomy car) for the trip home. Only by squashing all the passengers into the back and using the front seat and footwell as extra luggage space, could the car be persuaded to cope with all we'd been able to shoehorn into the Alfetta's boot.

But when only the driver is present, and the car is relieved of the excess weight its space invites, then once again there's no mistaking the stable it comes from. Engine noise is the big giveaway: although it's a comfortable car, it isn't particularly quiet in this department. The twin-cam chatter, and that unmistakable raucous Alfa exhaust boom, such music to the enthusiast ear, can still be heard in full song. It accelerates quickly, provided you can master the lower changes in the five-speed box, and it corners beautifully. Read what *What Car?* had to say about it: 'The car has an uncanny feeling of hugging the road at all times, no matter how hard the car is being driven. Alfa Romeo designers have also managed to soften the ride over previous Alfettas without upsetting the handling—thus the 2000 is a car which feels if anything too soft to be sporting, and yet corners as if on rails.'

There are some irritating points however: the instrument panel, though nicely located in the driver's line of sight, is a triumph of stylish graphics over efficiency. For me, the fact that the needles for speedometer and rev-counter moved in different arcs made the instruments difficult to read—on the smaller gauges, the combination of white needles against a strongly contrasting blue background and white figures made them hard to see in a quick scan. Reading the instruments became a much more deliberate job than the instantaneous glance which is all that should be needed on a high-performance car.

The ventilation is good: and for shorter drivers the driving position is comfortable. Once again, however, Italian manufacturers seem to be guilty of refusing to acknowledge that some drivers don't have short legs and long arms, and taller drivers did complain of less than perfect comfort behind the admittedly adjustable wheel. The finish on the test car was good, and the interior was generally a great deal more comfortable than on many Alfas from the past—though other writers have complained of variable quality as well as uncomfortable differences in the standards of suspension adjustment.

Certainly one area where the Alfetta 2000 has gained over some previous models is its comfort as a long-distance motorway express. The fact that this has not harmed its qualities as a cross-country fast tourer is remarkable—only the need to drop down to the awkward-to-find second gear on some very slow corners could disturb the essential rhythm and balance of driving over a long and otherwise difficult journey.

Alfa Romeo Alfetta 2000 GTV

This version of the sleek Giugiaro coupé is now the only one available in Britain: the 1.6 GT is no longer to be imported, as it competes too closely with the new Giulietta in its 1.6 version and even more closely with the brilliantly successful Alfasud Sprint in its larger 1.5-litre form. The body is still an eye-catcher, even though the car has been around for several years: and though it looks sleek and compact, it offers a fairly generous allowance of headroom and legroom for rear-seat passengers, compared with other designs of this type.

From an engineering point of view, there is little to separate the GTV from the 2000 saloon. There is the same soft suspension, allied to the same high standard of roadholding—the same driver comfort (for those not so tall drivers, at least), and the same agile responses. The steering is as quick and as lively as ever—and the gearbox unfortunately still as difficult to get used to. Yet much seems to depend, as it does in the suspension department, on the way in which the individual car was set up. There's no reason on earth why the gearbox on the GTV test car should have felt any different from that on the saloon—yet it did. It was immeasurably smoother, easier, more precise and faster to use—still a long way from the excellence of the old direct change, but streets ahead of those on earlier Alfettas. If this represents a progressive refinement, as Alfa engineers claim, and it isn't merely the luck of the draw or the work of an unusually perceptive and painstaking mechanic, then there is real hope for the rear-gearbox concept. At the moment, this seems to be the biggest problem which may postpone its real benefits being appreciated—one unexpected virtue of an appalling winter was the way in which it demonstrated how the balance of the GTV made it infinitely more tractable and controllable in icy conditions than my old nose-heavy Spider had been, for example.

Surprisingly, the character of the car seems entirely different. Perhaps because of the shape, perhaps because of the gearbox, driving the GTV seemed much closer to handling the Giulias or the 1750s. It started easily, accelerated with real fire in its belly, cornered with panache and stopped reassuringly quickly. The finish seemed up to scratch—apart from the Alfa badge on the rear lid, which dropped off the first time the hatch was closed, everything stayed in place and fitted well. Sadly, many complaints seem to centre on the expensive extras—sunroof and electric windows, for example—fitted to the more costly Strada version (UK market) rather than to the basic GTV.

But there was one more pressing irritation. The original GTV had a rev-counter set in front of the driver, and all the other instruments in a centre console. This bit of racing car wish-fulfilment didn't make sense on the open road, where speed limits come as important as engine speeds on routine journeys, and the rev-counter and speedometer have been juxtaposed. But why, oh why, couldn't they stick to the perfectly adequate, functional and attractive instrument layouts of the earlier cars, instead of switching to this irrational, bizarre and distinctly non-ergonomic alternative?

Alfa Romeo Giulietta 1.6

For the present at least, the Giulietta is only being imported to Britain in its larger version, and the 1.6 fits neatly into the gap between the Alfasuds and the Alfettas. (At the time of writing the 1.8TI had not been announced.) It's an unusual looking car with a sharply-etched wedge shape ending in a high bootline and a flicked-up spoiler at the tail—at first sight, many thought it ugly, but it's aerodynamically efficient, and its purposeful stance and crisp contours soon begin to appear quite handsome.

Again, the pedigree and philosophy behind the model is so similar to its larger sisters, that the Giulietta behaves like them too. Its engine starts as easily, but demands the same wait for everything to warm up thoroughly that all Alfas insist upon. The steering is lively and precise, the suspension soft but well located and the gearchange fits somewhere in between the Alfetta saloon and the GTV (at least, so far as the test cars were concerned) for ease of action. Some drivers complained of stronger understeer rather than the neutral handling of the larger cars: this could be due to the less powerful engine, but individual discrepancies in suspension setting-up may be more blameworthy, since other testers have hailed the roadholding as excellent. For example, *Motor Sport* thought the balance '. . . quite marvellous and taut. Nothing seems to upset it, whether there be bumps in mid-corner or unexpected mud from a farm tractor. I thrashed the test car round a route which wouldn't have been out of place on a *Motoring News* road rally and its behaviour was impeccable. There is quite a lot of roll, yet it isn't sloppy, and the car reacts beautifully to sudden changes of direction.'

Unfortunately, not everyone found the driving position as comfortable as on the larger cars, though here again it's probably the tallest drivers who come off worst. Again, the instrument layout is eccentric—though the nacelle is placed in front of the driver, the fact that the rev-counter and speedometer needles now rotate in opposite directions seems to produce entirely unnecessary distraction. The room in both front and rear seats is generous, though here the boot space suffers as a result: deep rather than wide or long, it cannot compare with that of the Alfetta saloon.

Visibility, though, is very good. The car is quiet in some respects, noisy in others: 'Hard acceleration is accompanied by that rasping musical mixture of induction and exhaust roar unique to Alfa, an exciting urgency of tone which is always pleasurable, never offensive and disappears when the throttle is only lightly applied' is how *Motor Sport* put it. 'A little tyre noise disturbs the peace, as does the typically Italian exhaust note though,' said *What Car?* It all depends on your point of view.

Ventilation was less effective than on the Alfetta. Wet winter conditions seemed to defy all the system's efforts at demisting for an awfully long time. But in the departments where the long tradition of sophistication of design are important—in the engine and the suspension in particular—the car has produced some extravagant praise in quarters usually better known for merciless criticism of any mechanical or behavioural shortcomings. 'It is not the splendid little SOHC [sic!] engine, but the vehicle's roadworthiness, that makes the Giulietta what it is: it is the combination of steering, roadholding, braking, ride quality, comfort, aerodynamic stability and superb road-following ability that makes it a paragon.' That was *CAR* magazine. 'A little charmer, producing excellent performance from its modest capacity, allied to handling, roadholding, braking and general character which make it an absolute joy to drive.' Likewise *Motor Sport*. And finally *What Car?*, in a test comparison of four sports saloons: 'Driving the Giulietta over long distances is an easy and relaxing task . . . at the end of a long journey in the RS2000 the driver is a tired, shaken wreck.'

Facts and Figures

Subjective impressions, however experienced and however numerous the testers, are not enough on their own. The proof of the design is in the hard figures, and this table sets out some of the more important measurements on which the cars making up our test sample can be compared.

ENGINE

	Price (late 1978) £	Valve gear	No. of cyls	Bore (mm)	Stroke (mm)	Capacity (cc)	Power (bhp)	Speed (rpm)	Length (in)	Width (in)	Height (in)
Audi 100LS	4890 (1977)	sohc	4	86.5	84.4	1984	115	5500	184	70	55
BMW 320/6	5944	sohc	6	66.0	80.0	1990	122	6000	172	64	55
BMW 525	8174	sohc	6	71.6	86.0	2494	150	5800	174	67	56
Fiat 131 Supermirafiori	3748	dohc	4	84	71.5	1585	96	6000	167	65	55
Fiat 132 2000	4595	dohc	4	84	90	1995	112	5600	172	65	54
Ford Capri 2.0	4211 (S) 4980	sohc	4	90.8	76.95	1993	98	5200	173	67	51
Ford Escort RS2000	3901	sohc	4	90.8	76.9	1993	110	5500	162	62	55
Mercedes-Benz 230	7981	sohc	4	93.8	83.6	2307	109	4800	186	70	57
Peugeot 504 TI	4927	ohv	4	88	81	1971	106	5200	177	67	57
Porsche 924	8199	sohc	4	86.5	84.4	1984	125	5800	164	66	50
Renault 20TS	5153	sohc	4	88	82	1995	110	5500	178	68	56
Rover 2300	5910	sohc	6	81	76	2350	123	5000	185	70	55
Saab 99 Combi	5570	sohc	4	90	78	1985	100	5200	174	67	57
Volkswagen Scirocco GLS	4720	sohc	4	79.5	80	1588	85	5600	152	64	52

For comparative Alfa Romeo models see Appendix 2

DIMENSIONS

PERFORMANCE

W'base (in)	F. Track (in)	Rear T. (in)	Wt (lb)	Boot (cu. ft.)	Tank (gall)	Front head-room (in)	Front leg-room (in)	Rear head-room (in)	Interior width (in)	Top speed (mph)	Standing ¼ mile Time (sec)	Speed (mph)	Average fuel consumption (mpg)
105	58	57	2530	23	12.7	36–40	36–45	34	58	108	18.8	75	28.8
101	54.6	55	2458	16	12.8	37	32.39	34	52	110	17.8	78	22.5
104	55.8	57.3	2970	22	15.5	35–38	30–41	34·5	54	115	18.2	80	21.6
98	54	52	2318	14	11	37·5	37–41	34	55	105	18.5	77	25.5
101	52	52.5	2520	12	12	37	33–41	35	53	103	20.4	76	24.4
101	54	53	2273	11/19	12.7	35	37–42	31	52	108	18.0	77	26.5
94	50.8	51.8	2206	10.3	9.4	38	36–41	32	50	106	18.5	79	22.0
110	58	57	2956	14.7	14.2	35	35–43	34	52	102	20.5	68	21.7
107	56	55	2710	19.2	12.3	36–38	35–41	34	56	106	18.0	77	27.2
93	54·5	53	2500	7/11	13.6	37·5	38–46	29	55	121	16.8	82	23.9
105	57	57	2587	14/49	13	36	37–44	33	56	104	19.0	72	26.8
111	59	59	2778	19/35	14.5	35	35–40	35	53	105	19.6	78	24.6
98	55	56	2800	13/53	12.1	35–37	34–41	34	55	102	19.3	74	26.1
94·5	54.7	53.1	1764	12/31	9.9	36	34–40	31·5	54.7	105	18.3	74	29.2

Appendix 5
PRODUCTION FIGURES
1950 TO 1977

1950	6 cars	6	1900 Berlina
1951	1228 cars	1220	1900 Berlina
		8	1900 Sprint
1952	3556 cars	3107	1900 Berlina/TI
		353	1900 Sprint (1st series)
		91	1900 Cabriolet
		5	1900M
1953	5411 cars	3115	1900 Berlina/TI (1st series)
		289	1900 Sprint
		2007	1900M
1954	3321 cars	2807	1900 Berlina Super/TI Super
		649	1900 Berlina/TI
		299	1900 Sprint (2nd series)
		154	1900M
		12	Giulietta Sprint
1955	5807 cars	2709	1900 Berlina Super/TI Super
		248	1900 Super Sprint
		4	1900 Berlina Primavera
		1415	Giulietta Sprint
		1430	Giulietta Berlina
		1	Giulietta Spider
1956	11,724 cars	1644	1900 Berlina Super/TI Super
		314	1900 Super Sprint
		286	1900 Berlina Primavera
		6348	Giulietta Berlina
		1855	Giulietta Sprint
		252	Giulietta Sprint Veloce
		1007	Giulietta Spider
		18	Giulietta Spider Veloce
1957	16,671 cars	1524	1900 Berlina Super/TI Super
		270	1900 Super Sprint
		10	1900 Berlina Primavera
		8940	Giulietta Berlina
		2115	Giulietta Sprint
		458	Giulietta Sprint Veloce
		1268	Giulietta TI
		2048	Giulietta Spider
		32	Giulietta Spider Veloce
		5	Giulietta Sprint Speciale (SS)
		1	Giulietta Sprint Zagato (SZ)

1958	20,557 cars	157	1900 Berlina Super
		15	1900 Super Sprint
		5773	Giulietta Berlina
		9948	Giulietta TI
		1504	Giulietta Sprint
		401	Giulietta Sprint Veloce
		1552	Giulietta Spider
		835	Giuletta Spider Veloce
		11	Giulietta SS
		319	2000 Berlina
		62	2000 Spider
1959	23,181 cars	6	1900 Berlina Super
		4428	Giulietta Berlina
		10,599	Giulietta TI
		3606	Giulietta Sprint
		363	Giulietta Sprint Veloce
		1773	Giulietta Spider
		368	Giulietta Spider Veloce
		195	Giulietta SS
		787	2000 Berlina
		1056	2000 Spider
1960	36,605 cars	17,019	Giulietta TI
		5123	Giulietta Berlina
		5558	Giulietta Sprint
		539	Giulietta Sprint Veloce
		3893	Giulietta Spider
		1203	Giulietta Spider Veloce
		200	Giulietta SS
		61	Giulietta SZ
		1074	2000 Berlina
		1930	2000 Spider
		5	2000 Sprint
1961	37,391 cars	20,705	Giulietta TI
		5292	Giulietta Berlina
		4962	Giulietta Sprint
		884	Giulietta Sprint Veloce
		2744	Giulietta Spider
		270	Giulietta Spider Veloce
		742	Giulietta SS
		112	Giulietta SZ
		619	2000 Berlina
		410	2000 Spider
		651	2000 Sprint

1962	34,887 cars	16,445	Giulietta TI
		1474	Giulietta Berlina
		1157	Giulietta Sprint
		261	Giulietta Sprint Veloce
		1182	Giulietta Spider
		70	Giulietta Spider Veloce
		213	Giulietta SS
		36	Giulietta SZ
		128	2000 Berlina
		48	2000 Sprint
		7026	Giulia TI
		3702	Giulia Sprint
		3145	Guilia Spider

1963	48,654 cars	11,499	Giulietta TI
		330	Giulietta Berlina
		289	Giulietta Sprint 1300
		27,624	Giulia TI
		178	Giulia TI Super
		3388	Giulia 1600 Sprint
		848	Giulia Sprint GT
		3875	Giulia Spider
		620	Giulia SS
		3	Giulia TZ

1964	53,968 cars	1282	Giulietta Sprint 1300
		5244	Giulietta TI
		21,237	Giulia TI
		323	Giulia TI Super
		106	Giulia GTC
		17	Giulia 1600 Sprint
		10,839	Giulia Sprint GT
		11,947	Giulia 1300 Berlina
		1945	Giulia Spider
		290	Giulia Spider Veloce
		676	Giulia SS
		62	Giulia TZ

1965	57,929 cars	329	Giulietta Sprint 1300
		1	Giulietta TI
		9304	Giulia TI
		602	Giulia GTC
		10,053	Giulia Sprint GT
		13,384	Giulia 1300 Berlina
		285	Giulia Spider 1600
		801	Giulia Spider Veloce
		103	Giulia SS
		42	Giulia TZ
		21,072	Giulia Super
		406	Giulia GTA
		769	Giulia GTV
		766	Giulia 1300TI
		12	Spider '4R' Zagato

1966	59,314 cars	15,616	Giulia Super
		21	Giulia GTA
		23,465	Giulia 1300TI
		6901	Giulia GTV
		3363	Duetto Spider

		5054	Giulia TI
		292	Giulia GTC
		162	Giulia Sprint GT
		1208	Giulia 1300 Berlina
		3176	Giulia GT 1300 Junior
		1	Giulia SS
		4	Giulia TZ
		51	Spider '4R' Zagato

1967	76,779 cars	20,030	Giulia Super
		903	Giulia TI
		1304	Giulia 1300 Berlina
		61	Giulia GTA
		6541	Giulia GTV
		2958	Duetto Spider
		13,020	Giulia 1300 Junior
		27,916	Giulia 1300TI
		1	Giulia TZ
		29	Spider '4R' Zagato
		2243	1750 Berlina
		919	1750 GTV
		854	1750 Spider Veloce

1968	97,182 cars	7332	Giulia Super
		32,498	Giulia 1300TI
		12,732	Giulia GT 1300 Junior
		82	Giulia 1300 Berlina
		29	Giulia GTV
		3	Duetto Spider
		320	Giulia GTA 1300 Junior
		1840	Giulia Spider 1300
		332	Giulia 1600S
		28,619	1750 Berlina
		11,621	1750 GTV
		1227	1750 Spider Veloce
		141	1750 Berlina (USA)
		147	1750 GTV (USA)
		259	1750 Spider Veloce (USA)

1969	104,300 cars	17,394	Giulia Super
		31,994	Giulia 1300TI
		15,674	Giulia GT 1300 Junior
		136	Giulia 1300 Berlina
		12	Giulia GTA
		1600	Giulia 1600S
		82	Giulia GTA 1300 Junior
		840	Giulia Spider 1300 Junior
		22,697	1750 Berlina
		10,159	1750 GTV
		1199	1750 Spider Veloce
		727	1750 Berlina (USA)
		640	1750 GTV (USA)
		1146	1750 Spider Veloce (USA)

1970	107,989 cars	15,412	Giulia Super
		26,447	Giulia 1300TI
		13,694	Giulia GT 1300 Junior
		294	Giulia 1300 Berlina
		1	Duetto Spider

4452	Giulia 1300 Super
566	Giulia 1300 Junior Zagato
525	Giulia Spider 1300 Junior
8	Giulia GTA 1300 Junior
283	Giulia 1600S
29,968	1750 Berlina
13,454	1750 GTV
658	1750 Spider Veloce
282	1750 Berlina (USA)
519	1750 GTV (USA)
1426	1750 Spider Veloce (USA)

1971 122,651 cars

17,253	Giulia Super
681	Giulia 1300TI
15,359	Giulia GT 1300 Junior
3	Giulia 1300 Berlina
22	Giulia GTA 1300 Junior
39,190	Giulia 1300 Super
749	Giulia Spider 1300 Junior
358	Giulia GT 1300 Junior Zagato
16,519	1750 Berlina
5629	1750 GTV
734	1750 Spider Veloce
600	1750 Berlina (USA)
1151	1750 GTV (USA)
1211	1750 Spider Veloce (USA)
15,416	2000 Berlina
6949	2000 GTV
811	2000 Spider Veloce
2	2000 Berlina (USA)
2	2000 GTV (USA)
12	2000 Spider Veloce (USA)

1972 99,197 cars

10,497	Giulia Super
80	Giulia 1300 TI

6968	Giulia GT 1300 Junior
15	Giulia GTA 1300 Junior
24,938	Giulia 1300 Super
584	Giulia Spider 1300 Junior
184	Giulia GT 1300 Junior Zagato
4495	Giulia GT 1600 Junior
928	Giulia Spider 1600
99	Giulia 1600 Coupé Zagato
74	1750 Berlina
8	1750 GTV
9	1750 Berlina (USA)
18	1750 GTV (USA)
7	1750 Spider Veloce (USA)
33,035	2000 Berlina
12,134	2000 GTV
1893	2000 Spider Veloce
1055	2000 Berlina (USA)
1164	2000 GTV (USA)
1012	2000 Spider Veloce (USA)

1973 509,105 cars
to (average:
1977 101,821 cars
 each year)

16,620	Giulia 1300 Super
40,332	2000 Berlina
17,300	2000 GTV
18,275	2000 Spider Veloce
303	Giulia 1600 Coupé Zagato
102,960	Alfetta Berlina
68,000	Giulia Nuova Super 1300
29,800	Giulia Nuova Super 1600
21,974	Alfetta GT 1.8
12,197	Alfetta GT 1.6
31,267	Alfetta GTV
57,475	Alfetta Berlina 1.6
52,000	Alfetta Berlina 1.8
34,212	Alfetta 2000 Berlina
3832	Giulietta 1.3
2558	Giulietta 1.6

Acknowledgements

It's awfully difficult, when coming to the end of a long and complex project like *Alfissimo!*, to be sure to remember all the people who gave so much help at each different stage. Perhaps the fairest way is simply to thank everyone involved, from my own family for putting up with the noise of the telephone and the typewriter and the long hours of midnight-oil burning to all those who came up with information, photographs, ideas and suggestions along the way. In particular though, I'd like to record a very real debt to all my friends at Alfa Romeo SpA in Milan, to Alvarez Garcia, Ray Corsi and Neil Verweij, to Engineers Garcea, Mazoni and Fedi for taking time to answer hours and hours of obscure questions and last, but most definitely not least, to Barry Needham at Alfa Romeo (Great Britain) Limited for all his help in making this book possible at all.

Finally, I know that the publishers would like to thank Michael Lindsey, Editor of the Alfa Romeo Owner's Club magazine for his enthusiastic assistance.

On the photographic side we would have been nowhere without the manufacturer's own special library, the Centro di documentazione Storica Alfa-Romeo. They supplied many, many prints of their own and those of others such as Carrozzeria Bertone, Farabola, Giorgio Lotti, Publifoto and Touring Superleggera whose copyright they own.

Many others supplied prints too; these are listed alphabetically. Thank you all.

Alfa Romeo Inc (of North America), Attualfoto, the author, *Autocar*, Hugh Bishop, Jeff Bloxham, Neill Bruce, Peter Coltrin, Michael Frostick collection, Robin Gedye, Martin Holmes, Reinhard Klein, Michael Lindsey collection, London Art Technical, Jean-Francois Marchet collection, Peter Marshall of the Alfa Romeo 1900 Register, Simon Moore, Tim Parker collection, Carrozzeria Pininfarina, Cyril Posthumus collection, and H. P. Seufert.

Index

A

Abarth, Carlo: 117

Agnelli, Giovanni: 8

Alfa Romeo cars: 24HP: 9, 10, 11, 12, 14

12HP: 9, 11

40–60: 10, 11, 13

1914 GP car: 14, 15, 16

G1: 15, 16, 17

RL: 17, 18, 24, 25

P1: 18, 20

P2: 21, 22, 23, 24, 25, 27, 28, 33

RLTF: 23

6C 1500: 24, 26, 27, 28, 37

6C 1750: 27, 28, 30, 31, 32, 37

8C 2300: 30, 31, 33, 36, 38

Tipo A: 32, 33

Monza: 32, 33

P3: 33, 35, 36, 39

6C 2300: 37, 38, 39, 41, 42, 44, 47

8C 2900: 39

GP V12: 41

GP V16: 42, 75

Alfetta GP: 42, 75, 77, 92, 195, 259

S10: 43

S11: 43

Tipo 162: 43

Tipo 163: 43

Tipo 512: 43, 162

6C 2500: 43, 45, 46, 47, 48, 49, 50, 52, 53, 54, 55, 58

Gazzella: 48, 49, 52, 55, 60

Freccia d'Oro: 53, 59, 61

4C 1900: 58, 59, 61, 62, 63, 64, 65, 66, 67, 69, 70, 71, 77, 83, 92, 93, 94, 101, 105, 106, 107

6C 3000: 60, 82, 195

1900 TI: 69, 70, 71, 77, 88, 91

6C 2500 Coloniale: 72

1900 M: 72, 73, 74, 75, 91, 94

1900 Sprint: 77, 80, 91, 96

Disco Volante: 80, 81, 82, 83, 85, 86, 91, 94, 101, 102, 103, 161

6C 3000 C50: 83

6C 3000 PR: 83

1900 Super: 86, 91, 92

BAT: 94, 96, 97, 101, 103

2000 Sportiva: 102, 103, 104

Tipo 750 Competizione: 117, 118

Giulietta: 105, 106, 107, 112, 113, 117, 118, 131, 132, 133, 139, 140, 142, 144, 153, 154, 159, 161, 165, 200

Giulietta Berlina: 108, 109

Giulietta Sprint: 110, 111

Giulietta Spider: 112, 113, 114, 129

Giulietta Sprint Veloce: 114, 116, 125, 140

Giulietta Spider Veloce: 116

Giulietta TI: 120, 121, 122, 123, 125, 133, 160, 166

2000 Berlina: 125, 128, 130, 131

2000 Sprint: 128, 130, 131

2000 Spider: 128, 129, 130, 131

Tipo 103: 154, 155, 157, 158, 159

Alfasud: 158, 253, 254, 256, 258, 273, 277

Giulia TI: 153, 157, 159, 160, 161, 162, 165, 166, 167, 169, 170, 184, 194

Giulia Sprint: 165, 178, 179

Giulia Spider: 165, 179

Giulia SS: 170

Giulia Sprint GT: 172, 174, 175, 177, 178, 182

Giulia 1300 Sprint: 178

Giulia 1300 Berlina: 179

Giulia GTC: 181, 182, 183

Giulia Super: 180, 181, 183, 240

1600 Spider/Duetto: 183, 184, 185, 186, 187, 188, 208, 224

Giulia Sprint GTV: 186, 187, 188, 189, 205, 224

GT 1300 Junior: 189

1750 4R Zagato: 190, 191, 192, 225

Giulia TI Super: 193

Giulia TZ: 193, 195, 200, 201, 202, 203, 205, 207, 213

Giulia GTA: 206, 207, 208, 211, 212, 215, 231, 233, 238, 239

GTA 1300 Junior: 211, 212, 233

Canguro: 213, 214

Scarabeo: 214, 215, 217, 218

Tipo 160: 215

1750 (1968): 222, 224, 225, 227, 237, 239, 243, 264